THE
PROTESTANT
REVOLT

Road To Freedom For American Churches

JAMES DeFOREST MURCH

Foreword by

EDMUND A. OPITZ

CRESTWOOD BOOKS
Box 2096
Arlington, Virginia 22202
1967

CONTENTS

gratis

124645

EDMUND A. OPITZ

Edmund A. Opitz is a senior staff member of the Foundation for Economic Education and book review editor of *The Freeman*. He is an ordained minister, a board member of the Congregational Foundation for Theological Studies, and coordinator of the activities of The Remnant. This is a nationwide fellowship of ministers predominately conservative or libertarian in their political and economic outlook. Mr. Opitz is a founder, and serves as the Hon. Secretary of The Nockian Society, an informal group of people interested in the work of Albert Jay Nock, American essayist and editor of the original *Freeman*.

Mr. Opitz took his college major in political science, with a minor in economics. He went on to get a theological degree, was ordained in the First Parish in Beverly, Massachusetts, and spent nine years serving three parishes in two states. During one pastorate he taught at Harrisburg Academy in Pennsylvania; during another, he was an instructor in government at Curry College in Boston. In World War II he served in India as a Red Cross Field Director.

He is the author of a book, *The Powers That Be*, dealing with the application of religious principles to economic and political problems, and the co-author of another on similar themes, *The Kingdom Without God*. Mr. Opitz also wrote the challenging chapter "Churches in Politics" in *Your Church—Their Target* (Crestwood). He has written the introduction to two other books and several short studies such as "Problems of Church and Society," and "Perspective on the Natural Law." His numerous articles and reviews have appeared in various publications: *The Freeman, Faith and Freedom, Christianity Today, National Review, The Contemporary Review, Modern Age, The Crozer Quarterly, Vital Speeches*, and others.

FOREWORD

"How often has public calamity been arrested on the very brink of ruin by the seasonable energy of a single man!"

Edmund Burke

NEWTON'S THIRD LAW OF MOTION still holds on the level of inanimate nature: To every action there is an equal and opposite reaction. In human affairs, however, free will may tilt the equation to one side or the other. An aroused personal reaction to a challenge may generate a response which is of greater moment and far richer in promise than the original action. The "action" analyzed in this book is a consequence of the secularist penetration of organized religion during recent generations. The extent of this secularization may be gauged by two of its effects: the emergence of weird theologies which deny the supernatural ("God is dead," "Christian atheism"), and the efforts of politically-minded churchmen to shape the churches into an ecclesiastical power bloc which would reduce religion to a mere instrument of revolutionary social change. The "reaction" is the encouraging lay and clerical response and resistance to this secularization and its effects, a story fully told here for the first time.

5

One hears the clash of arms in the background as he reads this book; it is of the arena as well as of the study. James DeForest Murch has been a sturdy warrior for the faith for many years, and a close student of it; he is a master of his material because he has participated in the events and pondered them as well. And he speaks out bluntly. A rebellious people, Isaiah wrote, would tell their prophets to "speak unto us smooth things." Not so Jim Murch, who preaches the Word with the bark on it. I am put in mind of Albert Jay Nock's journal entry for November 5, 1933: "One gets an awful surfeit of mush-and-milk in the current writing about public affairs. It reminds me of the preacher who told his people that 'unless you repent, as it were, and, as one might say, have a change of heart, you will be damned — so to speak — and, in a measure, go to hell.'" Nothing of this sort here!

The author and I do not see eye to eye on all matters; we come out of different religious backgrounds, our perspectives vary. And some readers may sharply disagree, for this is a controversial book. But it is an indispensable volume for everyone who is trying to make sense out of the turmoil in the churches; the outlandish theologies, the bizarre actions of prominent churchmen, and the new power ploy which seeks to hitch the church to the welfare state.

THE FORGOTTEN MAJORITY

One consequence of the rise of secularism and the politicalizing of religion is the growth of organizations, agencies, and councils designed to bring ecclesiastical leverage on society. Chief among these is the National Council of Churches, whose operations are here analyzed, and those of the World Council as well. But the bulk of the book is devoted to the Protestant bodies which are outside the National and World Councils, far superior numerically to those within. These are people, by and large, who do what the world expects Christians to do: They seek to know and do the will of the Father; they try to live by the Protestant ethic of industry, thrift, and personal responsibility; they dwell in charity with their neighbors; they keep the Commandments; they tell the truth; and so on. Quiet, unspectacular living is not news, and so the doings of the immense majority of people never get into the papers, nor into the history books either. But we know they are there, because no society can hang together which lacks this substratum of "right thinking and well doing." These people and their churches are given their due in this book.

We are informed that the tares will be found growing among the wheat until the last harvest. The world left to its own devices just naturally gravitates toward the dogs but, in God's good providence, there is always just enough saving health in a remnant to keep it from striking bottom. The world appears to follow what some wry humorist labeled Murphy's Laws: (1) If something can go wrong, it will. (2) When left to themselves, things go from bad to worse. (3) Nature always sides with the hidden flaw. (4) Whenever things seem to be going better, you have overlooked something! The Humanist doesn't find these "laws" funny; but the Christian has been saying all along that this is a fallen world, that it won't come out right, and that he hasn't been commissioned to run it!

Man is a rebel against the human condition, and it is the flaw in fallen human nature that makes him so. The Great Rebellion has been on ever since man entered the human estate. It has assumed as many forms as man's *hubris* has devised to deny his creaturehood and assert his autonomy. Liberalism — as the word is used by Great Societarians — is the most obtrusive manifestation of the Great Rebellion today. Liberals have the upper hand in Church and State and Academy — as well as in most opinion molding media. They may win next week, or next year. But we know they will defeat them-

7

selves in the end because the grain of things runs — ultimately — in other directions.

The Christian hope is not that men will some day achieve a perfect society, for "here we have no continuing city." Heaven, another dimension of being, cannot be established on earth. A generation ago Dean Inge foresaw "a reversion to political and external religion, the very thing against which the Gospel declared relentless war." It is not that Christianity regards social progress as unimportant, Inge goes on to say; it is a question of how genuine improvement may occur; "The true answer, though it is not a very popular one, is that the advance of civilization is in truth a sort of by-product of Christianity, not its chief aim; but we can appeal to history to support us that this progress is most stable and genuine when it is a by-product of a lofty and unworldly idealism."

SELF-CONTROL BEGETS SOCIAL FREEDOM

It is in the nature of the human condition that men are forever seeking, (a) an inner order of the soul, and (b) an outer order of society. The inner and spiritual liberty proclaimed in the Gospels must seek to realize itself and find proper expression in outer and social freedom. Christianity penetrates society and creates the appropriate political and economic structures by means of Christian persons who are citizens or magistrates. Thus, over the centuries, did Europe become Christendom — by the slow seepage of Gospel ideals into institutions, customs, conventions and laws. A civilization, Christian in its norms, was actualized. But it was no utopia; nor was one promised.

The utopian scheme is a secular version of the Kingdom of God, inspiring the belief in our time that a perfectly ordered social life will be possible as soon as political power is centralized and the wisest and best men operate the government according to an ideal blueprint.

The map of the universe these trends supply is guaranteed to lead us astray. Yet these trends are popular, and people who are always attracted to the latest fashion in ideas climb aboard the bandwagon. The Church is *in* the world, presumably, to witness to a quality of life that is not wholly *of* the world; it judges the things that come and go from the vantage point of a set of enduring values. The Church is not dedicated to wealth, power, or fame. These things are not bad in themselves, but the Church has another set of purposes, every one of which is aimed at cherishing and nourishing that elusive thing called "the soul," for whose proper ordering each person is accountable to his Maker. In terms of this main function, religion has taken on many other chores that have implications for even such seemingly remote provinces as politics and economics. These, however, are incidental to its main task, which is to remind man, in season and out, who he really is and what he may become; and this task, in every age, involves some resistance to "the world." Christianity can never be coextensive with any society or culture.

Most churches and most ministers are bending every effort in this direction; their effectiveness may be questioned, but not their intentions. The fantastic thing is that wealthy and powerful ecclesiastical organizations, seconded by articulate theologians, are doing their utmost — which is considerable — to promote and further the currently fashionable secular trends!

"SALVATION" BY COMPULSION

The Kingdom of God has been secularized into utopia-by-politics. The idea of the two cities — the City of God and the City of Man, Jerusalem and Babylon — has been central to Christian social thought from the earliest days. But no longer.

9

If politicians and a few other people will only take the advice of these ecclesiastical evangels of an earthly paradise, the Kingdom of God on earth will be due any minute.

Christians have always felt an obligation to improve the natural and social orders, but they have never until now equated a perfected social order with the Kingdom of God. This Kingdom was regarded as another dimension of existence, another realm of being, not simply an extension of our present set-up. But the late Bishop G. Bromley Oxnam told the Fifth World Order Study Conference in 1958 that Christians should "so change the planet that when our first visitors from Mars arrive they will find a society fit to be called the Kingdom of God."

There is a consistent pattern in the social changes taking place in this country and all over the world. We witness a trend toward the expansion of the political, coercive sector of the nation at the expense of the private, voluntary sector. The end result of this trend is a society run from the top by political direction and command; with no private sector immune from political interventions. This is authoritarianism, benign in some countries, tyrannical in others. The tyrannical version, Communism, has attracted some ecclesiastical support and still does; the benign version, domestic welfarism, attracts a great deal more. The aim of powerful churchmen is to mobilize the influence of religion and the churches behind every statist proposal — as if social reform and revolution were the end and religion a mere means!

The preoccupation of Liberal churchmen with political action has encouraged a certain laxity of thought in the theological domain. Not only is the reasoning less rigorous than it needs to be, but the Liberal mind has shown an unbecoming hospitality to extravagance of utterance, if only it pretends to novelty. We are treated to a series of "new" theologies and "new" moralities, whose latitudinarian sentiments are designed to betoken the breadth of mind and easy tolerance of mature people in a world come of age! Now it is true that history records some unseemly theological disputes which dissipated that love for the brethren to which we are enjoined. Worse still, churchmen in power have on occasion invoked the secular authority to guarantee doctrinal purity and punish deviations from the reigning orthodoxy. There is no warrant in Scripture for this kind of action, and ample warrant there for freedom of conscience.

Theological hassles are not the order of the day; there is no widespread concern to maintain creed and doctrine in pristine purity. This does not mean, however, that the True Believer mentality has disappeared; to the contrary, it is more virulent than ever, and it has more effective means to enforce its will. The Liberal Creed is not theological, but political and economic. It runs something like this: "I believe in the Welfare State and the Planned Economy; I believe in Social Security, Urban Renewal, Foreign Aid, the United Nations, and Medicare." Now many thoughtful citizens dissent from one or more of these propositions — which taken together comprise the Great Society — not because they don't want to see people better off but because they are convinced that the ends proclaimed cannot be reached by the means employed. The *general* welfare is not upgraded by political interventions which take from some to give to others; this makes everyone worse off, in the long run.

SECOND CLASS CITIZENSHIP FOR DISSENTERS

Besides being uneconomic, the Liberal program is also unjust. The rationale for the Welfare State is: Somebody's program at everybody's expense. The great mass of people have not been converted to Liberal orthodoxy in economic and political matters; they are unbelievers, and so they must be punished for holding beliefs deemed to be incorrect. Of course these present-day heretics are not burned at the stake, but neither were most heretics during the Ages of Faith. Most heretics then merely

11

suffered confiscation of property and certain civil disabilities — just as today. Those whose convictions do not permit them to endorse Social Security, Urban Renewal, Foreign Aid, and all the rest are nevertheless forced to help pay for these projects. A portion of their income and property is taxed away from Conservatives and Libertarians and used to further the Liberal program, which is that much less these people have for their own programs. Dissenters from the Liberal Creed do not have equality of rights with those in power. If this kind of thing were occurring in the religious realm everyone would acknowledge a serious breach of religious liberty; it is no less serious as a breach of civil liberty. Liberalism generates a body of second-class citizens as an intrinsic part of its operation.

These are some of the features of the thing which has emerged in our midst. If we don't like them we have no one to blame but ourselves, laymen and clergymen alike. The Church is people; not other people, us! During the course of the past several generations things have been done that should not have been done, while other things have been left undone. There has been indifference, sloth, preoccupation with other concerns. Defections have created a vacuum, so to speak, into which dubious ideologies have seeped. These ideologies have found embodiment in people and programs, and together they constitute the challenge we face. Part time or half-hearted resistance will not avail; the effort must be a heroic one, for, as Edmund Burke wrote, "When once things are gone out of their ordinary course, it is by acts out of the ordinary course they can alone be reestablished." With God's help, we may make it!

Edmund A. Opitz

JAMES DEFOREST MURCH

James DeForest Murch is an ordained minister of the Christian Church (Disciples of Christ). He has especially served in the field of religious journalism having been managing editor of the Standard Publishing Company, manager and editor of *United Evangelical Action* (official organ of the National Association of Evangelicals), and managing editor of *Christianity Today.*

He is the author of over 20 books, among which are *Christian Education and the Local Church, Christians Only* (a history of the Christian Churches and Churches of Christ), *Cooperation without Compromise* (a history of the National Association of Evangelicals), *Teach Me to Pray, God Still Lives, Church-State Relations: the American Way,* and *Teach or Perish.* Dr. Murch wrote "Reds and the World Council of Churches" as a chapter in *Your Church — Their Target.*

A strong believer in backing up his beliefs by aggressive Christian action he has served in many capacities in such national organizations as the International Society of Christian Endeavor, the National Sunday School Association (President), International Convention of Disciples of Christ, National Association of Evangelicals, National Religious Broadcasters (President), the Evangelical Press Association (President), and the National Society Sons of the American Revolution.

Dr. Murch has received honorary doctorates from Northwest Christian College (D. D.) and Milligan College (Litt. D.). His Alma Mater, Ohio University, recently gave him its Distinguished Service Award for attainments in the field of religion. He is a fellow of the International Institute of Arts and Letters and holds membership in a number of honorary fraternities and societies. He has for many years been listed in *Who's Who in America.*

He is also Consulting Editor, Crestwood Books.

13

INTRODUCTION

AMERICAN PROTESTANTISM is at the crossroads.

It must decide today whether it will take the road to freedom and the full realization of its traditional ideals, or whether it will succumb to the revolutionary liberal ideas of a monolithic super-ecclesiasticism and take the road to oblivion.

It must decide whether it will continue to espouse the God-ordained theology of the Holy Scriptures, or accept the so-called "new theology." The basic tenets of this heresy are those of Paul Tillich interpreted by such men as John A. T. Robinson and James A. Pike. They hold that God is to be identified with the depths of human consciousness and that he is immanent, of the earth earthy; not a transcendent God of supreme authority.

It must decide whether it will continue to live by the morality of the Ten Commandments and the Sermon on the Mount, or by the "new morality." This delusion holds that all ethics are situational and relativistic, but governed by the eternal attribute of love (whatever its creators may conceive that to be). The summary of the new morality is "permissiveness with love." This doctrine is already wreaking terrible havoc in sex relationships throughout the nation.

15

It must decide whether it will continue to honor the mission of the Church set forth in the Great Commission or become identified in the "new evangelism." This fallacy calls for the rejection of the sin-salvation thesis; for man's identification with the social changes which are occurring in the modern world; and for the enlistment of the Church as a power structure in the conflicts of race, class, politics and nations through involvement in demonstrations, riots, sit-ins, strikes, lobbying and legislation.

It must decide whether it will continue to work and pray for Christian unity in the spirit of Christ's prayer in John 17, or join in the frenetic drive for a "new ecumenical church." Does Protestantism want to see the restoration of the Church that Jesus built, or the creation of a socio-politically oriented Super-Church controlled by a clerical hierarchy with unlimited centralized power?

The night is far spent, the day is at hand when Protestantism must decide which road it will take.

Already the road to the left is being traveled by a very considerable number of so-called Protestant denominational and interchurch leaders. The virus of Liberalism is spreading at an alarming rate and we are beginning to see the results in American life.

THE PROTESTANT ETHIC

America is not utopia, but reflect on the American achievement. Our American culture for the past 200 years has been proudly called "Christian" and even "Protestant." It was based on a universal belief in the sovereignty of God, the divinely revealed law of God, the God-given freedom of the individual and the overruling direction of Divine Providence. Coupled with this was the conviction that by God's help any worthy ambition was within the range of achievement. For over three hundred years America was a land of open opportunity. Wide stretches of territory and great natural resources were unclaimed. Beyond new horizons and new frontiers lay hope of riches and a new life. Nothing could "keep a good man down." In this climate God-centered persons prospered and material progress was greater with each succeeding year.

In the "game of life" there were certain accepted rules. They began by taking God into account. His moral code must be obeyed. Respectability included going to church on Sunday and engaging in no worldly pleasures or business on God's day. Most leaders of community life had high regard for the clergy, paid their church dues, read their Bibles at least occasionally, prayed and did a little church work. Prayer before a business deal was not an uncommon practice. All the blessings of life were considered the gift of God. A rich man was considered a special mark of God's favor. There was even a Thanksgiving Day each year in which the whole community assembled in some church or churches to thank God for its material growth and prosperity.

Then, there was hard work. Slothfulness was considered a sin. It was believed that genius was at least half due to a full day's work. Self-denying workers seldom looked at the clock and were willing to labor sixteen hours a day if that were necessary to achieve a worthy goal.

Honor and integrity were prized possessions. It was believed that shrewdness and ambition were good but not the sacrifice of virtue. "A man's word was as good as his bond." The friend dependable and true, the adviser honest and fearless, the competitor just and chivalrous were characteristics of American business at its best.

Freedom of the individual and his God-given constitutional rights were either respected or demanded. Individuals were free to earn a living and climb their ladders of success in their own way. They could choose their own professions or change them at will. They could exercise their genius for making or manag-

17

ing money in any lawful way. If by dint of superior skill or intelligence a man chose to live better than his neighbor he could do so and his neighbor was free to excel him if he could.

Merit was the best qualification for advancement and success. Whether the man was poor, underprivileged or unknown, or wealthy, cultured and socially fortunate, his merit was recognized for what it was and usually rewarded.

Thrift was the hallmark of all worthy men. As soon as a young man began to earn money he began to save a portion of it. It was considered a good rule to put away a dollar out of every ten earned. Even the schools taught the habit and each child had his own savings account. It was believed that at some point in life these accumulated savings might either be the nucleus for starting a business or making a rewarding investment, or providing an "umbrella for a rainy day."

This so-called "Protestant ethic" reached out beyond the business and industrial life of the nation. It was responsible for the emancipation of the slaves during the Civil War of 1861-65. The state papers of President Abraham Lincoln during that dread period of our national history often read like pages out of the Bible. During the "Golden Age of the Sunday School" (1900-1916) moral right instead of political expediency often determined elections and motivated such movements as woman's suffrage and prohibition of the manufacture and sale of alcoholic beverages. The Protestant ethic called for humility and repentance when America was known to be in the wrong, for solving problems of ignorance, disease and poverty, for helping the "little people," the hungry, the helpless, the homeless, the friendless and the oppressed.

Consider now what has happened to the American dream. Today with the advent of modern liberal leadership in every phase of our national life we have accepted the Freudian ethic. We have expelled God and the Bible from our philosophy of education and rejected biblical moral and spritual standards in dealing with human problems. Egged on by leaders in the "new

Protestantism" we have produced a generation of teachers who regard man as a human animal which may be influenced only by external stimuli or experiences. They reject fixed standards of value judgments for the guidance of human conduct. They affirm with absolute conviction that there are no absolutes, no God-given rights, no ultimate truths. With liberal Protestant collusion we have taken God out of the public schools, prohibited prayer, Bible reading and instruction in morals and ethics. New generations are coming on who have no intelligible conception of an omnipotent and benign Supreme Being who has laid down certain immutable natural laws, endowed men with certain inalienable rights, and revealed unchallengeable basic rules of human conduct. They have no dependable criterion for evaluating right and wrong. And now what have we?

THE DEBACLE OF LIBERALISM

In the *family* all the Judeo-Christian mores are under fire. Marriage is weakened by the growing belief that sexual deviations and premarital intercourse are justifiable. Common-law marriages are no longer thought sinful since physical union is believed to make a couple one. Intercourse, once sacred to the marriage chamber, is condoned wherever and whenever the compelling inner attitudes and motives of the participants appear to be mutually desirable. Divorce is considered a necessity in the search for compatibility. Discipline of children according to a moral or religious code of conduct is considered repressive and destructive of balanced mental and physical development. Parental authority is considered a relic of tribal culture.

In the area of *human welfare* many believe that rational thinking and social revolution are the only hope of mankind. With one foot in humanism and the other in science, modern programs of mental health bypass religion and deal with men as human animals. Security cannot be earned, say the experts, it must be achieved by government through the redistribution of wealth and the maintenance of mankind in reasonable comfort on economic levels which do not vary too widely. With a great show of concern, public monies are provided for the unfortunate only to be used for the creation of new social problems. For example, unwed mothers often use relief checks to entice professional gigolos into becoming fathers of more children so that comfortable living may be provided at public expense.

In *government* the sovereignty of God is being denied. The moral or natural law given by the Sovereign of the universe to all mankind has hitherto been considered basic to the fundamental and statutory law of the nation. It has been generally agreed that primary law is founded by infinite wisdom and goodness on essential righteousness which never varies and requires no amendment or alteration. Courts now tend to repudiate this concept and see the province of jurisprudence as wholly contained within the framework of man-devised law suited to the social mores of the times. Self-evident truth is bypassed for the rule that all concepts are relative and subject to change. Everywhere laws are being written to eliminate the old and incorporate the new. The foundations of constitutional government are being shaken.

In *business* there are unmistakable signs of moral sag. A prominent executive in a recent luncheon conversation said, "I find that things have come to such a pass that when you remind businessmen that what they do is unethical by the old standards they simply shrug their shoulders and reply, 'Well, by the old rules perhaps, but it's legally permissible, so what?' Thousands of chiselers operate on a scale ranging from paltry deceptions of padding their tax returns to grandiose schemes on an international scale for tax avoidance. Bribes, price fixing, secret commissions, cutbacks, splits and dubious payoffs are common. A businessman who refuses to go along with such practices is called a 'panty-waist' and a 'relic' of the 'horse and buggy days.' "

In *labor* unscrupulous leaders feather their nests with a lion's share of the dues of the toiling masses. Gangsters who use murder and boycott as their weapons control crucial labor organizations, thus endangering the national defense and human welfare. The voices raised for Christian social justice are smothered in the self-seeking, capitalist-hating, power-mad propaganda that builds bigger unions at the expense of the public.

In *international relations* historic ideals of justice are being abandoned for methods of expediency. The bargaining method, the method of compromise, is superseding the mighty power of moral principle. In the first decade of the twentieth century many of the major nations of the world had signed a pact to outlaw war, only to see the world's bloodiest war fought to an inconclusive advantage. Now a ruthless cold war threatens to sap the vitals of Western civilization. Genocide continues to be practiced on a wide scale, whereby whole cultures are being wiped out. To use Professor Sorokin's phrase, "mankind's questioning of all dogma has led to the demoralization of all peoples of all religions and those who have no religion." The ensuing easy materialism is no match for the fanatical zeal with which atheistic and materialistic Communism promotes its ends, even to the use of brutality and extermination.

In *culture and the fine arts* God and morality are generally missing. Illegitimacy has captured the legitimate theater. Of the thirty-five thousand motion pictures unveiled in the last twenty years hardly a score had religious plots and most of the rest were subversive of public or private morals. Painting, once patronized by the Church, has catered to the prurient interest or degenerated into impressionism. Great religious music has received no major contribution for decades while jazz, rock-and-roll and the rhythm beats of the Hottentots have captured the popular interest.

It would take a whole chapter to delineate adequately the effect of liberalism on *religion* in general. Prayer has become a reflex influence or an escape mechanism. The Bible is widely believed to be of human origin to such an extent that it is no longer accepted as the revelation of God's will for man and the ultimate written authority for faith and life. God is viewed as being little more than the personification of the best in human relationships. Since conditioned reflexes determine all our acts, there can be no such thing as sin. Christ is still acknowledged to be a great moral leader but the idea of His being God manifest in the flesh or Redeemer from sin is considered an antiquated theological aberration. The evolving Church is busy adjusting itself to changing times and human needs. No wonder Ben Hecht, writing in *Esquire*, observed that "we need a new god for the space age" and that "the most amazing event to enter modern history has been generally snubbed by the chroniclers — it is the petering out of Christianity."

CHOOSE YE THIS DAY

This abandonment of the Protestant ethic both in the church and in the nation has contributed to what Dr. John A. Mackay calls "the pervasive sense of emptiness that marks our American culture today." Charles Peguy calls the modern man who is the product of this permissive generation, a "monster of uneasiness" and the easy victim of all sorts of subversive doctrines and movements.

Unless the people and the churches who are really Protestant revolt against their liberal leadership America will join with pagan nations in entering what historian Arnold Toynbee calls a "post-Christian era" in the history of the world. If the Protestant Christian witness is finally divorced from cultural identification with American institutions, if it is no longer heard in the pulpits of American churches, if it is no longer taught in American schools, colleges and universities, if it is suppressed by Councils of Churches and invisible Ecclesiastical Establishments, we are headed toward a new period of Dark Ages when Christians will have to return to individual witness in a hostile environment and pay in blood, sweat and tears for their apathy, cowardice and faithlessness.

In the Old Testament story of Elijah we read how this great crusading prophet put to rout the heathen priests of Baal on Mount Carmel. But when Queen Jezebel threatened to punish him by cutting him in pieces like a sacrificed animal, he ran and hid. At Horeb Jehovah put some of the old faith back into Elijah's heart and revealed to him that seven thousand Israelites had not bowed the knee to Baal. So the campaign went on until the heresy of Baal was purged from the land.

More than seven million American Protestants have not forsaken the biblical tenets of Protestantism. Indeed, by conservative count there are over thirty million who have no relationship whatsoever with the National Council of Churches and another ten million in denominations related to the Council who are thoroughly disillusioned with its policies, its programs and its leadership.

It is the purpose of this book to reveal to the American public the long-suppressed facts about the Protestant church situation in the nation, particularly the revolt against the Councils of Churches, and the constructive efforts being made to restore Protestantism to its former glory and power.

We hope to delineate the rise of the new Protestant spirit, the courageous revolt against liberal tyranny in practically all Protestant communions across the nation, and the growing need for united Protestant Christian testimony and action, to the end that Christ may be glorified and that His will may be done in our day and time.

American Protestantism is at the crossroads. Choose you this day which road you will take!

I

THE LIBERAL ESTABLISHMENT

IN THE BEGINNING of our treatise it needs to be made clear that there is a liberal ecclesiastical establishment which sets the tone for and influences the direction of modern institutional Protestantism.

As to "liberal" the word comes from Latin *liber,* meaning "a free man." Liberalism, in its best sense, means consciousness of liberty and resistance to any attempt on the part of constituted authority to exert artificial pressure or regulation of the rights of the individual. Against such imposition true liberalism must array its forces, whether it be in the field of morals, religion, intellectual activity, social relationships, economics or politics.

But in our day the word has been warped and twisted so that a liberal is one who, especially in the fields of political economy and theology, contends against the protection of the rights of the individual. The liberal today has sold out lock, stock and barrel, to regimentation and control in church and state. Whoever fails to fall in line and wishes to exercise his God-given liberties is called a Tory or a Reactionary. The highest virtue claimed by modern liberalism is "tolerance." Not tolerance of the Tories or the Reactionaries or their doctrines or practices, but a sort of moral relativism, an elasticity of thought which springs from the belief that there are no fixed standards of right and wrong. To the modern liberal there is no such thing as "moral accountability" for one's acts, whether it be in the matter of rearing children, punishing criminals, dealing with Communists, or taking vows for the Christian ministry. Modern Liberalism has its roots in scientific naturalism. More will be said about this later, but for the present this definitive statement will suffice.

As to "establishment," the word was originally applied to the official status of Anglicanism in Great Britain as the "established" church — the communion recognized and supported by the government. As time went on, Britons included religious, civil and cultural authority, revolving around the nobility, the public school system, the great universities — the effective governing class of England — under this term.

As we have come to use the word, an establishment is a sort of informal junta by which a community of interests or institutions is guided in all things that matter. The modern establishment is not organized in the usual sense of that term; it does not major in coordination or planning, although it would engage in such measures if those procedures were thought to be necessary. It is the product of a cultural, social, theological or political ideology imbibed from a select coterie of educational institutions. Gradually, as cream comes to the top of a can of milk, the elite who hold common views and seek common aims get to know one another and to work together. Because of their status and influence they exert great power. Members of the Establishment know where they stand on major issues before the issues come up, because their "so-called" Liberal ideology supplies them with a whole agenda of set answers. They are in constant demand in academic circles, civic institutions, churches, government, foundations and social affairs. They naturally develop a common idiom and a portfolio of tactics. Their advice and counsel are often sought and often followed. Anyone who observes, analyzes and realizes what is going on in the churches is bound to come to the conviction that there is an empirical thing in existence which is Liberal and which acts concertedly to achieve common ends in every channel of activity

26

embraced in the Protestant complex of denominations and institutions.

An interesting confirmation of the fact that a Liberal Protestant Establishment actually exists came recently from Professor Paul M. Harrison of Princeton. He was a participant in the Oberlin sessions of the Consultation on Church Union embracing major Protestant denominations (about which we shall learn later) and presented a sociological *"Analysis of the Participating Communions."* The document pointed out in some detail that there is a difference between legal authority and *actual power* in church government. Said the report:

". . . Given the disparate nature of authority and power in the participating denominations it can be reasonably hypothesized that one of the most effective instruments for sustaining the denominations and formulating denominational polity is also one of the most difficult to define. In secular political literature it has been called "The Establishment" . . . The Establishment appears to be a functional necessity in each of the denominations. The first order of business of every informal Establishment meeting is to deny the existence of the Establishment. The leaders of the Establishment maintain that real denominational power rests with the people, the local congregations, the regional officers, the national executives, the General Assembly, the General Council or the Presiding Bishop. But . . ."

The remainder of this section of the report then went into a limited description of the way the Establishment really works in the participating denominations represented at Oberlin. Dr. Harrison said that there is a little coterie of businessmen, professional clergymen, professional laymen, ecclesiastical executives and theologians of various persuasions (except "fundamentalists") who get together from time to time and decide what the program of the denomination will be. They are supported by two or three "big men" in the public eye, some representatives of the social elite and a handful of affluent folks who can undergird the budget. This small body of "key men" can hold the balance of power in executive and board meetings and exert the necessary influence to assure the election or appointment of the "right people" to all important positions in the ecclesiastical machine. The Establishment is made up of near-conservatives and almost-radicals who co-operate to discover non-irritating approaches to controversial issues and know what "wires to pull" to get approval in "representative" bodies for the policies and progress which are "in the best interests of the churches." Dr. Harrison then disclosed the fact that at the national level the Conservative-Liberal theological controversy of the 20's and 30's gave the Establishment some terrible headaches for a time but, he said, it "was eventually bridled by the Establishment." And he might have added, in favor of the Liberals.

It is interesting to see how the Liberal Establishment works. A whole book could be written on the subject but for our purposes we shall consider very briefly some developments which have taken place in the theological, socio-political and ecclesiastical areas of American Protestantism.

IN THE AREA OF THEOLOGY

What Liberalism has done in the field of theology is basic to an understanding of all else that has transpired in the rape of American Protestantism. It has challenged the "faith once for all delivered to the saints." It has refused to accept the authority of the Holy Scriptures and the historic creeds of Christendom and has projected its heresies into every root and branch of the Christian Church.

Theological Liberalism was born at the beginning of the Nineteenth Century. The apostle Paul characterized a similar apostasy in the First Century of the Christian Era as "another gospel" and branded it with his anathema. Following a period in which the world had been largely influenced by the rationalistic philosophies of David Hume, Immanuel Kant,

Georg Wilhelm Friedrich Hegel, and Auguste Comte, there emerged a new secularism and scientism. The former produced Karl Marx's *Communist Manifesto* and World Communism. Scientism gave new impetus to the study of the natural sciences with many salutary benefits to humanity, but an unfortunate by-product was a tragic contempt for spiritual things. In the great universities of Germany scientific objections to the basic doctrines of the Christian faith gained such credence in intellectual circles that theologians were forced to re-examine their traditional views. Since many of them were pure professionalists in the field of religion, they lacked faith to meet scientific naturalism with biblical truth. Such men as Schleiermacher, Ritschl and Troeltsch abandoned to the new culture strategic supernatural elements of the Christian faith. The "German rationalists" then proceeded to accommodate abstract Christianity to scientific naturalism.

Let us clarify what we mean by theological Liberalism. Basically, it denies the entrance of the creative power of God in the origin of Christianity, whether it be in the Virgin Birth, the miracles of Christ, the resurrection of Christ or the inspiration of the Word of God. Liberalism, as the term is here used, is an attempt to accommodate Christianity to modern scientific naturalism. Wherever scientific objections may arise from the details of the Christian religion, liberalism abandons to modern culture the inspiration of the Bible, the unique deity of the Person of Christ, the atonement for sin and a personal resurrection. On the other hand, liberalism retains the general principles of Christianity in "the good life," "the aspirations of the soul" and "the struggle for a better world."

It is not possible because of space limitations to analyze the various teachings of liberal theology today, but we can give a few suggestions as to landmarks in recognizing the liberal. No two liberals are alike, but their general principles are the same. They all act upon the application of evolutionary naturalism to

Christianity. The Bible, according to the liberals, is the historical record of the developing religious consciousness of one
people. That is a far cry from the Christian teaching concerning
the Bible as the Word of God and the record of that revelation
as inspired.

Concerning Jesus, the liberal does not want to have a religious relationship. He does not accept Jesus as one to be
worshiped. He does not accept the subjective-objective view
of man in his relationship to Jesus. He merely accepts Jesus
as an example, a prophet, a teacher and a moral pioneer. He
is willing to accept the religion of Jesus so that he can come to
God as the man Jesus came to God, but he is not willing to
accept the biblical revelation about Jesus, namely, that Jesus
is the Son of God, and Saviour, and the object of our worship.
What the liberal fails to recognize is that this same teacher and
moral leader claimed to be sinless and that He also had a
Messianic consciousness in which even in the Sermon on the
Mount He said, "In that day I will say unto you: depart from
me ye workers of iniquity." He also said, "Hereafter ye shall
see the Son of Man sitting on the right hand of power, and
coming in the clouds of heaven." Caiaphas declared that He
was guilty of blasphemy when He made this claim, yet that
claim cannot be expunged from the narrative.

The cross, as a substitutionary sacrifice for the liberal, is
merely the thought form of that generation in which the truth
of the love of God was expressed. The liberal claims that the
same truth was expressed in dialectic by the scholastics, by
doctrine in the age of the reformers and will be expressed dif-
ferently in our age, probably by the sacrificial life. The liberal
says that the eternal thing is the truth and that the category or
form of expressing that truth changes with different generations.
Hence the New Testament interpretation of the cross of Christ
is not the final one for the liberal.

Miracles, for the liberal, are merely the legendary clothing
of a great man. They are the age's high estimate of one who

left a tremendous impact upon his contemporaries. In order to express the greatness of his personality they clothed him with miracles, but the miracles really did not occur.

The gospel, for the liberal, is utterly changed from the means of reconciliation with God, or the redemption of the soul from sin, or the liberation of man from the bondage of evil to a sense of filial piety, or brotherhood, of mutual understanding and of betterment. In the gospel, for the liberal, there is no mention of the cross or if it is mentioned it is only as a way of sacrificial living.

The church, according to the liberal, is an organization for human betterment. It is no longer the assembly of called out people who are redeemed, the body of Christ, the organism of which He is the Head, and which enjoys mystical union with Him. The church becomes a movement akin to a radical party in the historical destiny of social development. The Communist Party is the vanguard of the social revolution. So the church is the vanguard of the spiritual betterment of mankind. One can easily recognize the difference between this and the Christian gospel.

The doctrines of the church and of Christianity as revealed in the incorporation papers of Christianity are utterly repudiated by the liberals and new doctrines are substituted for them.

That liberalism and orthodoxy are entirely incompatible is recognized by the leaders of both camps. As Dr. Charles Clayton Morrison, late editor of the liberal *Christian Century*, in an editorial entitled "Fundamentalism and Modernism: Two Religions," said:

> There is a clash here as grim as between Christianity and Confucianism . . . . The God of the fundamentalist is one God; the God of the modernist is another. The Christ of the fundamentalist is one Christ; the Christ of the modernist is another. The Bible of the fundamentalist is one Bible; the Bible of the modernist is another. The church, the kingdom, the salvation, the consummation of all things—

these are one thing to fundamentalists and another thing to the modernists. . . . Which is the true religion? . . . The future will tell.

Every area of the thought life of America was rent with controversy.

Philosophy, under the impact of the new naturalism, veered away from idealism to materialism. Whatever affinity philosophy had for religion came from the idealistic school. Materialism employing only a truncated reason has always been the breeding ground of atheism, humanism, naturalism, and all forms of skepticism; employing experience it produces sensationalism, naturalism, empiricism, experimentalism, positivism and pragmatism. Released from evangelical thought patterns the philosophers in church schools boldly proclaimed Christianity as a philosophy. The idealists, without a mooring in religion, repudiating the supremacy of matter, led their pupils into a plethora of Ideas, Ultimates, All-Wills and Absolutes. The materialists, emphasizing science and the scientific method with their evolutionary correlatives, produced a new generation of atheists, rationalists and pragmatists.

Psychology veered from the purposive school to the mechanistic school. The turn to liberalism in church-related schools opened the gate to those who believed that man is an animal and that human conduct consists of mechanical responses to nerve stimuli, that man's actions are the result of natural impulses over which he can exert no psychic or spiritual control. While many nominally Christian professors held to a modified form of naturalism, they still were quite free in declaring that "mind is incapable of recognizing truth from error, is limited in its ability to make moral choices" and that "the greatest good for the individual and society is achieved through the establishment of desirable nervous reflexes." Prayer, according to the naturalists, was a universal habit of the human race growing out of the common desires of the mind, which has a reflex influence capable of conditioning conduct. Every moral and religious practice was robbed of its spiritual reality.

Education, taking its cues from the new philosophy and psychology, discarded the Bible and the Christ of the Bible. God-centered education was exchanged for a man-centered process. God's will was no longer the basic norm. Man's mind became the measure of all things. The absolute truth of God's revelation to man was scrapped for relative truth. Human social welfare became a matter of primary concern. The goal of education was no longer to fit men to live in harmony with the will of God. Education, in the new view, is an instrument by which the developing and changing person may continue in the quest for certainty. Genuine values and tenable ends and ideals can be found only within the movement of experience and not from authority, human or supernatural.

This virus of theological liberalism has penetrated all the phases, functions and institutions of Christendom, resulting in a tremendous defection from the things which Christianity through the centuries had most surely believed.

The churches show a marked decline in spiritual power. Many pulpits are occupied by liberal ministers who lack conviction and passion because they have abandoned the Gospel that is "the power of God unto salvation." Real conversions are rare. Young men are not volunteering for the ministry or the mission field. The man in the pew has his doubts that Christianity is the true religion. In the office and in the social realm he finds a world dominated by pagan ideas. From without, the churches are beset by the perils of atheism, humanism, communism and statism; from within, by secularism, sectarianism, pharisaism and liberalism.

IN THE SOCIAL ORDER

Having abandoned a biblical Christian theology the Liberal

Establishment turned its attention to visionary plans for the amelioration of the material woes of mankind and the creation of a new Utopia—the Kingdom of God on earth.

The idea of a Utopia is as old as the family of man. A perfect state of things existed briefly in the Garden of Eden. It appears in the *Timaeus* of Plato and is fully developed in his *Republic*. The idealized description of Sparta in Plutarch's life of Lycurgus belongs in the same class. Sir Thomas More's *Utopia*, which describes an ideal commonwealth whose inhabitants exist under perfect conditions, set a new fashion in literature. In the writings of Thomas Hobbes, Sir Robert Filmer and Jean Jacques Rousseau an ideal state of society is described. Ideal commonwealths have been set up hundreds of times by idealists, socialists and communists—only to fall because of the defects of human nature.

But the Liberal Establishment does not read history. It has substituted a Social Gospel for the Christian Gospel which is the "power of God unto salvation"; a new gospel which is man-centered, not God-centered.

The Liberal Establishment believes that "Christianity is a life and not a doctrine"; it is a life or an experience that has doctrine merely as its symbolic intellectual expression, so that while life abides the doctrine must necessarily change from age to age.

This belief involves the most bottomless skepticism that could possibly be conceived; for if everything we say about God or about Christ or about the future life has value merely for this generation, and if something contradictory to it may have equal value in some future generation, then the thing we are saying is not true even here and now.

The Establishment makes "the worth and dignity of man" *the one basic principle* upon which both religion and democracy are founded.

While the worth and dignity of man is, in its proper relation to the doctrine and the lordship of Christ, a Christian principle, Protestants believe it is not *the basic principle* for social reasoning and action. When made basic it leads to humanistic and unchristian conclusions.

The trouble with these advocates of the Social Gospel is that they make the well-being of humanity their ultimate end, while the Bible Gospel makes it the glory of God. Dorothy Sayers deals incisively with this mode of thinking when she says in *Creed or Chaos*:

> Man cannot make himself happy by serving himself—not even when he calls self-service the service of the community; for "the community" in that context is only an extension of his own ego. Human happiness is a by-product, thrown off in man's service of God. . . . God is nobody's instrument. . . . It will not do to let the same sin creep back in a subtler and more virtuous-seeking form by suggesting that the service of God is necessary as a means to the service of man. That . . . would end by degrading God to the status of a heathen fetish, bound to the service of a tribe, and liable to be dumped head-downwards into the Water-butt if He failed to produce good harvest weather in return for services rendered.

However, the Social Gospel has now become the chief concern of most of the major Establishment-controlled Protestant denominations in America. Their journalism is filled with it. Their pulpits proclaim it. Their schools teach it. It is determining the pattern, the direction and the dynanism of their programs. Their call for life commitment is largely in terms of the Great Society.

Theologically these denominations hold that the church in the modern social order is the community of the committed to which God has given the task of direct participation in the life of the New Humanity. The gospel is said to stand in judgment of the old mores and the old social order: our economic injustice, our racial prejudice, our inhumanity to man, our hatred of our fellows and our moral dogmatism. As Colin Williams has said in his *What in the World?*:

The place of the community of Christ is at the perilous moving edges of change where Christ is offering men a participation in the life of the New Humanity.

In this situation it is held that the church must devise new forms of fellowship, witness and service; it must find modes of corporate presence in the political, economic and societal sectors of modern life so as to release the "Presence of Christ" which can change contemporary society.

This new jargon is only a smoke screen for something very similar to the Social Gospel disseminated by Walter Rauschenbusch and his disciples 50 years ago. Rauschenbusch attacked the individualism of orthodox Christianity and contended that Jesus was primarily concerned with social reform. He assailed liturgical complacency, pietistic sentimentalism and personal evangelism and accused the churches of commitment to a pseudo-religion consisting merely of Bible reading and hymn singing, with emphasis on "pie in the sky by and by." He condemned the profit motive in business and advocated socialism and government monopoly as the solution of America's social wrongs.

Albrecht Ritschl, a theological product of German idealism, was a major influence in Rauschenbusch's thought. The Ritschlian emphasis upon the community (moral collectivism) was particularly vital to the Social Gospel. Salvation, for Ritschl, was not to be interpreted in terms of a future life but in terms of service in a this-world kingdom of human goodness. In fact, Ritschl was convinced that God was not interested in saving the individual as such. Rauschenbusch, who possessed a deeply religious spirit, parted company with Ritschl at this point. For him "Christ," "redemption" and "the Kingdom of God" were essential to the saving of the social order. He saw the "Presence of Christ" and the "pervasiveness of the Kingdom" at work within the "social organism." Rauschenbusch frequently used Paul's analogy of "the body of Christ" to justify the "organism of society" as a basic concept. He saw the mystical, invisible church as synonymous with the visible, organized church and secular society and would admit no sharp separation of church and state. Furthermore, he saw the mission and role of the contemporary churches being accomplished in the world as a whole, which he believed to be the comprehensive arena of "the saving works of God."

When Rauschenbausch's dream of a redeemed society failed of realization through the moral and spiritual impact of his Social Gospel, he turned in his latter days to an almost exclusive demand for state intervention in economic and social life. Something of his disillusionment about God and the moral order has been carried over into the new Social Gospel in American Protestantism. Few modern liberals assume that a moral order is written into the nature of things. A crass pragmatism has invaded their ethics. Their "gospel" exhibits a definite trend from God to man and a collectivist trend from the individual to the group, accompanied by an eagerness to use political methods to achieve "the will of God." In this situation there is increasing liaison between church and state and a growing conviction that if there is ever to be a Great Society it must come largely through government. In liaison with left-wing political forces the Liberal Establishment is calling for social revolution sparked and forced by Big Government. All the old patterns are being torn up. Rugged individualism and capitalism, the right of a man to own his own property and his own business and to manage it as he sees fit without governmental interference, are being challenged and may well be outlawed. Advocates of the Social Gospel are saying, "The profit motive is dead." They see it standing "bankrupt, shivering and shaking as the chill winds of economic revolution bear down upon it." They call upon the churches to make profit a sin and upon the state to provide for the welfare of all its citizens by increased taxation.

The Social Gospel is little more nor less than Socialism. It calls for public ownership of all significant sectors of public life, such as banking, transportation and communications. In practice, it means the government ownership of the major means of production with consequent power to dispose of the fruits of labor. It means the cancellation of plans and programs which have been developed by individual and corporate incentive, the establishment of new quotas for factories, fields and mines, assignment of jobs, fixing of wages and hours of labor and the terms under which they may exchange. A few men exercising inordinate political power will then ride herd on the masses. The individual will no longer be permitted to exercise his God-given rights.

It is only a step from this to Communism. This is why the Liberal Establishment is friendly toward the Soviet Union and is constantly encouraging pronouncements to the effect that "Communism as an economic program for social reconstruction has points of contact with the social message of Christianity as in its avowed concern for the underprivileged and its insistence on racial equality. . . ." If we are to develop an economic order which will express the spirit of Christ, who came "not to be ministered unto but to minister," the primary test of production and distribution must not be a private advantage but the common good. A Christian spirit must find appropriate economic forms to fulfill its basic purpose of the greatest service to human need.

Says the Social Gospel, the church must support a planned economic system in which maximum social values shall be sought. It demands that co-operation shall supplant competition as a fundamental method. Industrial democracy is a goal comparable to that of political democracy. Both are relative terms. There is more than one way of making progress toward their realization. In one stage of development co-operation through collective agreements between the representatives of managers and workers, counseled by technical experts, may be most advantageous. Even in this elementary form of industrial relations the right of individual workers to organize and be represented by counsel or agents of their own free choice must be recognized as fundamental. In another stage participation by workers in management may be possible and desirable. In another workers might provide their own capital and assume full responsibility; in still another the Government might assume to exercise the powers of ownership, control and management for the common good.

In the present situation, therefore, one of our emerging objectives is a clearer definition of public and private as applied to business and industry. Could we not agree that natural resources and basic industries belong in a different category from enterprises in which a limited portion of the population has any concern?

(Of course "basic industries" mean power, transportation, credit, forests, all coal, iron, copper, etc.)

All of which means that the Liberal Establishment in effect is committed to the following objectives: (1) The scrapping of the profit motive, (2) the elimination of competition and the creation of a system of co-operation which will allow for government planning, (3) the placing of all natural resources under public ownership and control, (4) "co-operation" in economic life through state planning, and (5) a softening of our relationships with communist states.

The tragic thing about Protestantism's growing abdication of its moral and spiritual sovereignty and its concern for the salvation of the individual is that modern society is now plunging into what promises to be the greatest moral debacle in history. With all the church's talk about the Kingdom of God on earth, America is in an advanced state of moral decline which, if continued, will lead inevitably to the "City of Decay" and the "Valley of Doom." The Liberal Establishment is advocating lawlessness in the arena of civil rights; treating crime as a disease and not as sin; protecting the rights of criminals and disregarding the plight of their victims; destroying individual responsibility in favor of social consensus; and accepting economic and political corruption as justifiable means for the advancement of good ends. Never has the line between good and evil been as blurred and indistinct as it is today. Never has America been nearer destruction.

IN THE ECCLESIASTICAL AREA

The greatest undertaking of the Liberal Establishment is in the ecclesiastical area. Taking advantage of the deep desire in the hearts of millions for a united church, it is proposing the creation of One Church for One World—a global ecclesiastical empire that can rule the world.

The late Methodist Bishop G. Bromley Oxnam, who was unquestionably the major motivating influence in the Liberal Establishment of his day, can be given credit for first envisioning this crowning achievement. Dr. Oxnam is rightly given credit for drawing up the blueprints for the National Council of Churches and the World Council of Churches, both of which he headed as president before his death.

In his book, *On This Rock*, Bishop Oxnam set forth the blueprint American ecumenists are using. His Super-Church bypasses all the basic tenets of evangelical Christian doctrine. He sneered at "apostolic succession, immersion, ritual, episcopacy, second blessing, ruling elders and much more" which are barriers to church union. The plan would be to first effect inclusive co-operative Protestant action in the realm of Church functions. Next, to create an ecumenical ministry. The bishop himself said he would be glad to be re-ordained under this system:

I would gladly kneel in a service of mutual sharing in which the blessings of the differing ordinations might be conferred upon me. It would be for me a sacred and heart-warming moment to have the hands of Harry Emerson Fosdick placed upon my head and the independence of the Baptist tradition symbolically passed to me; and similarly to receive from Henry Sloane Coffin the rich traditions, the clear thought, and the democratic spirit of the Presbyterians; from Henry Knox Sherrill all that lies in the concept of the historic episcopate; from Rufus Jones, if he were still with us, the insights of the silences, the concerns that come from intimate communion with the Eternal; and to have bestowed upon me as blessings all that the others who might participate possess.

Then the picture emerges:

United action in many fields would follow rapidly. Our foreign or overseas missions could become one with the world organization and fellowship. We could have a common hymnal. There could be a Protestant daily paper. With what strength we could take up the modern media of radio and television and use them for the glory of God! Visual education would cease to be the sorry attempt of amateurs to enter a field callling for the highest art. A united Protestantism could summon the talents of the greatest artists of the earth, and from the screen would come the message of our Lord. There could be a united system of higher education, unitedly supported, in which we could train the lay leadership of our church, the teachers for our colleges and universities, and in united theological seminaries, the ministers of the church.

During this stage of development brotherly co-operation with the Greek Catholic (Eastern Orthodox) churches would be maintained; then union with the eastern church would be put through. At this juncture, the Bishop prophesies:

The union of American Christianity would electrify the world and accelerate the trends toward union in every continent.

Finally, the Bishop said, it will be possible

to kneel before a common altar (with the Roman church), beg forgiveness of the Christ for disunity, and, sharing in the Bread and Wine

41

of Holy Communion, rise in His Spirit to form the Holy Catholic Church to which all Christians may belong.

The creation of this ecclesiastical power structure is now well along. The Liberal Establishment is committed to the achievement of unity through compromise. They have experienced such radical changes in their own beliefs in the past fifty years that they are somewhat disillusioned as to the possibility of attaining unity through an acceptance of their views. They see denominational differences as sinful and believe they must be eliminated through a turn from theology to history, sociology and ethics. Liberals see church differences as the result of social traditions, the basic cultural heritage of a people, as well as political and economic interest; not as the result of profound spiritual forces at work in the hearts of men and commitment to the commands of the Gospel. This element in the leadership of the Ecumenical Movement believes most member churches are far enough along in their historic development that they are beginning to recognize the strength of the secular world and are in the process of rethinking their beliefs in the modern social and cultural frame of reference. It is believed that the churches are ready to compromise their traditional beliefs to achieve a position of mobility, adaptivity and universal acceptance. Liberalism is ready for compromise in theology. This compromise may be effected by a synthesis of Catholic, Conservative Protestant, Liberal Protestant, Radical Protestant, Neo-Orthodox and Anglican concepts of essential Christianity.

A more practical approach, which would bypass the interminable controversies over polity, doctrine, orders and institutions, is the new "Commonwealth Plan." It is based on the British idea of a Commonwealth of Nations in which each nation is considered sovereign, yet all are bound by treaties to safeguard their common interests, and their spiritual unity is symbolized by common allegiance to the Queen of England.

42

The Archbishop of Canterbury gave approval to such a scheme in his sermon in All Saints Anglican Church in Rome on the occasion of a visit to the Pope. He intimated that the Anglicans and the Romanists might at some future day be two of the churches of varying rites in this Commonwealth of Christendom. Bold prophets see the Pope as the head of the "Commonwealth." This is a long-range dream today but it may soon be realized if Ecumenical progress continues to gather momentum.

Once firmly established this global ecclesiastical empire under the guidance of the Liberal Establishment could commit the churches to any political doctrine it proposed. It already acts through committees and commissions and in publicity releases assumes to speak for all of Protestantism—committing its people, without their knowledge or consent, to pressures for or against political issues. These acts of moral imperialism would only be magnified in a united Church, with its organizational ramifications in all parts of the world. In liaison with internationalists in philanthropic, humanitarian, political, social, cultural, educational and religious circles they could guide the course of nations and rule the world.

Some years ago Dr. Liston Pope of Yale said, "Only Protestant churches willing to function in pressure group fashion will be able to make an impact on social and political problems in the world today." His dictum is the doctrine of the Liberal Establishment as it moves toward building One Church for One World. With its socio-political obsession it considers the Bible to be nothing, historic creeds to be nothing, religious scruples nothing, conscience nothing except they can be turned to the achievement of ecclesiastical socio-political Power. It is ready to make common cause with all classes of men, to honor the rites and festivals of all faiths, to give aid and comfort to their idolatries, to dethrone all revealed truth, and to inaugurate a latitudinarian infidelity in order to create a semblance of the Kingdom of God on Earth. When once

43

the earth has come to acknowledge the embodiments and representatives of such an ecclesiastical and hierarchical system, it will be nothing more in the sight of God than an iniquitous apostasy which might well be labeled Babylon the Great.

The tyranny of the Liberal Establishment becomes more apparent in the life of the American churches every day. But there is a remedy that can be evoked against it. This we shall hope to discover as we "reason together."

II

THE GROWING SUPER-CHURCH

TO IMPLEMENT the concepts of the Liberal Establishment it was necessary to create a corporate medium through which it could exert effective control over Protestant churches and their functional agencies; in other words, a Super-Church.

The Federal Council of Churches of Christ in the U.S.A. (founded in 1908) eventually became that medium. In its earlier years it rendered Protestantism yeoman service in the fields of temperance, social welfare, international and inter-racial good will. It encouraged sane evangelism. Both evangelicals and liberals co-operated with more or less enthusiasm in these enterprises. The lines of theological, sociological and political thought, however, became more and more distinct through years of research, study and conflict. While the FCC maintained an "inclusive" policy with regard to membership, it tended in practice to become "exclusive" with regard to its leadership. Dr. Harry Emerson Fosdick, acknowledged liberal, said in his *Adventurous Religion* (1926) that "the liberals are gaining ground, and if not stopped now, will soon be in control." His prophecy soon came true and the FCC lost its appeal to large segments of evangelical Protestants.

The Federal Council not only forsook strictly evangelical Protestantism, but it took on a neo-Catholic stance. Its approach to the solution of social problems became essentially humanistic. A "Social Creed" adopted in 1908 and revised in 1932 reflected a left-wing socialist philosophy. So far afield did the Council venture that in 1935 U. S. Naval Intelligence branded it as "radical," "socialist," and "pacifist." *Newsweek* in 1941 spoke of it as "a virtual monopoly" seeking to exert ecclesiastical authority over its members and restraining the freedom of non-co-operative denominations. Its public image was so revolting that thousands of conservatives withdrew. The liberals and moderates who remained in the Council began to realize that some new form of interchurch co-operation was essential if the fast-ebbing confidence of its constituency was to be maintained.

Under the leadership of Dr. Luther A. Weigle, of Yale, a committee was set up (1939) which adopted the strategy of merging all the major co-operative enterprises of American Protestantism, taking advantage of the confidence and status they enjoyed, and creating a single corporate agency which liberals could control. The respective councils involved were the Council of Church Boards of Education, the Foreign Missions Conference of North America, the Home Missions Council of North America, the International Council of Religious Education, the Missionary Movement of the U. S. and Canada, the United Council of Church Women, and the United Stewardship Council. After several years of high-handed ecclesiastical diplomacy, the National Council of the Churches of Christ in the USA was formed in Cleveland, Ohio, November 28 - December 1, 1950.

This move sounded the death-knell of free functional co-operation and instituted a system of ecclesiastical control and federative action in education, missions, social welfare, and other areas of church life. It created a growing liberal-controlled Super-Church which increasingly dominates American Protestantism.

National Council leadership vigorously denies its Super-Church status. If they did not, they would invite a wholesale insurrection from conservatives loyal to the traditions of their participating denominations. In due time, when the Establishment's brainwashing program has achieved its desired results, admissions can be made. Naive moderates and conservatives in parish leadership accept the present denial because they do not see any evidence that the Council is exerting governmental authority in their local churches; developing a new creed or liturgy; officiating in the observance of the sacraments of baptism and the eucharist; organizing parishes; establishing new churches; training and ordaining clergy; or doing locally any of the things usually associated with an ecclesiastical establishment.

What these naive people do not understand is that times have changed and that it is possible to have a Super-Church without the usual paraphernalia of traditional Protestant churches.

The modern Super-Church already in existence—

(1) claims no official authority over its constituent members although actually exercising that authority in subtle and invisible ways.

(2) has no detailed creed, because the Establishment has completely repudiated the idea that doctrinal unity is essential to centralized ecclesiastical government.

(3) makes no claim to apostolic or biblical authority since it repudiates both. It claims, rather, a direct relationship with the Holy Spirit which supersedes both.

(4) levies no financial assessments on local congregations, because its budget is underwritten by its constituent denominations.

(5) needs no members, because its central oligarchy rules through satellite councils and appropriate corporate bodies.

(6) does not baptize, for baptism is not essential to its membership or fellowship.

(7) has no liturgy or eucharist for the same reason.

(8) has no local churches or parishes because it can control all the local churches and parishes of its constituent members in all matters essential to its welfare.

(9) trains no clergy, because it supervises and controls all educational processes by which this work is done.

(10) does not bear the name of a church, because it is the channel through which the ultimate Ecumenical Church—One Church for One World—will be achieved. When that Church comes into full flower there will be no need for the National Council.

The National Council of Churches is not just a service agency or a federation of service agencies. It is definitely ecclesiastical in nature, authority, and program. It came into existence because (to quote its constitution) "in the providence of God, the time has come when it seems fitting more fully to manifest the essential oneness of the Christian Churches of the United States in Jesus Christ as their divine Lord and Saviour by the creation of an inclusive co-operative agency." It claims in its membership 34 denominations, comprising 41 million church members, 140 thousand churches, and 110 thousand clergymen. Its power may be noted by the affirmative response of its adherents to its pronouncements and the reaction it generates from those who oppose it.

ITS MONOLITHIC STRUCTURE

The Council is governed by a General Assembly meeting every three years. Each denomination is entitled to five representatives, plus one additional for every 100 thousand communicants or major fraction thereof. Then there is provision for additional members chosen by state, county, and city councils of churches. It is estimated that some 600 voting members can be constitutionally qualified. However, the much smaller General Board can do everything the Assembly can do except elect new denominations to membership or change the constitution and by-laws. The denominational and Council controls, checks and balances, action and interaction, are designed to allay denominational fears, but at the same time to deliver overall theological, educational, sociological, and political power and authority to the General Board which is dominated by left-wing liberal leadership.

The main functioning units of the Council are the Divisions, the Departments, the Joint Departments, the Central Departments, and Services. While much authority is given the various agencies, commissions, committees, and staffs, the General Secretary and the Vice-Presidents have the vote power to keep them in harmony with the liberal "party line."

The latest official listing of areas in which the Council operates includes: *Service Units*: Broadcasting and Films, Councils of Churches, Publication and Distribution, Public Relations, Research and Survey, and Lobbying. *General Units*: Church World Service, Evangelism, United Church Men, United Church Women. *General Christian Education*: Children's Work, Adult Work, Family Life, Curriculum, Leadership, Audio-Visuals and Broadcasts, Weekday Education, Religion and Public Education, Religious Drama, Camps and Conferences, Vacation Church Schools. *Higher Education*: Christian Colleges, Campus Christian Life, United Student Councils, Faculty Fellowships, Ministry, Student Volunteer and Interseminary Movements. *Missionary Education*: The Bible, Use and Understanding of the Bible, Lesson Syndication. *Christian Life and Work*: International Affairs, Pastoral Services, Racial and Cultural Relations, Social Welfare, Church and Economic Life, Worship and the Arts, Religious Liberty, Stewardship and Benevolence. *Home Missions*: Urban Church, Town and Country Church, Church Building, Migrant Work, Alaska, Indian Work, Home Missions Institutions, Missionary Personnel.

World Ecumenical Mission: Area Work in Africa, China, Japan, Philippines, Korea, Latin America, Near East, Southeast Asia, and Southern Asia; Christian Medical Work, Radio, Audio-Visual Education, Mass Communication, Rural Missions, World Literacy, Christian Literature, Personnel, Research, Union Churches. This amazing ecclesiastical bureaucracy grows with every passing year, forcing its tentacles of power into every conceivable area of church life. Always the philosophy in policy and program is unequivocally liberal and the personnel must parrot and act out the party line.

The following observances are actively promoted and very largely controlled by the Council: the Universal Week of Prayer, Church and Economic Life Week, Youth Week, Race Relations Sunday, Universal Day of Prayer for Students, World Day of Prayer, One Great Hour of Sharing, Easter to Pentecost, National Christian College Day, May Fellowship Day, National Family Week, Rural Life Sunday, Labor Sunday, Christian Education Week, Worldwide Communion Sunday, Churchman's Week, Men and Missions Sunday, World Order Sunday, Reformation Sunday, World Community Day, Stewardship Day, Share-Our-Surplus Week, etc. NCC news releases for newspaper, radio, television, and other public relations media are heavily weighted with liberal doctrines and propaganda.

The ramifications of the National Council now affect every sphere of life in the churches and in the nation. In its gargantuan influence it has gone far beyond an adventure in interchurch co-operation. It is without doubt a Super-Church the power and dominance of which are rapidly developing into full realization.

EDUCATION ITS STRONG ARM

Education is the National Council's strong arm. Through its

services for and controls over media of instruction and propaganda it is "brainwashing" American Protestantism and changing the course of thought and action in the churches.

Every conceivable branch of Christian education has been brought under the general supervision of the Council. To list only a few: Church Schools, Sunday Schools, Summer Camps and Conferences, Vacation Schools, Weekday Schools, Audio-Visual and Broadcast Education, the United Christian Youth Movement, Church Colleges and Seminaries, Ministerial Education, Leadership Education, National Denominational Executives, Directors of Christian Education, Professors, Pastors, Publishers, Research, Interseminary Assemblies, Curriculum, Newspaper Syndication, Bible Translation and Publication, and Religion and Public Education.

Council literature claims that it only renders "services" in these areas, but (to quote from an official directive), these services include the development of "basic philosophy and requisite programs" and the exercise of "such additional functions as may be assigned" by the divisional boards and division assemblies.

What is the basic philosophy which determines the nature and direction of the Council's educational programs in all the above areas? It is a humanism which puts man at its center, instead of God. It accepts a secularist, instead of a Christian world view. It sees truth as relative, never ultimate. It would secure freedom through lack of restraint rather than through obedience to God's revealed will. It sees intellectual and social attainment as an end, rather than the full-orbed life for the glory of God. While liberal educational leaders give lip service to Christian ideals they counsel objectivity and neutrality. They are crusaders for rational enlightenment and left-wing political action. They urge the claims of science, technology, power, and freedom of autonomous man above the clear teachings of God's Word as revealed in the Holy Scriptures.

In its service to Christian education in the local churches, the Council provides outlines for lesson study in the Sunday Schools and media for all curriculum building. Its curriculum craftsmen are committed to the doctrines of so-called "progressive education" which put the child at the center of the process rather than Christ and the Bible. They substitute "quest for truth" for indoctrination in the truth as revealed in the Holy Scriptures. They hold that "the new life" comes to the pupil as a result of the reconstruction of his experiences in a naturalistic environment. They emphasize the social aspects of biblical teaching and the building of a socialistic "Kingdom of God on earth," rather than individual salvation and a better world through Christian life and work. The NCC Department of Educational Development is the medium through which basic principles and patterns of curriculum are created. Some 200 educators are involved. Under Council leadership the enrollment of the church schools in America has steadily declined. There are now more children and youth without religious instruction in America than ever before in the nation's history.

Through the Council's Department of Higher Education it exerts massive influence over denominational colleges and universities. Each denomination, of course, has its own board or commission of higher education, but the Department frequently brings the heads of these bodies together and, through its staff, assists them in developing and projecting programs in harmony with the policies of the National Council. There are united campus programs for students, faculty fellowships, and other media for achieving liberal thought control. Much is said about "academic freedom," but it operates in a narrow frame of reference which excludes conservative, evangelical, biblical thinkers. Most institutions of higher education represented in the Council's constituency are committed to a left-wing social philosophy and have become breeding grounds for radical social action.

Only recently has the Council attempted to exert much influence in the crucial area of ministerial education. Now its department of ministry, vocational, and pastoral services is beginning to deal realistically with problems of seminary curricula, learning theory, research, evaluation, objectives, motivation, and long-range planning. It will not be long until the product of denominational ministerial training schools will be goose-stepping to the liberal ecumenical rhythm in theological education. But the Department is going even further. It is proposing a program of "continuing education for the ministry" with aims described as "personal, societal, and theological." Through the formation of professional societies, area training sessions, and regional ecumenical centers, the NCC clergy will be kept in line with Council policies and programs and directed in effective united action to achieve ecumenical goals.

Missionary education comes in for its share of Council control. The old Student Volunteer Movement, originally one of the most effective agencies for enlisting youth for service in the missionary task of winning the world for Christ, has been captured by Council leaders. However, it is a mere shadow of its former self and is being far outdistanced by evangelical agencies in recruitment of college students for mission services. Further consideration will be given this and other missionary problems in Chapter IV. Missionary education through the medium of literature is controlled by the effective Fellowship Press which produces books of high quality but with a definite liberal and socialist orientation.

Speaking of publications, the Council has an immense publishing program carried on by its Office of Publication and Distribution and through some seventy individual operating units. Each year many different types of literature, from small leaflets to casebound books, issue from Council offices. Its Office of Public Interpretation produces ideological publications, usually of leftist flavor. Then there are many periodicals that regularly spark Council programs and promote liberal doctrines. The

Office of Information spreads Council propaganda to the press and other news media through the nation.

The Bible is the most lucrative publication of the Council. Through special arrangements with Thomas Nelson and Son the Council maintains a monopoly over the Revised Standard Version. Income from this source finances many of the questionable ventures of the Council. Recently its Missionary Education Department has instituted radio, television, and newspaper programs in "The Use and Understanding of the Bible," which frequently reflect the liberal theological viewpoint and tend to undermine faith in the credibility and authority of the Holy Scriptures.

Reading lists are issued periodically. They act as a sort of *Index Expurgatorius* against conservative, biblical and/or evangelical literature. Sometimes these lists include books and tracts which are of a highly questionable moral quality, such as *Without Magnolias* which depicts an act of adultery between a Negro woman and a white man. The works of Langston Hughes, Victor Perlo, Herbert Aptheker, and W. E. DuBois, men with communist affiliations, have found their way into these recommended reading lists. This is not to say that many books of high cultural, philosophical, and ethical quality have not been recommended, but there is just enough of the dangerous and subversive to make the service of questionable value to the churches. (See pages 133-135.)

Finally, a word should be said about the Council's policy of opposition to the reading of the Bible and prayer in the public schools of the nation. Its Department of Religion and Public Education is responsible for this policy which plays into the hands of the atheistic, agnostic, humanistic, and secularistic forces at work in the nation to destroy the foundations of faith and morals in our social order.

This vast network of thought-forming media is full of dangers to American Protestantism and the whole American way of life as we have known it for 200 years. The Council therefore is an educational imperialism to be feared, opposed and contravened.

ITS LEFTIST POLITICAL POWER

The National Council of Churches has gone political in a big way. The radical alteration of the social order through political action appears to be its chief concern.

Its General Board in its Baltimore meeting in 1964 adopted a resolution calling on its member denominations to become more deeply involved politically. Said the document:

> Christian citizens cannot be indifferent to the denial of minority rights; to the impairment of the freedom of expression and religion; to foreign policies which could lead to nuclear warfare; or to policies that ignore our responsibilities to eliminate famine, disease, and ignorance in this country and abroad.

When the General Board met in Portland, Oregon, in 1965, most of its agenda was given to health, education, welfare, civil rights, and political action. The big headlines in the newspaper reports went to Dr. Colin Williams, executive director of the NCC Department of Parish and Community Life, who declared that Christian conversion without Christian social and political commitment can constitute "false witness." He branded churches that do not deal realistically (politically) with such major crises as race, poverty, changed patterns of family life, and urban decision-making as seeking "religious escape from Christ's demands." He called upon churchmen everywhere to shape a new revolution which would gear the Church to today's society. Throughout the meeting, God's "compassion and justice" found expression almost wholly in efforts to effect changes in the structure of the social order in the U.S.A.

This new jargon is only a smoke screen for something very

similar to the Social Gospel disseminated by Walter Rauschenbusch and his disciples fifty years ago. (See pages 36-39, III.) The modern version of this doctrine, and the one now widely accepted by National Council leaders, exhibits a definite trend from God to man and a collectivist trend from the individual to the group. In this situation there is increasing liaison between Church and State, and a growing conviction that if ever there is to be a Great Society it must come largely through government.

Dr. Ernest A. Gross, in a recent issue of *The Interchurch News,* outlined the ramifications of this politically socialistic policy throughout the organizational structure of the Council. It penetrates the Division of Christian Education and the Division of Home Missions, as well as the world-wide operations of the Division of Foreign Missions and the Department of Church World Service. Units within the Division of Christian Life and Work have important relationships to these sources of liberal propaganda, such as the Department of Racial and Cultural Relations, the Church and Economic Life, Social Welfare and Religious Liberty. The United Christian Youth Movement and the National Student Christian Federation, the United Church Men and the United Church Women have been infiltrated with left-wing socialist doctrines and harnessed to programs of civil disobedience and lawlessness in the name of social revolution. Putting all of this pattern together, the National Council has become one of the major political forces in the life of the nation. Effective lobbies are maintained in the Nation's Capital and in many state capitals.

Reams of political releases have been made to the American press, radio and television media of communication. The intimation always implicit in these releases is that they represent the view of 40 million American Protestants, when, in fact, more than 39 million of them were never even consulted about their opinions or convictions. When Council leaders have been faced with demands to justify their statements, all sorts of specious and hypocritical alibis have been offered to the effect that "the General Board has taken no official action." Nevertheless, the public is led to infer and politicos in government are led to believe that these are the political views of American Protestants. The following are a few of the public pronouncements that have been made in recent years:

Opposition to United States intervention in Cuba, Vietnam, and Santo Domingo.

Demand for U. S. recognition of Red China and her admission into the United Nations.

Condemnation of the House Un-American Activities Committee, the Senate Internal Security Sub-Committee, and the Senate Investigating Committee.

Approval of civil disobedience, participation in freedom marches, and law-breaking to promote social revolution.

Denial that the present struggle between the Free World and Communism can be viewed as a conflict between good and evil.

Opposition to prayer and Bible reading in the public schools.

Hostility to right-to-work laws in state and nation.

Repudiation of competition, free enterprise, and the profit motive in business and the approval of socialist economic doctrines.

Encouragement of the distribution of pornographic and obscene literature under the guise of advocacy of a free press and free speech.

Approval of racial intermarriage, sex freedom, birth control and flexible moral standards.

The most shocking of National Council political and social policies are those which condone or encourage Marxism. It cannot be accurately said that there are communists in the Council, but left-wing liberal leaders frequently follow "the party line"; and by their intensely vocal antagonism of right-wing doctrine intimate that the real enemy of society is not communism. In his most recent book, *Suicide of the West,* which brilliantly probes the liberal psyche, James Burnham makes it clear that "Liberalism is infected with communism in the quite precise sense that communism and liberalism share most of their basic axioms and principles, and many of their values and sentiments."

The close relationship of the National Council with the World Council of Churches, which is filled with communists from the churches behind the Iron Curtain, results in the necessity of entertaining delegations of communist-oriented churchmen. On these occasions naive Council leaders rejoice in the opportunities thus afforded to achieve what they call "the achievement of a united Christian witness unhampered by East-West political and ideological cleavages." Speaking of such events and also of the infiltration of communist literature from World Council lands, the late, eminent theologian, Dr. Emil Brunner of Switzerland, has warned American churches that they may well become the victims of communist socio-political propaganda in the name of ecumenicity.

During January of 1964, Czechoslovakian Professor Milan Opocensky, a self-confessed Marxist, toured college campuses in the U.S.A. presenting the communist line of "peaceful coexistence" and socialist endorsement. He was sponsored in this undertaking by the National Student Christian Federation, which is related to the Youth Department of the National Council of Churches. Scores of similar incidents could be cited which have been subversive of all that we hold dear in American social and political life.

It can be said without fear of successful contradiction that the National Council of Churches has no strong, clear testimony against Red communism, which is the world's most serious threat to Christianity and American democracy.

Every NCC constituent denomination is being asked to set up study groups and to carry the pattern of social revolution into its pulpits, its Sunday Schools, its various organizations, its press, its colleges and seminaries, its missionary agencies, and its plenary gatherings. Unless local churches and church leaders have the courage to stand up for the biblical, evangelical, and democratic way of life, and to "cleanse the temple" of this subversive propaganda, the Council will be able to achieve its leftist social and political aims in this generation.

DESTROYING THE FOUNDATIONS

To this point in our treatise we have dealt with the more apparent dangers in the National Council of Churches. But now we must come to grips with foundational matters — the issues that brought Protestantism into being and which are essential to its perpetuity and power.

National Council leaders have repeatedly denied that there is any theological significance in the affairs of their organization. They have until recently held that it is not appropriate for the Council to have a theology if it is to represent a variety of denominations with creeds of their own. It is apparent, however, to even the most casual observer that an organization cannot be a church organization without theological connotations.

When the Council was a complex of strictly Protestant denominations, it could be assumed that it held to the basic principles of traditional Protestantism. Such an assumption is no longer possible.

It may be well to recall the historic principles inherent in Protestantism:

Protestantism recognizes Christ as the sole and supreme Head of the Church and Lord of all.

It acknowledges the Holy Scriptures as God's infallible revelation of His will and the ultimate authority for the Church in doctrine, ordinances and life.

It teaches salvation by the justification of the individual and through faith in Christ.

It practices the universal priesthood of all believers and the right of private judgment.

It requires individual piety and the practice of social righteousness.

It emphasizes evangelism as the chief task of the Church and has sent its missionaries to the ends of the earth.

In its purest form, it insists on the separation of Church and State.

It promotes universal education, freedom of speech and worship, and all the larger freedoms which are the fruit of obedience to the will of God.

The only theological assurance given to the evangelical Protestant community that the National Council of Churches would adhere to the above principles is an item in its constitution which requires belief in "Jesus Christ as divine Lord and Saviour." This grudging minimal commitment is far less satisfactory than that of the World Council of Churches, which reads:

The World Council of Churches is a fellowship of Churches which confess that the Lord Jesus Christ is God and Saviour, according to the Scriptures, and therefore seek to fulfill their common calling to the glory of the one God: Father, Son, and Holy Spirit.

The National Council has dealt with the issue of the nature of Jesus Christ in the liberal theological direction. It has refused to speak of Him as God and Saviour or to move into the question of sin in either man or society, or into the doctrine of the Atonement. It has deliberately bypassed any expression of its commitment to the Holy Scriptures. The only clue to the theological stance of the Council or its leaders is in the actions of the Council or its various agencies which may express or imply some body of belief.

Most of the Council's pronouncements and actions are in the field of the social order. What do they reveal about its theology? A very definite liberalism. When a social issue is presented to one of its Commissions or to the General Board, it can be predicted ahead of time that their position will be liberal and leftist. Confronted with the necessity of giving some religious ground for their pronouncements and actions, Council leadership is being driven to the creation of a new theology.

At the July, 1965, meeting of the General Board in New York City, its General Secretary, Dr. R. H. Edwin Espy, told the representatives of the constituent denominations that the time has come for the development of a new Council theology. NCC's top administrator prefaced his statement by declaring that the Council has been consciously increasing its involvement in "the life of the world." This, said he, involves certain vague theological assumptions, but the Council has not expressed them in terms which the world can understand. Then he implied that the time has come for the Council to develop a theology of its own, over and above the theologies of its member denominations. It is interesting to note that the General Board, at its Portland (Oregon) meeting in December, 1964, asked for some kind of theological study of its secular involvements. No formal action was taken. But Espy, under questioning in New York, admitted that there was some kind of unofficial theological study already underway. This development will be watched with great interest.

Another clue to the theological stance of the Council may be found in the type of leadership it habitually chooses. In its early years it chose men like Harry Emerson Fosdick, Henry Sloane Coffin, Francis McConnell, and G. Bromley Oxnam for its key positions. Fosdick in *The Peril of Worshiping Jesus* said that "the divinity of Jesus differs from ours in degree, but not in kind." Writing an Iowa Sunday School teacher, he said, "Of course I do not believe in the Virgin Birth or in that old-fashioned doctrine of the substitutionary atonement and do not know of any intelligent Christian minister that does." This book could be filled with similar liberal declarations from each of those named above.

Today, men like James A. Pike, retired under fire as a Bishop of the Episcopal Church, dominate NCC leadership. The Bishop has declared his disbelief in the deity of Jesus; he scoffs at the doctrine of the Trinity; and boldly affirms that there are several passages in the Apostles' Creed which he does not believe. As to the Bible, he says, "The Church is not under the judgment of the Bible finally." His recent book is filled with views so leftist that it was a theological bombshell even to some liberals.

The Council no longer claims to be representative of American Protestantism. It has broadened its appeal to include all segments of Christendom and has lost its distinctive testimony for the evangelical Christian faith. Indicative of this fact is the following excerpts from a call to prayer by Dr. Samuel McCrea Cavert, one of the most ardent leaders:

Let us give thanks for the gifts and the graces of each great division of Christendom: for the Roman Catholic Church; its glorious traditions, its disciplines of holiness; its worship, rich with the religious passion of the centuries; its noble company of martyrs, doctors, and saints.

For the Eastern Orthodox Church; its secret treasure of mystic experience; its marvelous liturgy; its regard for the collective life and its common will as a source of authority.

For the Church of the New Jerusalem, with its insistence that the life of religion is to do good and that the Lord's Church is wherever men lead a life according to the precepts of charity.

For the Universalist Church, with its belief that all men shall in the providence of a loving Father God find richness of life and full salvation.

For the Unitarian Church, with its emphasis upon the freedom of mind and spirit to search for the truth of God, wherever it may be found.

There are still many thousands of thoroughly Protestant Christian laymen and ministers within the National Council, but they are increasingly unhappy under a leadership that denies the credibility and authority of the Holy Scriptures; that substitutes naturalism for supernaturalism; that prefers Freudian psychological treatments to the saving Gospel; that promotes a socialistic Utopia instead of the biblical Kingdom of God; that seeks truth in the vain philosophies and theologies of men rather than in the infallible Word of God. The hour is upon these Protestants when they must choose whom they will serve.

AND WHAT OF THE GOSPEL?

We also need to do a little clear thinking about the Gospel. It is one thing to say, "I want my preacher to preach the Gospel, not politics," and another to know what the Gospel really is. Some Protestants do not know enough about the biblical Gospel to be able to recognize the Liberal counterfeit of it when they hear it in the pulpit or read it in their church papers. The counterfeit is what is being used to brainwash Protestant churchmen into accepting and promoting left-wing socialistic and communistic concepts of a "better world" — the Kingdom of God on earth.

The proclamation of the Gospel of Jesus Christ for the salvation of lost and sinful men is the major task of the Church. With over 90 million in our nation unaffiliated with any religious body and for the most part strangers to the Gospel, a tremendous evangelical responsibility rests upon the churches of Christ in America. Add to this situation the fact that liberalism, humanism, and agnosticism have made appalling inroads within the churches themselves, and the conviction grows that the evangelistic task demands primacy in any vital interchurch concern.

It is passing strange, under these circumstances, that evangelism and missions are not dignified by division status in the structure of the National Council of Churches. Indeed, conversion of lost and sinful men is a concept that is looked upon with something akin to contempt. Bishop Pike, to whom reference has been previously made, has said that it is impossible to assert that "no one is saved except through the earthly Jesus Christ." He furthermore states that "the kind of god . . . who would limit salvation to a select group of people who happen to have heard 'the good news' and heard it well . . . is an impossible god. As to this god, I am now an atheist."

A *Time* magazine report (May 14, 1965) of the annual meeting of the NCC Commission on Evangelism in Atlanta, said, "Conversion, traditionally as basic to Christianity as prayer, is today a concept in evolution." The reporter then proceeds to draw a contrast between the old concept based on the Great Commission and the new idea being promoted by National Council leadership. Most quoted was Dr. Gerald Jud of the United Church of Christ. Among other things he said, "Old evangelism tried to get everybody in the ark. Today the church is trying to get the significance of God's love to people outside the ark." He held that it would be a healthy sign if the churches reported no growth whatsoever in numbers, but spent its time converting the baptized heathen in their membership — the millions of comfortable Christians who have no social vision and live by ethical principles no longer relevant to our changing times. Billy Graham's kind of evangelism came in for drastic criticism, and all revival-style preaching was condemned as ringing hollow in the ears of educated and enlightened people.

What has happened to bring about this change in an organization that used to enthusiastically promote "preaching missions" and talk about the "conversion of the world in this generation"? The fact is that National Council leadership in the field of evangelism and missions has lost its motivation for carrying out the Great Commission.

Dr. Harold Lindsell well states the motivating factors which for 2,000 years have made the Christian Church a mighty evangelizing force in the world:

(1) Belief that the Bible is the infallible Word of God;

(2) that the Gospel is centered in the atonement of Christ, His bodily resurrection and that every Christian is under orders to evangelize the world;

(3) that man is lost in sin, corrupt, guilty, threatened with eternal punishment, called to repentance, obedience and forgiveness of sin;

(4) that it is impossible to be saved through non-Christian religions; and

(5) that the Church is a redemptive fellowship which is separate from the world and the spirit of evil, but willing to identify itself with lost mankind for the purpose of evangelization. The thrust of Christian evangelism and missions involves proclamation (*kerygma*), service (*diakonia*), fellowship (*koinonia*), and teaching (*didache*).

On the other hand, liberals (1) disown an authoritative Bible, (2) make evangelistic theory God-centered rather than Christ-centered, (3) reject the idea that man is lost in sin and can be saved only by accepting and obeying the Christian Gospel, (4) see at the core of all creeds and religions a nucleus of religious truth and in the human soul an inalienable religious intuition comparable to the Christian faith, (5) accept establishment of God's Kingdom—a redeemed society—as the mission of the Church. Therefore, liberals believe that the primary business of the Church is the interpretation of the Christian religion in such a way as to renew and revitalize human beings and the fabric of human society with creative ideals and energies. They hold that the Church should be freed from the obligation of preaching a distinctive Gospel for the purpose of converting individual souls so that it can co-operate with all agencies (whether they be Christian or not) for social improvement and the building of a better world.

There are still thousands of ministers and lay members of

the churches committed to the National Council program who maintain their biblical evangelistic beliefs and practices, but their churches are being slowly but surely infiltrated and "brainwashed" by the liberal concept of evangelism through literature, visual aids, conferences, and study groups. The approach is so cleverly veiled with biblical words and phrases that the average person is unaware of the liberal poison which will inevitably destroy all conviction and motivation for the salvation of the lost.

Church growth is steadily diminishing among the major denominations affiliated with the Council. Losses are covered up in talk of mergers and interfaith co-operation. Drives for new church members in suburban areas, while resulting in "encouraging gains," when analyzed prove to be largely made up of laymen who switch denominational allegiances and amount to little more than "ecclesiastical cannibalism." Many churches in today's mobile America are so busy absorbing transfers that they are little concerned with the "forgotten man" who is perishing in sin and needs a Saviour. The tragic fact is that the growth in church membership in America is failing miserably to keep pace percentage-wise with growing population.

In striking contrast to this is the rapid growth of churches outside the Council orbit, such as those of the Southern Baptists and the rapidly burgeoning Church of Christ. Pentecostal and Holiness denominations report large ingatherings. Were it not for this amazing evangelistic surge, there would be little hope for stemming the tides of unbelief in America.

A word should be said about Christian missions — evangelism in foreign lands — sustained by the Protestant denominations in the U.S.A. Here the same blight of liberalism in the National Council of Churches is wreaking havoc. The term "evangelization" is almost synonymous with "humanization" in its vocabulary. The shockingly liberal philosophy of missions so effectively expressed by Dr. W. E. Hocking in his *Rethinking Missions* as far back as 1932 is now widely accepted. The

Ecumenical Movement is forcing the abandonment of denominational missionary work through mergers into regional interchurch bodies controlled by liberal leaders. Eventually all the old church mission boards and societies and their distinctive testimonies will be scrapped. The so-called "younger churches" and national councils of churches in foreign lands are taking over the work formerly done by American missionaries. The only relationship with America will be monetary. American churches will be expected to furnish "foreign aid" while liberal, left-wing nationals determine the policies and programs of the churches. So-called "confessionalism" will be destroyed and superseded by a nebulous "ecumenical theology" which is to emerge from studies and conversations now going on. Missions will be replaced by a comparable zeal for "one church in one world" and eventually for a "parliament of religions" in some sort of world socialist utopia.

Here, again, the hope for winning the world to Christ, by the preaching of the powerful Gospel of Jesus Christ and the salvation of lost and sinful men, is increasingly dependent upon those Protestant forces outside the orbit of the National Council of Churches. According to the latest official figures available, the American churches working through the Division of Foreign Missions of the National Council had 8,342 missionaries on foreign fields. In contrast, the evangelical Protestant churches outside the Council had 20,144 missionaries abroad.

In view of the rapid growth of atheistic communism and the multiplication of false religions, together with the attendant corruption and debauchery in human society, there is increasing need for the dissemination of the evangelistic message of the Cross and the spiritual renewal of the Church. The churches that are still committed to the fundamentals of the evangelical Christian faith and have the conviction that Christ alone is the hope of salvation for all men everywhere, need to move forward evangelistically with greater zeal and determination than ever, looking to God for the resources, the guidance, and the strength essential to accomplish His purpose.

SHORT CUT TO CHURCH UNION

The Liberal Establishment has recently become quite restive because the National Council of Churches has not moved more rapidly and effectively to become the great central ecclesiastical and political power structure it originally envisioned. Something drastic is now being done.

As a short cut to speedier realization of their dream Dr. Eugene Carson Blake, then Stated Clerk of the United Presbyterian Church in the USA, and the notorious Bishop James A. Pike of the Protestant Episcopal Church, conceived the idea of launching the Consultation on Church Union, outside the aegis of the Council but closely enough allied with it to assure its tacit approval. The 1960 NCC General Assembly was to meet in San Francisco. On the Sunday before the gavel fell opening the first session of the Assembly, in Bishop Pike's neighboring Grace Cathedral Dr. Blake issued a dramatic call for Church Union in the presence of a great audience which included all the top brass of the Council. The press gave it front-page headlines across the nation. All Protestantism was duly impressed.

After the Blake-Pike proposal was considered by proper denominational channels, representatives of the Episcopal, Presbyterian and Methodist churches met in Washington, D. C., in April, 1962. Here they officially formed the Consultation on Church Union (COCU) and laid the groundwork for the great adventure. Since then other denominations have been added to the original triumvirate upon invitation: The United Church of Christ, the Christian Church (Disciples of Christ), the Evangelical United Brethren Church, the Presbyterian Church in the US, the African Methodist Episcopal Church, the African Methodist Episcopal Zion Church, the Christian Methodist Episcopal Church and others.

In COCU's Dallas meeting (1966) a blueprint of the new Super Church was devised. Many compromises in doctrine and practice were proposed. A Report of the proceedings was issued under the title, *Plan for Church Union*, and formally presented to the governing bodies of the participating denominations. By COCU's next meeting (1967) in Boston, it became apparent that many obstacles and delays might block quick official approval. So another and more drastic short cut to immediate central power was proposed.

As this volume goes to press the strategy of the Liberal Establishment seems to be: Get approval of COCU denominations to create a temporary over-all central administrative and planning body which will draft united policies and programs and direct allied action until full consummation of The Plan is feasible. Under the new scheme there will be no immediate changes in denominational organization or personnel—only a commonly-accepted understanding that the central body will "call the shots." Revision of constitutions and by-laws, changes in traditional doctrines and practices will come much, much later, after the sheep have been duly brainwashed and conditioned for quiet acquiescence to the inevitable. Behind-the-scenes implementation of the new strategy is in actual process already, and previews of the system are said to be most encouraging to the Establishment.

FOREIGN DOMINATION DEVELOPING

The connection of the National Council of Churches with the World Council has implications which American Protestants need to carefully consider. The World Council, with headquarters in Geneva, Switzerland, was created largely through American Liberal leadership. It was born in Amsterdam, the

Netherlands, in 1948 and its structure was created in Evanston, Illinois, in 1954.

The Council began as pretty much a Protestant-oriented body, but as it has developed through the years it has tended to abandon Protestant principles. Eastern Orthodox Catholics are now in the majority numerically, and coupled with Episcopalians, Anglicans, and other political and liturgical cousins, dominate the WCC today. While the bulk of its financial underwriting comes from America, Americans are swallowed up in foreign ideologies, including communism.

The National Council of Churches is now but one of the many national units of the World Council which are being restructured into national churches that will eventually constitute the huge World Commonwealth dominated by a foreign hierarchy.

This is really the ecumenical pattern of restructure being followed to create One Church for One World. Some 500 theologians are now engaged in considering the conditions and issues which prevent church unity. More than 50 different kinds of unity talks are now going on in 35 nations (31 being conducted across confessional lines) looking toward the eventual creation of new national churches on the general plan of the new Church of South India.

The National Council of Churches is rapidly becoming an appendage of the World Council. There is a close relationship between the two bodies. Geneva, Switzerland (headquarters of the World Council), pretty largely dictates to New York the broad theological, sociological, and international political ideology which is passed down to American churches through the NCC. The great world confessional bodies such as the Lutheran World Federation, the World Methodist Council, the Baptist World Alliance, the Alliance of Reformed Churches Throughout the World Holding to the Presbyterian System, the World Convention of Churches of Christ (Disciples), the Lambeth Conference of Bishops of the Anglican Communion, and the

Eastern Orthodox Episcopate — all have significant relations with the World Council and have a regularly scheduled world conference in which their officials participate under WCC leadership. There are many American church bodies participating in these organizations which are not yet members of either the NCC or the WCC, which are slowly being conditioned to accept the idea of One Church for One World in terms of World Council devices.

In recent years foreign communist and Catholic influences have been increasingly felt in the World Council. With the entry of the Russian Church (50 million members), the Bulgarian Church (6 million members), the Rumanian Church (13 million members), and the Polish Church (400 thousand members), the Eastern Orthodox constituency in the Council was boosted to nearly 100 million. The Eastern Orthodox churches with 17 members on the Central Committee now constitute the largest confessional segment in the Committee, which is the authoritative policy-determining, program-making, and action-directing body of the organization. Coupled with other Catholic-type churches (such as the Anglican, Old Catholic, Coptic, Mar-Thoma, and the newly formed nationalistic ecumenical churches such as the Church of South India), this means that the Council has definitely broken away from its original Protestant anchorage and its Western heritage.

This brief survey would not be complete without reference to the official approaches being made by Geneva and Rome looking to the eventual unity of all Christendom. The Pope has designated the new Secretariat for Christian Unity, under the direction of Cardinal Bea, to conduct all phases of the rapprochement with Geneva. On the other hand, the World Council has designated certain official agencies to deal officially with Rome. Optimistic ecumeniacs prophesy that there will be union with Rome within 200 years. Whatever may be left of the Protestant testimony in the WCC will be, by that time, utterly lost.

71

American Protestants simply cannot afford to be aligned with the World Council and/or the National Council of Churches. Many are revolting against them for the following ten reasons:

(1) Setting themselves up as potential ecumenical ecclesiasticisms they have refused to adopt as a basis of fellowship the absolute minimum of basic evangelical Christian doctrine. They have committed themselves to the institutional concept of Christian unity and united Christian action.

(2) The Councils have admitted into their membership a host of "liberals" and "catholics" who are committed to theologies, philosophies, and ideologies which are definitely anti-Christian in the biblical sense.

(3) They have created organizations which to all intents and purposes are ecclesiastical oligarchies in which real control rests with a coterie of men committed to the above principles foreign to evangelical Christianity.

(4) The ramifications of the Councils are such that they are now functioning as a "Super-Church," bringing pressures and/or exerting controls over both member and non-member churches and denominations. Protestants are being forced to take protective measures to insure unfettered liberty in preaching the Gospel and carrying on their church programs.

(5) Their concept of the nature of the Church, the character of Christ, and of other essential Biblical doctrines is so inadequate and/or heretical that even tacit approval of it constitutes disloyalty to the "faith once delivered to the saints."

(6) They have adopted an approach to Christian unity which is un-Protestant, un-Biblical, and, therefore, un-Christian.

(7) They are seriously affecting the development of distinctly evangelical foreign missionary work and are secularizing and socializing the whole missionary movement in all the churches.

(8) They are encouraging leftist social revolution and the advance of World Communism through active meddling in national and international politics.

(9) Growing involvements with the hierarchies of the Eastern Orthodox Catholic and the Roman Catholic churches is destroying the distinctive Protestant testimony.

(10) They are deliberately omitting and shamefully neglecting to preserve and perpetuate within their corporate entities the values and liberties inherent in historic Protestantism.

III

A CRUCIAL ISSUE

PROTESTANTISM in its purest and best tradition has stood for the separation of Church and State. It has frowned upon the corporate presence of the Christian Church in political, economic and societal sectors of life. It has claimed sovereignty only in moral and spiritual realms. So crucial has this issue become in modern-day Protestant church life in America that it requires special treatment in a separate chapter.

Protestantism in its purest and best tradition has given primary consideration to the saving power of the Gospel of Christ in the lives of individuals. It has not been unconcerned about the social order. The greatest social and political progress in the world has been achieved in Protestant lands, but Protestants have held that such progress cannot come by Church-directed sociological experimentation, scientific exploration, philosophical speculation, psychological or political pressures while individuals are guilty of abnormal debaucheries, moral leprosy or degenerate lust. Advocacy of social changes and readjustments in human relationships is futile while the cleansing and renewal of individuals are neglected. Protestantism has held that it is a debasing credo which says that the individual does not matter, and that the saved-or-lost relationship with God and man is immaterial.

Protestantism in its purest and best tradition has stood for freedom. In America this doctrine has been demonstrated in many amazing ways. Edmund Burke, who spoke before the English Parliament in behalf of the American colonists, observed that they had a very deep sense of personal independence, and that the rootage of this individualism was their religion. "Religion," said Burke, "always the principle of energy, in this new people is no way worn or impaired; and their mode of expressing it is also one main cause of this free spirit. The people are Protestants, and of that kind which is most averse to all submission of mind and opinion. This is a persuasion not only favorable to liberty, but built upon it. . . . The dissenting interests have sprung up in direct opposition to all the ordinary powers of the world, and could justify that opposition only on a strong claim to natural liberty." Burke saw the American Protestant emphasis on liberty as spiritual in its roots and branching out into secular liberties beyond those enjoyed in the mother country.

PROTESTANTISM UNDER ATTACK

Today these basic Protestant principles are under fire by the leadership of practically all Protestant denominations related to the National Council of Churches. We are witnessing the brutal reality of a movement to build a centralized ecclesiastical power structure which has as its goal the mounting of a socio-political revolution for the creation of a Church-dominated Utopia. Planners of the One Great World State believe that if education and persuasion cannot bring men to bow to the yoke of the single sovereign aims of the Church and the State, then force must be used. The ecclesiastical planners see the possession of legally enforceable power, both temporal and spiritual, as the ultimate goal of the ecumenical movement.

The 1966 Conference of Church and Society, held in Geneva, Switzerland, produced the prospectus of this new world order. It is now being taught and implemented from the pulpits and

in the church school classrooms of American Protestant churches related to the National Council of Churches. The Report of
this important conference calls for political and social revolution and for the erection of a system of world socialism under
a supranational government.

In these churches, with total disregard for the principles and
laws of the Constitution of the United States, their members are
being taught that they should no longer seek to save individual
souls and improve individual characters, on the assumption that
good people will produce good government and a good society,
but that they should be primarily concerned for the structure of
society and become consciously and actively involved in politics.
In this socialistic educational program churchmen are being
advised that this political involvement will at times confront
them with situations in which the use of constitutional methods
of political action will not be enough and that the use of violent
or non-violent revolutionary action may be necessary.

Quoting the Geneva prospectus: "In cases where legislation
violates an acceptable constitution, and no speedy means of
legal relief are available, the Christian may be called to civil
disobedience (sit-down strikes, passive disobedience or deliberate violation of laws). In cases in which the constitution itself
is inadequate, the Christian is called to work for its amendment
in the interest of firmer guarantees of human rights. Where
such changes are impossible, the Christian may come to the
conclusion that he has no alternative but to violate the constitution in order to make possible a better one. . . . Laws may
be defied in the defense of the constitution, and the constitution
may be defied in defense of human rights." Moving from
relativism to confusion, then to anarchism and nihilism, the
Geneva document asks "whether the violence which sheds blood
in planned revolutions may not be a lesser evil than the violence
which, though bloodless, condemns whole populations to per-
petual despair." The document fails to explain satisfactorily

the exact circumstances under which revolution is essential. There is only the sweeping statement that this is so and there is no censure for professional anarchists and agitators.

Thus every effort is being made to transform the corporate Church into an agitating, propagandizing, lobbying political institution in support of a detailed program of social reform. The clergymen who are promoting this effort are guilty of initiating a new clericalism. Historically, clericalism was a form of political power exercised by the Church in Roman Catholic countries. So repressive was it in Europe that the founding fathers of the United States determined to bar it to America by the adoption of the First Amendment to the Constitution guaranteeing the separation of Church and State.

Clericalism has been defined by Dr. John A. Mackay, former president of Princeton Theological Seminary, as follows: "Clericalism is the pursuit of power, especially political power, by a religious hierarchy, carried on by secular methods and for the purpose of social domination. . . . The goal of clericalism is to exert a decisive influence upon the representative spheres of public life in the interests of the Church's secular power. Clericalism seeks to shape the policies of the State, the composition of government departments, the expression of opinion, the appropriation of funds, the forms of entertainment. The purpose of achieving this goal involves the use of pressures which are linked to subtle forms of intimidation where resistance is offered."

The new clericalism in America is based on a faulty diagnosis of the ills of society. Consequently it proposes the wrong remedies. Its chief remedy is socialism — the achievement of the good society by legislative action and administrative fiat. Liberal clerics utter their pronouncements with a "Thus-saith-the-Lord" finality and expect their naive flocks to comply with meek submissiveness to all their directives. They will not admit that there is any tenable position on economic and political matters other than the nostrums they peddle. This is an unfortunate situation largely because it destroys the inalienable right of free men to arrive at their own conclusions by reason, logic and intuition. Free men do not like to submit to the ready-made ideas of clergymen who are often totally ignorant of practical economic, social and political facts, merely because they have had a revelation from Above or some directive from National Council of Churches or denominational headquarters. Dr. Walter Judd, for many years United States congressman from Minnesota, put it this way: "I don't want the church working in politics. I don't want political action by the clergy and by ecclesiastical bodies. I do want political action by Christians. It isn't the job of the church to say what should be done. It is the job of the church to *change men and women* and send them into society and into politics to help change government."

The grassroots revolt against this action-centered political secularism is growing everywhere in American Protestantism. Thinking men and women are restudying the nature and mission of the Church as set forth in the New Testament and in the history of Protestantism. What does the record show?

The Church of the First Century faced a world basically similar to ours. There was a big government in the Roman Empire. There were the problems of civil rights, poverty, slavery, class discrimination and oppression of all sorts. Hot memories of the Maccabean revolt still stirred fanatical rebels to plot against Gentile oppression. The Dead Sea Scrolls speak of Bar Kochba, the revolutionist, whose uprising brought final destruction to the Hebrew nation by Roman armies. What was the stance of the embryo church in the midst of this situation?

John the Baptist came preaching the coming Kingdom. What sort of Kingdom? In his audiences were the Zealots, the freedom-fighters of that day. John made it clear that the Kingdom he envisioned was not of this world and that the coming Messiah was not a candidate for the throne of a new Hebrew state. Still the Zealots cried for political action.

At the beginning of His earthly ministry, Jesus Christ, in the synagogue at Nazareth, said, "The Spirit of the Lord is upon me, because he has anointed me to preach good news to the poor. He has sent me to proclaim release to the captives and recovering of sight to the blind, to set at liberty those who are oppressed, to proclaim the acceptable year of the Lord". At the heart of His ministry was concern for individuals in need. The same concern is reflected in Matthew 25 in Christ's description of the Last Judgement. When it came to dealing with the nature of the Kingdom He proposed to set up, He made it clear that it was to be in the world but not of the world. This was a shocking disclosure to the Zealots and all those who conceived His Messianic purpose to be the political restoration of the Davidic Kingdom and the destruction of Roman rule. Citizenship in Christ's Kingdom was contingent on a "new birth," so graphically described in His dialogue with Nicodemus in John 3. Christ's confrontations with the political forces of His time were marked by moral suasion and submission to authority, while declaring the whole counsel of God. When He became a victim of these temporal powers, many thought that His ministry had failed, yet the impact of His divine personality and His moral and spiritual teaching upon the political and social community was so great that nothing in the world was the same afterward.

Those who followed in His train adopted His teaching and His way of life. They preached a saving Gospel; they made disciples; they baptized, taught and trained them; they witnessed and practiced Christ's redemptive and compassionate love before all the nations. They made no appeals to political leaders for the settlement of national or international problems or the adoption of codes designed to bring universal peace. They did no lobbying for social legislation in the senate of Rome or the council at Athens. They organized no crusades or marches demanding the amelioration of racial, economic or political ills. They joined in no political campaigns and supported no particular messiahs promising new utopias for the underprivileged masses. Yet the world was literally "turned upside down" for God. The "Christian Era" in world history came into being as the natural result of the changed lives of individuals.

Then, in the Third and Fourth Centuries of the Christian Era a subtle change began to take place in the life of the Church. Church and State were wedded under Roman Emperor Constantine. Bishops fawned before his throne. The metamorphosis which took place is definitely comparable to that which is being promoted today by Protestantism's liberal clergy. Politics came to dominate the concerns of the Church and so obsessed the lives of its leaders that it eventually sought to control all nations. No ruler could assume power without Church approval. No king or emperor could be crowned except by a prelate of the ecclesiastical establishment in Rome.

During the Middle Ages, the Church sought to control the minds of men and there was little genuine progress. Every generation lived as did its forebears. The amount of food that could be raised set population limits. A large proportion of the people died in recurring famines. Few people went to bed at night with full stomachs. During those centuries there lived many great scientists, followers of Hero of Alexandria and Archimedes, and many others. These men had great minds. Had they been free to implement their concepts, they would undoubtedly have changed history. But when a Copernicus, or a Galileo, or a Leonardo da Vinci appeared he had to contend against authoritarian efforts of suppression. The Middle Ages, instead of being referred to as the "Dark Ages," might well have been considered the "Age of Enlightenment," potentially. But the Church exercised such rigid control over the minds of men, their lives and their activities, that it was impossible for great minds to accomplish their objectives.

Then, in the early part of the Sixteenth Century came the Reformation. Calvin, Luther, Zwingli, Farel, John Knox, and their contemporaries, left the Roman Catholic Church and initiated the great Protestant Movement. They believed that the Church should not bind men's consciences. They defined conscience as an attribute of the soul and held that neither the Church nor any other institution should interfere with it.

The unique characteristic of Protestantism, as visualized by those early Reformers, was that the Church should not become corporately involved in economic, social and political affairs, but that the true mission of the Church should be ecclesiastical. And so, thereafter, in the Protestant Western World, men were enabled to exercise their initiative, ingenuity, resourcefulness and inventiveness. Machines gradually came into use and with them labor was greatly able to increase its productivity. Starvation, which had controlled the population in the Middle Ages, was itself brought under control.

Luther, Calvin and other Church leaders of that day did not look upon themselves as reformers, but rather as restorers. They sought to restore the Church as it existed in the First, Second and Third Centuries — a Church that was patterned after the teachings of Scripture. As time went on, the new leaders of the Church were no longer content to adhere to the principles laid down by their Reformation fathers; rather, they sought more and more power over the lives and activities of the people. They did not hesitate to exploit the Church by forcing the State to enact laws that were in accord with their own ideological concepts.

This condition became so bad in Britain that in 1640, the English Parliament called together 121 of the leading biblical scholars of England and Scotland, and, after adding to this group 30 of their own most trusted members of Parliament, assigned them the task of determining what constituted proper government for the Church, based on the teachings of the Bible.

This group, known as the "Westminster Divines," held conferences which lasted for five and one-half years. Over 1,100
all-day meetings were held. In each of these more than an hour
was devoted to prayer. Many of the conferees came long dis-
tances, and the only means of transportation was by stagecoach.
It was necessary, furthermore, to leave their families during a
period of civil strife in order to do God's work. They truly
made great sacrifies, but their efforts were rewarded. The
completed documents — which were unanimously approved,
except for one vote — consisted not only of the form of Church
Government and Discipline but also the Confession of Faith,
the Larger and Shorter Catechism, and a Directory for the
Worship of God.

These documents laid down a pattern which has had a profound influence on Protestantism, both from the standpoint of
Church government and sound doctrine. Basic to Church government was the directive that synods and councils should
handle or conclude nothing but that which is ecclesiastical.
Basic to sound doctrine was the directive that the Church must
adhere to that which the Bible teaches about Christ and the
revelations of the prophets.

The Church has many responsibilities, but there are two
which are basic — one positive and the other negative. If the
Church violates either one of these basic principles, it will
destroy itself. The first of these is that the Bible, both Old and
New Testaments, is the infallible Word of God. This is the
positive responsibility. The negative is that the Church must
not, as a corporate body, involve itself in economic, social and
political affairs. Protestantism has always recognized the principle that Christians, as individuals, have the responsibility to
involve themselves in these economic, social and political affairs
for which they possess competence. The true purpose of the
Church is to regenerate man. To fulfill this purpose the Church
must restrict its activities to the ecclesiastical realm. The Westminster Divines were probably the greatest biblical scholars of

all time. No group has had such a clear vision of what constitutes the mission of the Church. It is a strange paradox that so many of the prelates in modern-day Protestantism cannot resist the temptation to use such spiritual power as may be placed in their hands in order to control civil affairs. Their present grab for power, if persisted in, will inevitably result in mammoth Protestant schism.

Revolt against the new clericalism grows every day. Publisher Clifford P. Morehouse, lay president of the Protestant Episcopal Church's house of deputies, recently counseled all makers of church polity and program to "guard constantly against the great danger of confusing their personal predilections with the will of the Almighty". Similar counsel, largely unheeded, has come from the highly-respected Dr. David H. C. Read, minister of New York's Madison Avenue Presbyterian Church, "I find that there is something incomplete, lopsided, sometimes even false, about the new activism in the churches. Renewal of the church does not come from new forms of social action, however necessary these may be. It begins within. A church that sets out to do the works of God, spreading into every area of life, yet neglecting the living center of belief, is doomed not to renewal but to decay". A Church of England theologian, after visiting a number of the largest and most influential Protestant churches in America, remarked recently, "I have observed an almost frenetic devotion to social action. It would be tragically ironic if the church, grown skeptical about God's power to redeem society by transforming human nature, were to fall into the same ideological error as communism and attempt to transform man by altering his environment".

The lines are being clearly drawn. Will Protestantism continue to hold that the Church is in the world but not of the world, bearing witness to the saving and transforming power of the Gospel in the lives of men? Or will Protestantism come to think of the Church as of the world and seek accommodation to secular power for the achievement of so-called "righteous ends"? If the latter, it means that America will move, with Church sanction, toward a command society, organized and operated bureaucratically, employing all the instruments of authority of the political State. Such a development must inevitably result in a world despotism which the Church will contend is "enlightened and essential to the realization of the highest hopes of mankind".

Is this what American Protestants want?

Millions of them are saying "NO!"

IV

REBIRTH OF THE PROTESTANT SPIRIT

AFTER MORE THAN three decades of destructive FCC, NCC and WCC propaganda, open and subversive, American Protestantism has been so weakened and discredited in the public eye that, unless a massive crusade for its rebirth is speedily initiated, it will die.

Such a crusade is already in its incipient stages. It has arisen voluntarily from the grassroots of our society and is growing by leaps and bounds. It will be the purpose of this chapter to give a broad view of this revolutionary development. The facts disclosed here cannot be found in the secular press or in the kept religious press. A knowledge of them should hearten every true child of God and give new impetus for renewal, revival and advance.

Every thoughtful and unbiased American must admit that the American Protestant spirit is the spirit that has made America great. We are surrounded on all sides by the fruits of strong Protestant insistence that this land must express God's ideal of freedom—political, economic, social and religious. That freedom must under no circumstances be circumscribed by any power, whether it be governmental or clerical. We must not let this generation or coming generations forget by what price our liberties have been purchased. Nor must we fail to sound the warning voiced by James Russell Lowell who, when asked by Guizot, "How long do you think the American republic will endure?" answered, "So long as the ideals of its Founding Fathers continue to be dominant."

It is in the spirit of this freedom that thousands upon thousands of American Protestants are at long last comparing the teachings of Holy Scripture and the historic principles of Protestantism with the pronouncements and practices of the Councils of Churches and the Liberal Establishment which controls them, and arriving at some revolutionary conclusions.

True American Protestant Christians are resentful of the "God is dead" agnostic and nihilistic theologies being preached from their pulpits and are calling for unequivocal loyalty to the Christ and the Gospel on the part of their clergy.

They are tired of having aspersions cast on the authenticity and authority of the Bible, which Chillingworth called "the religion of Protestants." They are refusing to accept the opinions of men unbolstered by the "thus saith the Lord" of Divine revelation.

They are disgusted with a Liberal Social Gospel which would create a Utopia by radical mass movements and political pressures. They want to hear again about individual salvation which changes and transforms men's lives and makes them fit for fellowship with God.

They are rebelling against a clerical domination which treats them as sheep, demanding their complete acquiescence in the distasteful programs of a Super-Church. They remember that Protestants have traditionally practiced the priesthood of all believers and held to the right of private judgment. They resent being lumped into a mass of faceless automatons and delivered by the Liberal Establishment as "in favor" or "not in favor" of this or that social or political position, without ever bothering to consult them or to get their approval. When they read in the press or hear over radio and television that "the Christian Church believes and declares to the world" . . .

something they know that millions of American Protestants do not so believe and declare, they are inspired to revolt.

This revolution is clearly discerned in (1) the refusal of whole denominations to join the Councils of Churches, (2) open schisms resulting in the establishment of new churches and denominations, and (3) the burgeoning unrest within the churches affiliated with the Councils which is expressing itself in many ways.

Reference to the 1965 *Yearbook of American Churches,* which is published by the National Council of Churches, reveals that the Council then claimed 41,341,466 members, 38,483,805 of whom were Protestants. This same *Yearbook* reported that there was a total of 66,854,200 Protestants in the United States at that time. Let us examine these figures more closely:

The church bodies claimed by the Council fall naturally into three divisions or groups: (1) denominations with strong centralized polity such as the Episcopal Church, the Methodist churches and the Presbyterian churches; (2) denominations which have a Congregational polity, and (3) Eastern Orthodox Catholic churches which have no Protestant heritage. Members of denominations in the first classification may be claimed as valid constituents of the Council. Members of denominations in the second classification may or may not be valid constituents, depending on the policies of local congregations. Members in the third classification are not Protestants at all.

Only by the widest stretch of the imagination can the National Council claim a total Protestant constituency of 38,483,-805. Let us examine the membership of the local churches in the first classification: Episcopal, Methodist and Presbyterian polity permits the ecclesiastical authorities to demand acquiescence of individual churches and members to the official position of the Church on all matters theological and secular. Despite this, many of their members hold that the denomination has no moral right to interfere with their freedom of thought and action in controversial social or political matters. They repudiate its right to implicate them in the policies and programs of the Council.

In the Congregational bodies, involved in the second classification, each and every local church is, theoretically at least, a wholly self-governing unit, holding title to its own church property and with authority to fix conditions of membership, choose its own ministry and arrive at its own conclusions on socio-political matters. It follows that in a strictly congregational church no member can be made a member of, constituent of, or in any way be forced to affiliate with the National Council of Churches. The NCC in claiming total membership of these bodies in its statistical reports is committing a fraud upon the public.

The burgeoning unrest in these Protestant denominations officially affiliated with the Council can now be understood in its proper perspective. This protest is very real, threatening the peace and unity of their respective bodies and weakening the influence of the Council as a vital factor in the religious life of America.

Now to the denominations which are unaffiliated with Council. Their revolt against it is of long standing. They made their choice when they were invited to join and have steadfastly refused to acknowledge it as having the right to speak for American Protestantism in any way, shape or form. Chief among these bodies are the Southern Baptist Convention, the largest Protestant body in the nation; the Lutheran Church—Missouri Synod, the most rapidly growing Lutheran denomination in America; the rapidly growing Christian Churches and Churches of Christ; the burgeoning Pentecostal bodies; and the continuing Congregational churches. To the many millions of members of these bodies must be added the membership of scores of other Protestant denominations, to say nothing of the millions of members of Christian Science, Mormon and similar bodies which hold conservative views antagonistic to those of the Councils. This mighty host stands in utter repudiation of their policies and programs. In this complex of the churches, all of which are growing rapidly, we are witnessing a rebirth of many elements of the American Protestant spirit. In later chapters we shall deal more specifically with their progress on what we choose to call the Road to Freedom for the American Churches.

Then there is a vast area of revolt which is very difficult to reduce to authentic statistics. Anyone who travels the highways or explores the streets of our American cities has noticed hundreds upon hundreds of new church buildings, many of them of magnificent proportions, which bear such names as Bible Church, Peoples Church, Baptist Temple, Christian Tabernacle and Undenominational Center. None of these has any affiliation with any traditionally Protestant body. They are free and independent assemblies of Christians, most of which originated in protest against the doctrines, policies and programs of local churches which had departed from the orthodox Christian faith or insisted upon co-operation in the subversive activities of Councils of Churches. Their total membership must run into the millions. Add to these the bare and unadorned store-front churches and missions in the underprivileged areas of our great cities and the plain little rural churches where remnant groups carry on the work abandoned by older denominations, and you have other millions who are reflecting the true Protestant spirit and striving, as best they know how, to perpetuate "the faith once for all delivered to the saints."

It is, therefore, evident that there are far more American Protestants outside the National Council of Churches than in it. (See Appendix A.)

In this Era of Rebirth God has raised up many individual

leaders who without benefit of official sponsorship by any denomination are serving the new-born cause of Protestantism with distinction. Outstanding among these is Evangelist Billy Graham. Beginning to preach at the age of seventeen this North Carolinian of Southern Baptist background became an associate pastor of the Gospel Tabernacle at Tampa, Florida, and later succeeded Dr. V. Raymond Edman as pastor of the Wheaton, Illinois, Tabernacle. Impelled to an evangelistic career he was first associated with Youth for Christ, drawing great audiences wherever he went. In a wonderful revival in Los Angeles in 1949 Graham first came into national prominence because of the conversion of many Hollywood starlets, figures of the underworld, and athletic heroes. Today Graham and his mammoth crusades have become the rallying point for the masses who still want to hear the evangelical biblical Christian message. He is easily the most popular religious figure in the world. Wherever he goes the largest auditoriums and outdoor stadia overflow with eager listeners. Multiplied thousands have accepted Christ as their Saviour and the Kingdom of God has been immensely advanced. He bears no stamp but that of Jesus Christ and accepts the support of all those who love the Lord. Thus the true Protestant spirit is visualized for all to see and imbibe. He and his work are a living demonstration of the fact that it is not necessary to preach another gospel suited to modern socio-political mores in order to appeal to the masses. Employing every modern medium for the dissemination of the Gospel—radio, television, the cinema, the press, etc.—millions are being reached daily in the ever-enlarging ministry of this man of God.

The revolt against the Liberal Establishment and the Councils of Churches is expressing itself in ways too numerous to mention. For the most part they are constructive and are resulting in advance in every phase of Christian life and work. A general survey will be inspiring and helpful.

CHRISTIAN EDUCATION

Protestants believe that Christian education is committed to a philosophy entirely different from that of secular education or Liberal religious education. It sees the first aim of Christian education as the salvation of the soul and, secondly, Christian nurture. It must be God-centered instead of pupil-centered. It must enrich the capacity of the pupil to know God and to live in accord with God's will. The Christian educational institutions must accept a Christian philosophy of education, have a faculty thoroughly committed to that philosophy, a Christ- and Bible-centered curriculum, a student body willing to accept this philosophy and its aims, and to apply the Christian truth and ethic in all their relationships in human society.

When the Liberal virus penetrated Protestant church-related schools and colleges the mind of man was exalted above the will of God as revealed in the Holy Scriptures. Modern naturalistic science committed to the basic theory of evolution came to dominate the whole curriculum. Truth was held to be only relative and its validity depended upon the student's ability to assimilate, corroborate and verify. Religion became merely an escape mechanism and was eventually eliminated from serious consideration as an essential to the building of the good life. All authority, both human and divine, was condemned and replaced by the view that "genuine values and tenable ends and ideals are to be found only within the movement of experience."

The ensuing educational revolt resulted in the founding of hundreds of new liberal arts colleges, Bible institutes and seminaries across the land. A restatement of the historic American Protestant philosophy of Christian education soon appeared in a volume entitled, *Christian Education in a Democracy*, published by Oxford University Press and edited by Dr. Frank E. Gaebelein. These new institutions, linked with

91

the very considerable number of church-related colleges, universities and seminaries owned and operated by denominations outside the aegis of the Councils of Churches, constitute one of the most hopeful prospects for the perpetuation of the true Protestant spirit in our American life. In Appendix C many of these institutions are listed.

New Protestant theological seminaries and Bible training schools are crowded with thousands of eager students preparing for full-time Christian service. New Protestant day schools under parish or Protestant-community auspices are being organized at the rate of hundreds each year where the failures of public education to provide essential moral, religious, social and economic instruction are glaringly apparent. The older Protestant day schools (Lutheran, Mennonite, Episcopal and Adventist) are strengthened by this development.

Christian education in the local church served by Sunday Schools, Bible Schools and Church Schools had become infiltrated by study materials filled with Liberal theological errors, social gospel teachings and subtle attacks upon the American Protestant way of life. The blight of this wave of agnostic and humanistic "brainwashing" movement resulted in loss of enrollment and failure to carry on the true educational mission of the Church. Then came the organization of the National Sunday School Association to take the place of the old Liberal International Council of Religious Education and the rise of many sound area and evangelical denominational associations. Many new publishers of Sunday School materials "true to the Bible" arose. Their literature began to displace Liberal studies. Courageous evangelical teachers and leaders virtually went on strike until changes were made. Many denominations began to take a new look at their Sunday School literature to root out dangerous trends and to strengthen evangelical Protestant testimony. The greatest gains in Sunday School attendance and membership came in schools where the Bible was again exalted as their chief textbook and American Protestant principles were again taught. It is estimated that today there are twenty-five million enrolled in such schools across the nation. A new development called "The Expanded Program" of Christian education for local churches gives great promise for the future indoctrination of the total membership of Protestant churches on all the vital issues that confront them.

CHRISTIAN MISSIONS

The massive advance in Christian Missions is undoubtedly the greatest in modern Protestant history. American Protestantism has been largely responsible for most Christian missionary work throughout the world. The famous "Haystack Meeting" in 1806 gave impetus to the movement in America. Every Protestant denomination soon had its representatives preaching the Gospel and winning converts in most of the known world. Then came John R. Mott's great idea of united advance to "win the world for Christ in a generation," with the famous Edinburgh Conference in 1910 inspiring unprecedented inter-church co-operation. While the goal was not reached, the missionary cause was vastly enlarged and effectuated. Then came Liberal infiltration and *Rethinking Missions*, the report of the so-called Laymen's Foreign Missions Inquiry, spear-headed by Dr. W. E. Hocking of Harvard. This was the blueprint for compromise with the heathen religions and the revamping of Christian Missions in the spirit of Christ's Great Commission into what is now known as Ecumenical Mission. Evangelism and individual conversion was to be replaced by liberal social action and a parliament of religions which would bring in the millennium. Practically all the major denominations succumbed to the well-laid plans of the Liberal Establishment. Today the missionary enterprise, as represented by the Councils of Churches, has shrivelled to a mere shadow of its former glory.

Then came the revolt. The Southern Baptist Convention and several Lutheran bodies pulled out of the conciliar organization. Many smaller evangelical denominations, such as the Christian and Missionary Alliance, with large missionary operations, took an independent stance. Many mission Boards split, with evangelical elements setting up new Boards, such as the Presbyterian Board of Foreign Missions. Scores of new undenominational independent "faith" organizations came into being, such as the China Inland Mission. The Evangelical Foreign Missions Association, with over a hundred denominational boards, was formed for mutual aid. The Interdenominational Foreign Missions Association, with an equal number of "faith mission" Boards, came into existence. Scores of unrelated missions burgeoned into being, such as those of the Churches of Christ, with over 800 missionaries on the foreign field. Individuals felt "the call of the Lord" to go out unattached; while there were a considerable number of casualties in such efforts, many of them developed into strong missionary endeavors.

Today there are some 20,000 American Protestant missionaries at work around the world outside the orbit of the Councils of Churches. (See Appendix B.) While the conciliar foreign program dwindles, that of the new groups spreads by leaps and bounds. A growing maturity marks the new movement. In 1966 at Wheaton College a conference of its leaders drafted a significant statement concerning the proper place and task of Christian missions in a changing world. They came up with a Declaration which will probably go down in church history as one of the great Christian documents of our time. It contained pronouncements on Mission and Syncretism, Mission and Neo-Universalism, Mission and Proselytization, Mission and Neo-Romanism, Mission and Social Concern, Mission and Church Growth, Mission and Foreign Missions, Mission and Christian Unity, Mission and Evaluating Methods, and Mission and a Hostile World. Every sentence rang with old-time Protestant missionary conviction and intelligently expressed the spirit of mission as revealed in the Holy Scriptures. To the mission leadership of the Councils of Churches, Wheaton spoke as follows: "Prove your case from the Bible. We will obey whatever the Scriptures command. Why quarrel? Why should schisms rend the Body of Christ? Let us agree to be guided by Scripture!"

SOCIAL ACTION

American Protestants have always been interested in the social implications of the Gospel. They give primacy to the saving power of Christ in the life of the individual and hold that the chief concern of the church lies in the spiritual realm. In their best tradition, however, Protestants have been leaders in the application of the principles of Christianity to every aspect of life. Yet they are not prepared to give *carte blanche* endorsement to the socio-political program now being promoted by the Liberal Establishment and the Councils of Churches. They do not want the church in politics. They do not want the church to promote left-wing socialistic doctrines and activities and to play fast and loose with the communist conspiracy in the name of Jesus Christ.

After taking an overdose of social action philosophy and propaganda from the Liberal Establishment and the Councils of Churches, there came revolt. The first significant protest in the true Protestant spirit came when the National Lay Committee of the National Council, under the leadership of noted Presbyterian layman J. Howard Pew, resigned in 1955. It said to Council officials that it was evident that they wanted no real dialog with Christian businessmen, rather they wanted them to rubber stamp their left-wing ideas. Said The Chairman's Final Report: "Throughout our Committee's term of life it repeatedly brought to the Council's attention the seriousness of the problems involved in its issuance of controversial statements and studies in the fields of sociology, economics and politics; and the inherent danger in speaking to official Washington and the United Nations General Assembly in behalf of Protestantism on matters outside their field and for which they possess no mandate." The Report further stated that "the political adventures of the National Council in the fields of economic and political controversy will seriously hinder and not further Christian leadership in the pressing fields of evangelism, fellowship and education." This massive 316-page document had wide circulation and sparked a resistance movement in Protestant denominations and local churches which is still gathering momentum. As recently as May, 1966, Mr. Pew had an article entitled *Should the Church 'Meddle' in Civil Affairs?*, in the widely-circulated *Reader's Digest*, in which he continued his fight to keep the Church at its main task—the salvation and nurture of the individual.

In almost every major Protestant denomination lay committees are being set up to study the social action pronouncements of Councils of Churches and to report their findings through proper church channels. In Methodist, Episcopal and Presbyterian churches this development is the cause of considerable controversy. An independent committee created by a group of laymen in southern Methodist churches, called The Circuit Riders, has alerted thousands in all denominations concerning the dangers of NCC socialistic and communistic propaganda. There will be greater lay revolt as the issues become clearer and the liberal pressures more provocative.

But there is a constructive side to the revolt against the social action program of the Councils. The National Association of Evangelicals is engaged in formulating a philosophy of social action based on an orthodox biblical theology in the hope that American Protestantism will resume its traditional and proper role as a mighty force for righteousness in the nation. The NAE conferees believe that nothing less than such a testimony will be adequate for the cultural crisis which has overtaken the Western world. They seek to give Christians a biblical perspective of the needs of humanity in a changing world and a kind of social justice to meet them—a social justice which is inherent in the revealed righteousness of a sovereign God.

COMMUNICATIONS MEDIA

All major American communications media are either closed or are quite lukewarm to any Protestant news, discussions, viewpoints or propaganda which does not emanate from sources approved by Councils of Churches. Traditional Protestantism has thus been forced to create its own media in press, radio and television.

At first these were distinctly denominational and not of wide influence in the nation. The first major successful attempt to produce a journal of wide American Protestant appeal was *United Evangelical Action*, published by the National Association of Evangelicals. While it has persisted and presents an attractive appearance, it has had neither the necessary funds nor the broad interdenominational support essential to wide acceptance. *Christianity Today*, launched in 1956, has become the acknowledged spokesman for traditional American Protestantism. It is published fortnightly and has the backing of a group of well-to-do consecrated Christian businessmen. In its first year it had 40,000 paid subscribers. It quickly moved ahead of the *Christian Century*, the sophisticated opinion-moulding organ of the Liberal Establishment—both in influence and in general acceptance. Ten years later *Christianity Today* had a paid circulation of 152,000 and was still growing, while *Christian Century* marked time and, in the opinion of many, began to deteriorate in quality and effectiveness.

In the wake of these two pioneer journals came *Eternity, His, World Vision, Christian Life, This Day, Decision*—all high quality publications. *Decision* is the organ of the Billy Graham Association and has reached the phenomenal circulation (for religious journals) of over 2,000,000. An older magazine of quality, *Christian Herald*, serving the Christian home primarily, has on occasion spoken out boldly for traditional Protestant principles and action. More will be said about the remarkable metamorphosis of evangelical denominational journals into publications of real quality. There is something of the "house organ" in them; in their very nature this must be, but by and large they show a growing concern for the issues and answers in American Protestantism.

In 1948 the Evangelical Press Association was organized to serve the growing number of magazines and periodicals that were committed to traditional American Protestant principles. It was the answer to the Associated Church Press which, while not officially related to the National Council of Churches, was controlled by liberal leadership and geared into the Council program. ACP conventions were sounding boards for liberal philosophies and social action. Today the Evangelical Press Association numbers in its membership 150 periodicals with a total circulation of around 8,000,000 and is still growing.

Answering the call of thousands of churches in the major Protestant denominations for Sunday School and Church School literature "true to the Bible," many publishers of trustworthy materials came into being. They have grown to mammoth proportions. Among them are Gospel Light Publications, Scripture Press, Union Gospel Press, Standard Publishing, David C. Cook, and many others that might be mentioned. Their materials have displaced liberal "social gospel" literature which is being forced upon unsuspecting congregations by denominations related to the Councils of Churches.

A new breed of book publishers uninhibited by the Liberal Establishment is beginning to produce a distinctly evangelical American Protestant literature. Among these are Eerdmans,

Tyndale, Fleming H. Revell, Zondervan, Baker, Crestwood Books and Moody. Denominational houses such as Concordia, Broadman, Light and Life are making a worthwhile contribution far beyond their borders. So strong has been the evidence of growing importance of the broader Protestant market that Oxford, Prentice-Hall, Harper & Row and other first-rate secular publishers are beginning to ask for manuscripts from conservatives. Maybe the Berlin Wall can be cracked one of these days.

Now, for a word about radio and television. When Dr. Charles G. McFarland was executive secretary of the National Council and Frank R. Goodman had charge of its radio activities (1929), an attempt was made to sign up the major radio outlets of the nation in an iron-clad contract which would give the Council exclusive control of all Protestant radio broadcasts in America. This was an attempt by the Liberal Establishment, in a land of free speech and free exercise of religion, to bar all conservatives from the air waves. It failed because of organized revolt in which the National Religious Broadcasters, Incorporated, took the field in a vigorous advocacy of free speech and won its case in the Federal Communications Commission. NRB now numbers in its membership over 150 nationwide broadcasters including the Hour of Decision, the Lutheran Hour, the Old-Fashioned Revival Hour, the Light and Life Hour, Showers of Blessing, and the Christian Brotherhood Hour. Multiplied millions hear the Gospel in the old-time Protestant tradition, varied in interpretation, but basically biblical and evangelical. The Lutheran Church—Missouri Synod pioneered in television and "This Is the Life" is now the most popular program of its kind in America. Much remains to be accomplished in securing recognition from secular networks for the traditional American Protestant position on vital issues, but a break is visible in this area of communications media.

AMERICAN YOUTH

The brainwashing of American youth through agencies controlled by the Liberal Establishment and the Councils of Churches is little short of tragic. The Student Christian Centers at the doors of State-supported universities and colleges are hotbeds of faddist theologies, the new morality, socialistic and communistic political action and every conceivable left-wing movement. The Councils of Churches are condoning such activities in their youth ministries.

There is revolt in this area. American Protestant churches are increasingly certain that this is not the kind of guidance the youth of America must have if the future of the land is to be preserved and perpetuated according to the principles which have made America great. The Inter-Varsity Christian Fellowship is one of the agencies which is being used of God on over 350 American college campuses to counteract materialistic unbelief, pagan social mores, and provide spiritual reality and relevance. It had its origin in Cambridge, England, but early in its history leaped the ocean and has become a mighty power for good among American youth. Many conservative churches located adjacent to university campuses are organizing to provide various services to students. Churches of Christ have nearly 80 so-called "Bible Chairs" in which college-credit studies in the Bible are offered and counseling services are rendered. A number of these have adequate buildings with social facilities. Beyond the college campuses Youth for Christ carries on an amazing program. It grew out of a sincere desire on the part of many American Protestants to combat juvenile delinquency. YFC took over Saturday night, went to the largest public auditoriums available in metropolitan areas, staged musical and cultural programs along with an evangelistic appeal and won thousands of young people to Christ. There are, of course, many denominational youth groups and the traditionally evangelical interdenominational Society of Christian Endeavor which reach hundreds of thousands of youth. Evangelical Protestant colleges and seminaries are reporting unprecedented numbers of young men and women volunteering for full-time Christian service at home and abroad. When the challenge of the Christian Gospel is adequately presented to American youth they accept it and are ready to commit themselves unreservedly and sacrificially in their Master's service.

In this limited and inadequate attempt to give a sweeping general view of the concurrent rebirth of the American Protestant spirit many worthy efforts had to be omitted. They are legion. This development is little short of miraculous and is only a portent of what it is to be.

There is unquestionably a "sound of marching in the mulberry trees" (II Samuel 5:22-25) and the Lord will honor his people if they follow his leadership instead of that of a spurious Establishment that would destroy all that Protestants hold dear. Fully convinced and dedicated Protestant Christians, who grasp the cause-and-effect realities of history and know that times of religious declension and apostasy have always been followed by revival and advance, are certain of eventual victory.

V

BAPTISTS FOR FREEDOM

BAPTISTS constitute the largest Protestant family in the world that has refused to bow to the yoke of the National and World Councils of Churches. There are, all told, some 23 million Baptists in America and they are expanding everywhere.

This might be expected of a people who place such a high premium on "soul liberty." Baptists recognize no human authority and subscribe to no human creed. They maintain that every believer has "absolute liberty under Christ"; as a member of Christ's body he has the right to interpret Christ's will for himself. Their emphasis on the sovereignty of the individual has made a strong appeal to the common man and to the socially and economically disinherited.

Roger Williams is generally credited as being the man who brought Baptistism to America. He established the first Baptist Church in Providence, Rhode Island, in 1639. Originally a clergyman of the Church of England, he early became a "Separatist" and ardently espoused the doctrine of "soul liberty." His political philosophy dealt a telling blow to the English kings and the bishops of the "Establishment." In the quaint language of his *Bloudy Tenent of Persecution* he says:

(1) God requireth not a uniformity of Religion to be inacted by any civill state; which inforced uniformity (sooner or later) is the greatest occasion of civill warre, ravishing of conscience, persecution of Jesus Christ in His servants, and of the hypocrisie and destruction of mil-

lions of souls. (2) It is the will and command of God, that . . . permission of the most Paganish, Jewish, Turkish, or Antichristian consciences and Worships, bee granted all men in all Nations and Countries; and that they are only to be fought against with the Sword which is only (in Soule matters) able to conquer, to wit, the Sword of God's Spirit, the Word of God. (3) True civility and Christianity may both flourish in a State or Kingdome, notwithstanding the divers and contrary consciences, either of Jew or Gentile.

Williams drafted a charter for Providence and Rhode Island which guaranteed complete liberty of conscience to all men. As an ardent advocate of freedom he exerted a deep influence on the development of the American Baptist political and social philosophy and the American way of life.

E. Y. Mullins, noted Southern Baptist churchman, stated Baptist distinctives under six axioms: (1) "The theological axiom: The holy and loving God has a right to be Sovereign. (2) The religious axiom: All souls have an equal right to direct access to God. (3) The ecclesiastical axiom: All believers have a right to equal privileges in the church. (4) The moral axiom: To be responsible, man must be free. (5) The religio-civic axiom: A free Church in a free State. (6) The social axiom: Love your neighbor as yourself."

SOUTHERN BAPTIST CONVENTION

The largest single Baptist communion in the world consists of those churches which are related to the Southern Baptist Convention in America. They have steadfastly remained outside the aegis of the National Council and World Council of Churches.

The Southern Baptist Convention is a fellowship of 10,772,-712 members (1965) in 33,797 churches. Organized in 1845, the Convention has co-operating churches in all fifty states. The members of the churches work together in 1,184 district associations, generally along county lines, 29 state conventions as well as through the national body.

In the United States there are 29 separate national groups of Baptists, many of them quite small. Together, however, they account for 93,591 churches and 23,659,403 members. Only Roman Catholics have a larger membership. Approximately one out of five church members in the USA is a Baptist. More than one-third of the Baptist churches and almost half of the Baptist members in the country are related to the Southern Baptist Convention.

Until 1940 Southern Baptist churches were in 19 states, primarily in the Southern and Southeastern part of the nation. Expansion west and north in the past 25 years followed the tremendous population migration of World War II. Today, there are 1,696 Southern Baptist Churches with 440,401 members in the eleven Western states. There are now across the North, from the Great Lakes to New England, 1,806 churches with 379,981 members affiliated with the Southern Baptist Convention. Today, the fellowship of Southern Baptists extends from Key West and Cape Cod to Puget Sound and San Diego, and on to the Hawaiian Islands and Alaska. There are now Southern Baptist churches and missions north of the Arctic Circle in Alaska.

In those areas of concern which come within the purview of our study, Southern Baptists have spoken out with sincerity, insight and conviction. From a statement issued by the Committee on Baptist Ideals on the occasion of the 150th Anniversary of the first national Baptist organization in America, we quote:

On Individual Freedom: "Baptists cherish freedom of conscience and full freedom of religion for all persons. Man is free to accept or reject religion; to choose or change his faith; to preach and teach the truth as he sees it, always with due regard for the rights and convictions of others; to worship both privately and publicly; to invite others to share in services of worship and church activities; and to own property and all needed facilities with which to propagate his faith. Such religious liberty is cherished not as a privilege to be granted, denied, or merely tolerated—either by the state or by any religious body—but as a right under God."

On Citizenship: "The Christian is a citizen of two worlds—the kingdom of God and the political state—and should be obedient to the law of the land as well as the higher law of God. If a choice must be made, the Christian must obey God rather than man. He should be respectful to those who interpret and enforce the law; and he should participate actively in the life of the community, seeking to permeate social, economic, and political life with Christian spirit and principles. The Christian's stewardship of life includes such citizenship responsibilities as paying taxes, voting, and supporting worthy legislation. He should pray for those in authority and should encourage Christians to accept civic responsibility as a service to God and man.

"The Christian is a citizen of two worlds—the kingdom of God and the state—and should be obedient to the law of the land as well as to the higher law of God."

On the State: "Both church and state are ordained of God and answerable to him. Each is distinct: each has divine purpose; neither is to encroach upon the rights of the other. They are to remain separate, but they are to stand in proper relationship with each other under God. The state is ordained of God for the exercise of civil authority, the maintenance of order, and the promotion of public welfare.

"The church is a voluntary fellowship of Christians, joined together under the lordship of Christ for worship and service in his name. The state is not to ignore God's sovereignty or reject his laws as the basis for moral order and social justice. Christians are to accept their responsibilities for the support of the state and for loyal obedience to civil authority in all things not contrary to the clear will of God.

"The state owes the church protection and full freedom in the pursuit of its spiritual ends. The church owes the state moral and spiritual reinforcement for law and order and the clear proclamation of those truths which undergird justice and peace. The church is responsible both to pray for the state and to declare the judgments of God as they relate to government, responsible citizenship, and the rights of all persons. The church must take seriously and practice the principles which it declares should govern the relation of church and state.

"Church and state are both ordained of God and are answerable to him. They should remain separate, but they are under the obligation of mutual recognition and reinforcement as each seeks to fulfil its divine function."

On World Relations: "Jesus Christ came into the world, but he was not of the world. He prayed not that his people be taken out of the world but that they be kept from evil. His church, therefore, is to be responsibly in the world but not of the world. The church and individual Christians must oppose evil and work toward the elimination of all that corrupts or degrades the life of man. It must take a positive stand for righteousness and work earnestly to bring about mutual respect, brotherhood, justice, and peace in all the relationships of men and races and nations. It looks forward with confidence to the ultimate fulfilment of God's purpose in Christ for the world.

"The church is to be responsibly in the world; its mission is to the world; but its character and ministry are not to be of the world."

Southern Baptists support some 25 colleges and universities among which are Baylor University, Mercer University, Oklahoma Baptist University, University of Richmond, and Stetson University. In their six theological seminaries there are some five thousand young men studying for the ministry. The largest of these institutions are Southwestern Baptist at Fort Worth, Texas, with some 2,000 students and Southern Baptist at Louisville, Kentucky, with around 1,200 men enrolled.

The foreign mission Board reported 2,070 missionaries working in 61 countries in 1965. During the year 213 new missionaries were appointed. Of all Co-operative Program (undesignated) funds for Southern Baptist Convention causes, 49.28 per cent ($11,123,505) went to foreign missions in 1965.

The home mission Board sponsors work in the 50 states,

Cuba, Panama, and Puerto Rico. During 1965 the missionary force grew by 148 to a new high of 2,520, with most of the personnel employed under co-operative agreements with state conventions. Work is done with language groups, evangelism, church extension, pioneer and rural-urban missions, Negro Baptists, chaplaincy metropolitan missions and others. The Co-operative Program provided $4,365,353 for work in home missions in 1965.

The Sunday School Board has responsibility for publication of literature and books. It seeks to develop and promote educational programs which are helpful to 8,000,000 Sunday school students in some 34,000 local churches. It operates the Baptist Book Stores and the summer assemblies at Ridgecrest, North Carolina, and Glorieta, New Mexico. The Board has 1,325 employees, 763 in Nashville. The trade name "Broadman Press" which appears on its books and brochures is increasingly honored for the quality of its publications.

State conventions issue journals with a total circulation running into the millions, such as the *Baptist Standard* in Texas. The editorial stance of most of these periodicals is conservative theologically, sociologically and politically and they have tremendous influence especially in the Southern states.

In such a free church situation as the Southern Baptist fellowship presents, it is only natural that the virus of Liberalism has succeeded in penetrating some of their schools and churches. In a few cases this has led to divisions and withdrawals. The most notable example is the defection of Dr. Frank Norris and the First Baptist Church of Fort Worth, Texas, and his followers in an "independent" movement that now numbers 500 churches, including Temple Baptist Church, Detroit, Michigan, which claims to be "the largest Baptist church in the world." Such churches are usually rabidly opposed to the Councils of Churches and exert considerable influence in grassroots areas.

THE "NORTHERN BAPTISTS"

The Northern Baptist Convention, composed mainly of churches north of the Mason and Dixon Line, was early infected with Liberalism. Shortly before it changed its name to the American Baptist Convention it became a hotbed of left-wing propaganda.

The major source of its troubles was the extremely liberal University of Chicago which began its career as a Northern Baptist institution. It was created by Dr. William Rainey Harper and backed by Rockefeller millions. Harper was educated in German universities and became a rationalist of the first order. He gathered around him a coterie of liberals who soon came to positions of prominence in all areas of Northern Baptist life. They brought great changes in the organizational structure of the denomination and in its theological and social views. They set up a bureaucratic system of church government which deprived the local churches of many of the freedoms they had hitherto enjoyed. George Burman Foster and Shailer Mathews of Chicago led the forces of theological liberalism and Walter Rauschenbusch of Colgate-Rochester Theological Seminary led the forces of sociological and political liberalism. They said, "The church must be institutionalized to serve effectively in a day of institutionalism." They insisted that "the fundamental conception of a minister's education must be changed from that of a man with 'the Gospel message' to that of a leader of a social group with a definitely religious and moral function." Harry Emerson Fosdick, pastor to the Rockefellers, became the popular voice of the Liberal Establishment and effectively led its forces to control of the Convention.

Northern Baptist Liberals became outstanding leaders in the old Federal Council of Churches and the National Council. The influence of Walter Rauschenbusch had much to do with the Federal Council's left-wing socialistic pronouncements. Rauschenbusch's book, *Christianity and the Social Crisis,* became the

Bible of Liberals in the field of the social order. His how-to-do-it volume, *Christianizing the Social Order,* pilloried capitalism and the profit motive and told how this "wicked system" could be replaced by a co-operative commonwealth. Norman Thomas, the Presbyterian preacher turned political-party Socialist and perennial candidate for President of the United States, once said, "The writings of Walter Rauschenbusch had more to do with making me a Socialist than anything which I read in Karl Marx." His classes in Colgate-Rochester Seminary were filled with eager young men training for the ministry. He inspired them to abandon the traditional Christian Gospel and substitute for it what came to be known as the Social Gospel. These men became the leaders of leftist social efforts which have become the chief concern of the National Council and World Council of Churches. Like Rauschenbusch in his later years, they rejected the transcendence of God and identified him with humanity. They thought of God as the totality of the strivings of humanity and of his Kingdom as the ultimate achievement of an earthly Utopia. Many Northern Baptist pulpits became sounding boards for this heresy.

Northern Baptist Liberals must be credited with laying the groundwork for the undermining and destruction of evangelical Christian missions in and through the churches related to the Councils of Churches. A number of them were on the Commission of Appraisal which published *Rethinking Missions, a Layman's Inquiry After One Hundred Years.* The Rockefeller family underwrote the expense of the venture. This report reflected the thinking of the School of Comparative Religions, advocated a social gospel and denied virtually all the fundamentals of the Christian faith.

A fine example of the leadership Northern Baptists contributed to the Council was Edwin T. Dahlberg. When he was president of the Council he was on record in the files of the U. S. House Un-American Activities Committee as being affiliated with or in some way related to twenty-five organizations guilty of promoting efforts subversive to the government. He not only favored the social gospel doctrines and programs of the Council but helped to form and implement them. He endorsed *Rethinking Missions* and worked to bring all the mission boards of Council-related denominations under the Council's liberal control. More advanced than many in his thinking about the mission of the church in foreign lands, he looked forward to the day when in a parliament of all religions a religious synthesis might be achieved as a basis for One Religion in One World.

Conservative Baptists like W. B. Riley, Curtis Lee Laws, J. Whitcomb Brougher, J. C. Massee, John Roach Stratton, A. C. Dixon, W. B. Hinson, Cortland Myers and others fought vigorously for traditional Baptist beliefs and practices but with little success within the Convention. Soon new schools began to arise. Gordon College, Northern Baptist Theological Seminary, Eastern Baptist Theological Seminary and other institutions began to train a new generation of ministers true to traditional Baptist distinctives. They grew in power and influence but they were unable to dislodge liberal control of the Convention and its related institutions. Then came a series of defections.

PROTEST AND SCHISM

Many local churches and area associations deserted to the Southern Baptists. Minnesota, Oregon and Arizona State Conventions withdrew to become independent associations. The Swedish Baptist General Conference, which had a close affiliation with the Northern Convention, withdrew. With its 40,000 members, its Bethel College, its publishing interests, and its foreign missions operation, it set up its own separate denomination. Today under the name of Baptist General Conference it has a membership of 83,000 in 550 churches and has found a happy inter-church relationship outside the Councils of Church-es with the National Association of Evangelicals.

Next came the split-off of what is now known as the General Association of Regular Baptist Churches. It adopted the tradi-tional New Hampshire Baptist Confession of Faith as a basis of fellowship and called all Northern Baptists to join them in a strong testimony for "the faith once delivered to the saints." Today they number around 155,000 communicants in 1,200 churches and are growing rapidly. They repudiated all ties with the Councils of Churches and found inter-church relations with the American Council of Christian Churches.

A still larger schism came in Northern Convention ranks when the Conservative Baptist Association of America was formed at Atlantic City, New Jersey, in 1947. It announced itself as an association of Baptists who regarded the Old and New Testament Scriptures as the divinely inspired Word of God and therefore infallible and of supreme authority; and each local church as independent and autonomous, and free from ecclesiastical or political authority. It called "any sovereign Baptist church" to join them in their testimony. Today the CBAA has a membership of over 300,000 in 1,550 churches. They have renounced the Councils of Churches. Many of their local churches find their inter-church fellowship largely in the National Association of Evangelicals.

Probably as large a number of Northern Baptists as are included in the three new Associations mentioned above have quietly withdrawn and set up new independent Baptist churches which have no central denominational organization. They are strongly opposed to the Councils of Churches. What has hap-pened in the Northern Convention is that about half of its constituency has separated from its fellowship as a protest against its theological, sociological and political liberalism and its centralization of ecclesiastical authority.

WICHITA'S DECLARATION OF INDEPENDENCE

Yet still within the fellowship of the Northern Baptist Convention are hundreds of congregations which, putting their trust in the Baptist principle of the free, autonomous local church, have withdrawn support from the Councils of Churches and refused to support many of the agencies of their denomination. Gradually they are being disillusioned regarding the existence of that principle any longer in the ABC. An outstanding example of such congregations was the First Baptist Church of Wichita, Kansas, the largest ABC church in America. Its recent experiences have startled the nation.

Preston D. Huston tells the story:

"As the American Baptist Convention departed from its original purpose, the First Church in Wichita and the Convention grew further apart, although we contributed most of our $50,000 annual missions budget through the Convention.

"Within the congregation the seeds of schism were slowly planted. They were watered and nurtured by the complacency of a congregation that had become self-satisfied with the luxuries that years of sacrifice had provided, despite numerous warnings from the pulpit.

"Several Sunday School teachers were permitted to teach beliefs contrary to the faiths and practices of our church. In a few instances certain individuals gained positions of leadership that more qualified persons had refused.

"This small group wanted a closer tie with the American Baptist Convention and the National Council of Churches. The majority favored following a course of self-determination which had been so successful in past years. Then a group of ten concerned men set out to study the effects the National Council of Churches and the Ecumenical Movement were having on the American Baptist Convention. With strong leadership from Pastor F. B. Thorn, who held true to the church's slogan, 'Famous for the Gospel,' the church remained united, but the coals of unrest began to smolder.

112

"On January 2, 1960, Dr. Thorn announced he would retire later that year. New leadership was to be sought. Which direction would the church take in seeking new leadership? The church Advisory Committee had the responsibility to seek out the new pastor according to the Constitution. This committee, composed of various church committee chairmen and organizational presidents, was dominated by leaders of the small group who favored following the course of the American Baptist Convention and National Council of Churches. Most of these people had gained positions of responsibility through default of the congregation who paid little heed to the beliefs and positions of the people they elected, accepting them only on the basis of their availability.

"On February 8, 1960, the ten-man study group made a report to the Board of Deacons on the National Council of Churches. This report concluded that the Ecumenical Movement as advocated by the National Council of Churches had had an undue influence on the American Baptist Convention that was not in keeping with the faith and practices of the First Baptist Church. The Report was published in a brochure entitled, '*Why One Church's Conscience Spoke Against the National Council of Churches.*'

"The group urged that a resolution be passed to withhold funds from the American Baptist Convention in protest of their alliance with the National Council of Churches. The outcome of this resolution would then determine the type of pastoral leadership to be sought. On March 9, 1960, the congregation voted 1170 to 235 to withdraw financial support to the American Baptist Convention. According to Baptist custom, the course for the future was set. The majority had expressed their will.

"Upon invitation of officials of the American Baptist Convention, First Baptist Church sent a delegation to the Annual Convention at Rochester, New York, on June 2, 1960, to explain their position and to find a solution to their problem. This opportunity was not afforded. Instead, the delegation was insulted and discredited as a group of 'isolationists' and 'fundamentalists.' The situation then catapulted into a national scandal with sensational news stories in the national press.

"On July 13, the church voted to sever all ties with the American Baptist Convention. They did this in the full belief that a local Baptist Church was a pure democracy completely autonomous and self-governing. On August 3, 1960, the minority group, encouraged and supported by the American Baptist Convention and the Kansas Baptist Convention, filed a law suit against the majority. Their petition demanded that property and funds be turned over to the minority and that the defendants along with anyone who 'was similarly situated' be restrained from entering church property and from participating in church business affairs. They held that the majority had departed from original faith and practices of the church.

"The stakes now were extremely high. No longer was the dispute over the American Baptist Convention and National Council of Churches, but it hit at the heart of the Baptist beliefs: *That a local Baptist church was completely autonomous, and that a majority of the congregation had the right to determine with what outside organizations the church would co-operate.*

"The case was heard in Sedgwick County District Court starting May 2, 1961. After two and a half days of testimony, Judge Howard C. Kline found that the First Baptist Church was an autonomous body. Neither the ABC, nor the Kansas Baptist Convention had any control over it; the majority had acted within their traditional rights. The decision for the majority group was a victory for Baptist beliefs.

"But the victory was short-lived. The minority appealed their case to the Kansas Supreme Court. Just a year later, on May 5, 1962, the Supreme Court reversed the decision and awarded the property to the minority group. In making their ruling, the Kansas Supreme Court departed from the transcript of the district court trial and found definitions more commonly used by churches governed by episcopalian authority. Nevertheless, the decision held and the majority group refused to take the case to the U. S. Supreme Court. Two and a half years of strife was already too much. The doors of the great First Baptist edifice—one of the finest in the Midwest—were closed to those who had dared to stand for truth and freedom."

Then Dr. Thorn was recalled from retirement in Texas. He led in organizing the Metropolitan Baptist Church, now affiliated with the Southern Baptist Convention. Three years and six months following the Kansas Supreme Court decision the congregation moved into a new $2,000,000 sanctuary in downtown Wichita. Its growth now calls for an addition of 62,000 additional square feet of Sunday school space, a new chapel and a fellowship hall that will serve 1,000 people at church dinners.

The former church home occupied by the minority of the old congregation sees only 400 to 500 people meeting in the great sanctuary each Sunday. A pall of gloom hangs over the virtually deserted structure during the week — a monument to liberal tyranny and super-church domination.

Anyone capable of viewing the Northern Baptist Convention and the American Baptist Convention over the years, without bias and in proper perspective, would have to admit that this sector of Baptists has had a tragic record of losses which have left it little less than a shambles. The blame must be laid directly upon the Liberals who have controlled its extra-congregational organizations and ruthlessly imposed their policies and programs upon their trusting and unsuspecting brethren.

NEGRO BAPTISTS AND THE COUNCILS

The major Negro Baptist denominations are related to the National Council and the World Council of Churches. The Negro bodies are the National Baptist Convention of America and the National Baptist Convention, USA, Inc. The former has 11,400 churches and 2,700,000 members; the latter, 26,000 churches and 5,500,000 members. Despite the large number of communicants, the great mass of the Negroes involved know very little if anything about the Councils and their workings, and care less.

But in the Council-related Baptist churches are to be found many outstanding Negro liberals loud in their advocacy of anarchistic ideas. As an example we find Adam Clayton Powell, Jr., pastor of the Abyssinian Baptist Church in Harlem, which he claims is "the largest Baptist Church in the world." He is listed in the files of the U. S. House Un-American Activities Committee as involved in the affairs of 114 organizations subversive of the American way of life. His notorious conduct is a matter of wide public information. Another noted liberal is Martin Luther King, Jr., pastor of the Dexter Avenue Baptist Church, Montgomery, Alabama. Despite the favorable world-wide recognition given him when he was awarded the coveted Nobel Prize for advancing the cause of peace, he has been responsible for stirring up untold inter-racial unrest and disorder and giving aid and encouragement to many illegal and anarchistic movements detrimental to law and order throughout the nation. The National Council of Churches, in its so-called "Delta Ministry" and other similar projects, has aided and abetted Dr. King and his left-wing associates in their mischievous activities.

OTHER NON-COUNCIL BAPTISTS

Out of the 30 Baptist denominations in America only five are related to the Councils. The limitations of this volume make it impossible to describe all of those outside the aegis of the Councils. We have dealt with the Southern Baptist Convention, the Baptist General Conference, the General Association of Regular Baptists and the Conservative Baptist Association of America. Among the others are —

The American Baptist Association with 3,150 churches and 655,000 members. This is a fellowship of independent missionary Baptist churches distributed throughout the United States but with their greatest strength in the South.

The National Primitive Baptist Convention in the USA with 1,500 churches and 770,000 members. While this organization was not formed until 1907 the Primitive Baptists claim to be the original Baptists in the South and the only fellowship of Baptists that has maintained all New Testament church practices unsullied by modern innovations. They have avoided setting up extra-congregational Boards and Commissions for fear that such organizations would spell the beginning of centralization of power and ultimately lead to ecclesiasticism. Each local church is free under Christ and the Holy Scriptures to carry on its work without any outside direction.

The North American Baptist Association with 1,450 churches and 174,000 members. Most of its constituency trace their beginnings to the earliest Baptist penetration of the South, but the Association itself was formed in 1950. The main tenets of this group are the verbal inspiration of the Bible, the premillennial second coming of Christ, the complete autonomy of the local congregation which alone has the right to carry on missionary work.

The North American Baptist General Conference with 325 churches and 53,000 members. These churches emanate from German Baptist immigrants of more than a century ago. Many of them are still bilingual in their ministry. Although scattered throughout the nation, they are bound together by a common heritage, a strong spiritual unity, a Bible-centered faith and a deep concern for Christian missions.

The Free Will Baptists with 2,000 churches and 170,000 members. Most Baptists are Calvinistic in theology, but the Free Will Baptists are Arminian. In the northern part of the United States they were organized in 1727 by Paul Palmer. In the south in 1787 by Benjamin Randall. In 1911 many of their churches in the north affiliated with the Northern Baptist Convention. The present body is predominantly southern, although it claims churches in some 38 states.

While to "outsiders" the Baptist family seems hopelessly divided, there are basic doctrines held in common theoretically which give hope of closer unity and co-operation in the days ahead. Generally speaking, Baptist associations and conventions have no authority over one another or over the churches. They are voluntary and advisory bodies designed to elicit, combine and direct the energies of those who choose to co-operate in and through them. Baptists believe that Christian unity in the New Testament sense is spiritual harmony. It may express itself in voluntary co-operation for common ends through a variety of groups which need not in themselves be made tests of fellowship. Should such co-operation involve violation of conscience or compromise of loyalty to Christ and His Word as revealed in the New Testament, they shun it. It is the latter Baptist principle which has caused such a tremendous reaction against the Councils of Churches. Baptists are unwilling to pay the price of compromise of deeply-rooted biblical convictions that would be involved in such an association. They have been traveling the Freedom Road for centuries and they are not disposed to leave it to blaze paths in the Ecumenical Wilderness.

VI

EPISCOPALIANS FOR FREEDOM

IN GOLDEN GATE PARK, San Francisco, there stands a huge cross, marking the spot where the first Episcopal worship service was held on American soil by the chaplain of Sir Francis Drake in 1579. The first Episcopal congregation was established at Jamestown, Virginia, in 1609, a decade before the founding of Plymouth.

American Episcopalians are proud of these historical facts which they proudly cite as proof of their part in the formative movements of religion in early America. They like to tell how many leaders of the American Revolution were Episcopalians, beginning with George Washington, who became first President of the United States.

While they were conscious of their Church of England ancestry and fully acknowledge their kinship in basic theological beliefs and ecclesiastical polity, they insist upon identification as an American Protestant Church. The first significant step that was taken in their break with England was when they applied to the Maryland Legislature for a charter under the nomen, "Protestant Episcopal Church." In Connecticut the establishment of the American episcopacy was initiated when they elected Samuel Seabury as their bishop. They sent him to London for ordination at the hands of the Archbishop of Canterbury, according to their doctrine of Apostolic Succession. But when the Archbishop insisted on his taking the traditional vow of allegiance to the Crown, Seabury refused and got his ordination from the nonjuring bishops of Scotland in 1784. The break was clear and the Protestant Episcopal Church of America has since maintained its freedom from foreign domination. Liberals have repeatedly tried to have the name "Protestant" deleted from its name but to date have failed to accomplish their purpose.

It was a long time before American Episcopalians became reconciled to the doctrine of Separation of Church and State, but eventually they surrendered all their traditional privileges. In the metamorphosis that took place in America, the *Book of Common Prayer* was revised as were the Thirty-nine Articles of Religion. They still reflected, however, the conservative Lutheran and Calvinistic doctrines of the Reformation. In the development and growth of Episcopalianism in the United States it has become a center of wealth, culture, social and intellectual sophistication of tremendous influence in the life of the nation.

Latitudinarianism is the distinctive mark of the Church in America. It has, like its English counterpart, permitted three widely differing schools of thought to exist in its clergy and its ecclesiastical institutions. There is the "Low Church" which is predominantly evangelical and tolerates no departure from the essentials of the Christian religion, emphasizes "Gospel" preaching, and recognizes the validity of nonepiscopal ministerial offices. It is out of this sector of the Church of England that the Wesleyan Movement came, the ancestor of the Methodist Episcopal Church in America. In their moral standards they are strictly Protestant. They seek the consciousness of the supernatural not only in liturgy and ritual but in the divinely-guided experiences of everyday life. Then, there is the "High Church," commonly known as the Anglo-Catholic, which contends that it perpetuates the ideals of Pre-Roman Western Catholicism. Its advocates maintain that spiritual development can take place only within the Church through the Sacraments. The *American Missal* which is widely used is reminiscent of

Roman Catholic thought and practice. The third sector of Episcopalianism is the "Broad Church" which minimizes doctrinal differences and seeks a rationalistic approach to Christianity. It partakes of "High" and "Low," accepting the principles of liberal theology as basic to the unity of the Church. Through its "comprehensive policy" the Protestant Episcopal Church can include in its membership churchmen of practically all descriptions: the ritualist, the formalist, the biblicist, the pietist, the legalist, the moralist, the ecumenist and the rationalist. Because of this policy non-Episcopalians are constantly mystified as to what the Church believes, but confirmed Episcopalians proudly boast that theirs is the freest of all the free churches in America.

THE PIKE CONTROVERSY

This situation may help explain how a man like Bishop James A. Pike could rise to the position of notoriety and influence he holds in the Episcopal Church today. He is unquestionably a member of the Liberal Establishment, which would control American Protestantism. His relationship with the powerful American press and other media of communication enables him, under the cloak of the Church and in the name of Jesus Christ, to undermine not only the American way of life but the Christian faith of multiplied thousands.

Taking full advantage of the freedom Episcopalians enjoy, those who are opposed to the Bishop and his avant garde views and actions have moved against him.

In 1965 fourteen Episcopal clergymen of the diocese of Arizona petitioned the House of Bishops to challenge his faithfulness to the Christian religion and his office. There was a riffle of interest but it was smothered by the United Press International and the Associated Press. These news services announced that Pike had been cleared of heresy charges when in fact no specific charges had been preferred. The House of Bishops simply failed to "challenge his faithfulness."

Then in 1966 twelve bishops related to the American Church Union, an Episcopal body dedicated to maintaining the catholic faith in the Church, appealed to Pike to resign. So great was the grassroots revolt of Episcopalians across the nation against Pike that he resigned as head of the California Episcopal diocese, but doggedly held on to his status as a bishop of the Church.

Later on, in 1966, Bishop Henry I. Louttit of Florida headed up a group of 28 bishops who were prepared to lodge heresy charges against Pike before the House of Bishops. *Time* magazine for November 11 outlined the Pike heresies which were disturbing the Church. They included repudiation of the idea that Christ is God, that he was virgin born, that he is one with the Father and the Holy Spirit in the Trinity, that men can only be saved through him, that his atonement is essential to salvation, that his resurrection and ascension were historical and factual events, that the Bible is the Word of God and authoritative in doctrine and life, that the creed Pike repeated every Sunday in divine worship is binding upon him. The House of Bishops, fearing a revolutionary upheaval the like of which the Church had not seen in all the years of its history in America, persuaded the objecting bishops not to force a heresy trial. Instead, the House (after cocktails) approved a statement of principles that denounced Pike's theologizing as "offensive" and "irresponsible" but not serious enough to warrant a trial that might wound the Church. The latest information we have about this tragic situation is that Pike is demanding a full-fledged trial in which he can air his views. He has threatened to go as far as the civil courts to get it. The secular press is egging him on and lauding him as the adventurous prophet of a new day in Christendom. Meanwhile, the cancerous growth of his Liberal doctrines is eating at the heart of the Church.

More than any other thing the Pike controversy has served

to alert conservative bishops, rectors and vestrymen to the dangers inherent in the Councils of Churches. Pike has been their darling. When the Liberal Establishment was ready to propose the merger of the major Protestant denominations into one great American Ecumenical Church, the Bishop invited Dr. Eugene Carson Blake into the pulpit of his Grace Episcopal Cathedral in San Francisco to deliver the call to action. The plan immediately took the name of "The Blake-Pike Proposal" and was so designated until the name Pike became more of a liability than an asset. Pike has been identified in some way or other with most of the left-wing theological, sociological and political pronouncements of the National Council of Churches. Now every time Pike's name is mentioned Episcopalians ask, "What is the matter with the Episcopal Church? Why don't we withdraw from the Councils?"

THE COUNCIL ISSUE

So hot did the Council issue become in Virginia that Bishop Robert F. Gibson felt compelled to give a whole page to the problem of the Councils in *The Virginia Churchman*. He expressed himself as amazed at the extent of the unrest and confusion in the churches. In a studied apologetic for the Councils he absolved them from all guilt in their left-wing proclivities and called upon his flock to practice the Golden Rule and love their neighbors as themselves. He met none of the questions being raised with convincing documented answers and left the impression that the Church could never be wrong about its policies and programs. But the local parish leaders all over Virginia began withdrawing financial support from the official church agencies and passing resolutions denouncing the Councils of Churches. Women began to cease giving to the United Thank Offering and sought other channels of charity where their gifts would not be used in a social gospel frame of

123

reference. Virginia Episcopalians in many places are in open revolt.

In nearby Washington, D. C., the vestry of All Saints Church, one of the wealthiest and most prestigious in the Capital City, cut its annual contribution to the diocese in half — from $11,880 to $6,000 — as a protest against Bishop Paul Moore's activities in civil rights demonstrations and other social action programs of the diocese, the denomination and the National Council of Churches. In a resolution sent to all other parishes of the diocese, All Saints' vestrymen said, "Our laymen believing in the separation of Church and State do not want our contributions to the Lord's work used to propagandize the controversial state subjects such as 'fair employment,' sale or rental of private property, and termination of our nuclear defense experiments while other nations proceed with such development. Nor do we approve use of church funds or personnel to foster public demonstrations or marches that tend to breed disrespect for law and order and the property rights of others." Instead of supporting such things, the resolution said, the church should devote its money to "increased efforts on fundamental spiritual concerns" that affect the lives of its members and condition them to act as individuals in the application of Christian principles to all of life. Despite ecclesiastical pressures on All Saints' vestry, which brought about some adjustments, the Church is restive and threatens to take drastic action if diocesan leadership does not respond to its warnings. One of the most prominent figures in Washington, an All Saints' layman, said, "We are fed up with the actions of our suffragan bishop and his allies in the Council of Churches. We don't like his activities in the name of our church in the Delta Ministry, in the Home Rule movement for the District of Columbia, and in strong-arm methods of correcting social evils such as war, poverty and racial discrimination. Furthermore, we do not want to be identified with pronouncements of the National Council of Churches calling for the recognition of Red China, the withdrawal of our military forces from South Vietnam, attacks on the House Committee on Un-American Activities, trade with Communist countries and a policy of 'peaceful coexistence' with those forces which would destroy us as a nation. If the Bishop continues in the course he is now pursuing, he will arouse passions worse than those stirred in former generations by disputes over theological doctrine and be guilty of promoting the deepest schism ever precipitated in our church and in American religious life as a whole."

REVOLT IN TEXAS

In Houston, Texas, the rector of St. Thomas Church, Dr. T. Robert Ingram, shocked his congregation and the whole religious community by coming out strongly against the policies and programs of the National Council of Churches. In an interview featured by *The Houston Post* Dr. Ingram branded the Council as "attempting to control American churches like a beekeeper uses the queen bee to control a swarming hive. The queen bee of the NCC is one-worldism," he said. "They are all the time talking about world unity, one-world government and a one-world church. Their line is indistinguishable from that of world Communism in many respects. With a ruthlessness comparable to that of the Russian commissars they are forcing American churches to go along on the party line. If you don't you get stung!" Dr. Ingram and his vestry withdrew St. Thomas from all association with the Councils of Churches — local, state, national and world. He realizes that the Protestant Episcopal Diocese of Texas belongs to the State Council and the National Council, but St. Thomas has served notice on the diocese that there is one parish at least that is unalterably opposed to such a relationship. Dr. Ingram has founded two successful parochial schools and has promoted elementary school sacred studies all over the state. He is using his ever-increasing influence to halt blind allegiance to the Councils by churches of all denominations.

Also in Texas Dr. Paul Kratzig, an Episcopal rector, has organized a Foundation for Christian Theology which will seek through "Chairs of Theology" and "Educational Missions" to "define and counteract the influence of humanism as a substitute for Christian belief." The Foundation had its origin with concerned Episcopalians, both clergy and laity, but it is now appealing to Protestants of all denominations. Dr. Kratzig says it has become a necessity "in the face of mounting political and sociological activity on the part of churches affiliated with the National Council of Churches."

He says further: "The conservative point of view frequently is criticized as 'being against everything.' We are not against everything, we are for Christianity as a valid pursuit completely separate and apart from the socio-political trends of this or any other era. Through this Foundation we shall seek to define this positive, constructive and creative approach to fundamental Christianity. We shall not be oblivious to the needs of people but we shall deal with them in a totally Christian perspective."

Dr. Kratzig is author of a new book entitled, *The National Council of Churches and the Social Revolution*, which purposes to show that this organization is motivated more by sociological and political concerns than by concern for the primary mission of the Christian Church, and that these socio-political concerns are indeed inimical to the Church's primary mission.

"The Church is destroying its effectiveness in the world and its mission by attempting to go along with the revolutionary trend instead of providing a strong and stable fort in the midst of a changing world," Dr. Kratzig asserts, adding that hundreds of letters received by him from all parts of the United States indicate a growing "withdrawal of support from the Councils both financially and in terms of actual participation."

REVOLT IN LOUISIANA

Probably the most significant revolt against the National Council of Churches among Episcopalians was that of St. Mark's Church in Shreveport—the largest, wealthiest and most influential in the diocese of Louisiana.

The action of the church in withdrawing from the Council and calling upon the diocese and the whole Protestant Episcopal Church to withdraw was based on a 10-month study and investigation by a committee appointed by St. Mark's vestry. The committee was composed of some of the most distinguished citizens of the state and included: Joseph L. Hargrove, oil consultant and partner in the firm of Hargrove Oil and Gas Company; Henry Linam, prominent Shreveport oil operator and former president of Standard Oil of Venezuela; Charlton Lyons, Sr., Shreveport financier who has long taken leading roles in business, political and civic enterprises; John M. Madison, an attorney, vice president of the Caddo Parish School Board and active leader in Shreveport civic and legal organizations; Charles T. McCord, Jr., owner of the McCord Oil Company, president of Wilcox Crude Oil Corporation, and active in many enterprises for the welfare of the community; and James A. Van Hook, prominent attorney, former chairman of the Community Council and active worker in civic projects. These men had not only served their own faith well but all Protestantism and all Christendom. Their names and reputations constituted a hallmark of all that is honorable and respectable in our national life.

Their careful and thoughtful work produced a 12,000-word report, together with a 16,000-word appendix. So trenchant, comprehensive and convincing is this great document that a digest of it is given here.

After giving historical and statistical data on the Council, the report showed how the body is controlled. It pointed out that the General Board of the Council is the day-to-day governing body of the organization and is composed of representatives of the various constituent Communions selected at the national level. Membership varies at intervals, as the result of fractional voting, but usually there are a total of 173 votes. An extremely small representation is required for a quorum (20 votes) to conduct business for the General Board. Consequently, a mere eleven and a half per cent of the total voting membership of the General Board, if it is from twenty-nine and a half per cent of the Communions, is a quorum and can conduct business. Only 11 votes are required for a majority of such a quorum. Yet actions of the General Board are publicized as representing all Protestantism.

The Report described the General Board as a body created through a somewhat "nebulous" chain of authority that has resulted in only two representatives, each possessing only a half of vote, for all Protestantism in the state of Louisiana. Those representatives both are members of the National Baptist Convention, U.S.A., Inc., in Louisiana a Negro denomination.

POLITICAL MEDDLING

On examining past positions taken by the General Board, the committee found that all of the following pronouncements were approved as "representative of Protestantism" with less than a majority vote:

An agenda of what the United States government should do as action for peace.

An official position on the use of nuclear energy.

A protest against too much secrecy in the American government concerning control of armament and the use of space.

A statement on ethics in industrial relations.

A pronouncement dealing with health services.

In one instance the NCC issued a pronouncement on technical assistance to foreign countries as representing American Protestants, after a vote of only 31 for. There were six dissenting votes and no abstentions.

On another occasion the General Board issued a statement on federal aid to education, claiming it spoke for American Protestants. This pronouncement is particularly significant in that it is the only one of about 40 studied by the vestry committee, in which a majority of the voting membership was recorded. The pronouncement drew 87 affirmative votes, just one more than the majority, according to the report.

Delving further into past activities of the Council, the group uncovered numerous other pronouncements on "purely political problems" such as ethics in agriculture, international aid and trade, immigration and permanent universal military training which it opposed. All the pronouncements were issued as representing the thinking of American Protestants.

The Report notes that the NCC always acts in controversial political matters on the general ground that they involve Christian principles. However, the document questions the "right," either moral or constitutional, of the Council to determine the Christian position in any matters of political, legislative or governmental nature.

The vestrymen point up that there is no question of freedom of the pulpit. But they declare that by its political activities, the NCC has carried political discord into the many facets of Protestant Christianity, "building fires of destruction under the tenets of Christian Faith, Fellowship and Charity."

DANGEROUS PROPAGANDA

Elaborating on other ways in which it found the Council "harmful and dangerous," the committee indicated that the size of the organization's professional staff is largely responsible for far-flung activities of the NCC. And they expressed the opinion that the staff is controlled by a "hard core" of professionals, many of whom have never served pastorates.

According to figures obtained from headquarters, there is a total of 6,000 NCC employees including executive and administrative officials and personnel of the various departments and divisions of the Council.

The report points out that the number of persons on the staff enables the NCC to produce a tremendous amount of propaganda — professionally handled publicity, speeches, reports, General Board and Assembly pronouncements. In addition, workers are available for lobbying activities such as appearances before Congressional committees, the vestrymen noted.

And all evidence indicates that the propaganda follows lines set by the General Board, although presented as representative of the thinking of 39 million American Protestants, they concluded.

Discussing the charge of Communism within the NCC, the committee commented that to its knowledge, the Council never has been listed by the four major governmental bodies which investigate such matters: the House Un-American Activities Committee, the Internal Security Subcommittee of the Senate Judiciary Committee, the Attorney General's Office and the California House Un-American Activities Committee.

However, the report lists the following examples of utterances and activities of the Council as closely paralleling those of the Communist conspiracy:

Abolition of universal military training, abandonment of military alliances such as SEATO, seating of Red China in the United Nations, limitations on the House Un-American Activities Committee which would destroy its usefulness, repeal of McCarran Act restrictions on immigrants which serve to bar entrance of Communists to this country, condemnation of literature warning churches against Communist infiltration, encouragement of Harry Bridges' Citizens Victory Committee, and the like.

The report further pointed out that left-wing economists are engaged in studies on such matters as "The Ethical Aspects and Economics of Defense Spending and Disarmament" and "The Churches' Role in the Conservation of Natural Resources" which are a far cry from the major concerns which should occupy the minds of church leaders.

LOBBYING ACTIVITIES

Turning to other areas of criticism of the Council, the vestry committee reported that the NCC participates in activities which can only be defined as lobbying. And they indicated that examples of such activities include official opposition to right-to-work laws.

Reflecting the opinion that the "hard core" of professionals in NCC headquarters has extended its influence into every branch of the NCC, the report lashes out even at the United Church Women. The organization is the sponsor of such projects as the World Day of Prayer observance held annually in Shreveport and cities throughout the nation.

However, the vestrymen uncovered evidence recorded in the Workbook for the Fifth General Assembly, December, 1960, to support their theory. Says the record:

"Church Women have unitedly supported action to give meaning to their concerns. Testimony has been offered on the extension of the Reciprocal Trade Agreement Act and foreign aid. Statements have been entered on questions of immigration legislation, appropriations for UNICEF, and appropriations for the support of the UN Technical Assistance program. In order to finance economic growth, United Church Women has supported the establishment of the Development Loan Fund of the United States of America, and the Special Fund and the International Development Association of the United Nations.

Resolutions have been adopted asking that the Connally Amendment be repealed . . ."

The Committee called attention to the fact that the NCC, when criticized for non-religious political propaganda activities, hides behind the contention that "actions of the Board commit no one." The report says this statement literally is true and is set down in the Constitution and in other formal actions of the Board itself; but the pronouncements of the General Board are presented to the churches and the public in a manner to give the impression that they are representative of the thinking of all American Protestants. NCC activities and Board pronouncements could not gain any volume of publicity in behalf of Christianity or political causes otherwise. What a quorum of 20 on the Board decided—or a minority of 50 or 75—would not be "news" for any communications media or of interest to many people. It is the embracement of "American Protestants" that draws attention to the NCC activities and makes them important in the public mind and to the news media. Such deceit and dissembling is vigorously condemned by the committee.

In the 11 years since adoption of that Constitution the NCC may have achieved some of its aims in the purely Christian religious fields, said the report, but it also has become a national and even international propaganda machine in controversial political issues involving baffling problems in constitutional and statutory law and statutes which have split Congresses, created deep schisms within both major political parties, divided bar associations, resulted even in reversal by the Supreme Court of its own previous decisions, and provoked basic differences of opinion in groups everywhere, including Church congregations.

The NCC has done this in the name of Christianity and Christian unity, yet obviously the more controversial an issue the greater the cleavage of opinion concerning it.

Thus, instead of fostering Christian love and unity, the

NCC's course has been one to encourage and breed dissension among Protestant Christians and in their communions and churches over political problems having no place in the worship of God. The end result has been to weaken the confidence of American Protestants in their own clerical leadership and to divide them against each other in bitter disputes even within individual congregations. The effect of the NCC in its political activities thus has been to hinder rather than to help Christianity.

READING LISTS

A particularly damning section of the report has to do with the reading lists recommended to the churches by the Council. Said the committee:

"In 1957 a pamphlet titled '*The Negro American—A Reading List*' was published by the Department of Racial and Cultural Relations of the NCC. It contained a Foreword by Alfred S. Kramer, who was then Associate Executive Director of the Department. It contained, in addition to the Foreword, an Introduction, a Reading Guide, a list of 'Some Other Helpful Materials,' a list of 'Some Race Relations Organizations,' an Index of Authors, Addresses of Publishers, and lists of books for Primary Children (pre-school and grades 1-3), Intermediates (grades 4-6), Juniors (7-9), Seniors (grades 10-12), and Adults. In the introduction one of the compilers of the list urged: 'Read for enjoyment and information, remembering to note publication date. Read aloud to your children, or put the books where they will be picked up. Make recommendations to your children's teachers and to librarians. Share your copy of this list with friends. Urge church, PTA, and other organizations to circulate copies.'

"The list is bad for two reasons. First, some of the books are of highly questionable moral background. For instance, the NCC in a letter to our Rector in December 1960 especially recommended to the Vestry Committee the book *Without Magnolias*, by Bucklin Moon, as being representative of the list in that it was trying to show the moral climate in which Negroes live. . . . If this book is a recommended example, we wonder what the rest of the books must be like. Vile language is used in *Without Magnolias*. It depicts an act of adultery between a Negro woman and a white man in New York City, not only without an expression that this was immoral, but in such a manner that it was condoned; furthermore, the reader is led to feel sympathy for the participants, who experienced no remorse or qualms of conscience.

"Another book, *Color Blind*, by Margaret Halsey, is written in acceptable language, but devotes all of Chapter 8, pages 89-120 inclusive, to the subject of 'Sex, Jealousy and the Negro,' with discussion included on relative sex potentials of Negro and White males. Regardless of what Miss Halsey contends—and the Vestry Committee is not dealing with that point—why should such materials be included in the recommendations of churches?

"The question raised here is not one of Negro or White morals. But why should a tremendous church organization recommend to its communions and their Protestant members the use and distribution of a book couched in filthy and pornographic language? If the subject should be on the reading list, certainly there are books that discuss it in language of common decency.

"The second basic fault we find in the reading list is a strange affinity found between the Communist conspiracy and the authors whose work is cited. Miss Halsey has been listed as a member or supporter of certain Communist Front organizations. The author whose works are most numerous is Langston Hughes, who was identified before a Congressional Investigatory body as an active Communist. He is the author of a blasphemous poem the very reading of which condemns him as not just atheistic but anti-God. He is a member, sponsor or signer on numerous Communist fronts, on subversive committees and organizations.

"Another author is Victor Perlo whose book, *The Negro in Southern Agriculture*—recommended on this list—was published by International Publishers, the Communist Party's major publishing firm in this country. The Senate International Security Subcommittee describes him as 'an open propagandist for Soviet World conspiracy.'

"Herbert Aptheker wrote the recommended *A Documentary History of the Negro People in the United States*. He stated before the Subversives Activities Control Board in 1952 that he joined the Communist Party in 1939 and that the Soviet Union and Red China were on the side of peace but that he believed the Government of the United States was the center of war danger in the world.

"*Black Reconstruction*, by W. E. B. DuBois, was recommended. DuBois has long been actively associated with Communist organizations. In Peking, on the occasion of his 91st birthday, he was given a testimonial dinner by Vice Premier Chen Yi, at which he heaped praise upon Red China. For this occasion he, too, wrote a blasphemous poem, 'I Sing to China.' You will do well to read it if you are to understand our charge that these authors are out of place for Christian thinking and education."

Studies of lesser scope have been made by Episcopal churches in Arizona, Texas, South Carolina, Virginia and other states. This unrest is spreading throughout the nation and indicates that Episcopalians are taking a hard look at the Road to Freedom and emancipation from subservience to "kept" bishops and from the politically oriented hierarchy of the growing Super-Church. There is a deep desire for a return to the main business of the Church and the task it was founded to accomplish under Christ.

VII

METHODISTS FOR FREEDOM

THE METHODIST CHURCH is the mighty spearhead of Liberalism in American Protestantism. Out of this denomination came the blueprint for the National Council of Churches and the World Council, the inspiration and the basic principles for their leftist socio-political policies and programs, and their theological imperspicuity ranging all the way from the "personalism" of Borden Parker Bowne to the "God-is-deadism" of Thomas J. J. Altizer.

METHODISTS AND FREEDOM

It was not always so with Methodism. English John Wesley, its founder, while committed to a certain mysticism, enthusiasm and latitudinarianism, strongly urged the reading of the Scriptures, conversations, prayer and sound doctrinal preaching. He gave great prominence to moral discipline. English Methodism early developed a constitution and body of laws which governed the faith and life of the individual and the ritual and organizational procedure of local congregations and conferences. Wesley's idea of freedom was so strongly imbedded in his movement that it early led to Methodism's break with the Established Church. He insisted that the Christian is a free man and more or less the master of his own destiny within the Bible's ethical injunctions and the obligation he owes to his sovereign Lord. Pietism even to the point of perfectionism set goals of human behavior for Methodists far in advance of those held by most Protestants. Through personal conversion and holiness Methodism made a tremendous impact upon the social order, reducing the incidence of such social ills of English society as crime, intemperance, slavery and child labor.

Freedom was originally the hallmark of American Methodism. Wesley, completely ignoring Anglican ecclesiastical procedure, ordained ministers for the colonies, appointed Thomas Coke and Francis Asbury as superintendents, prepared a liturgy and articles of faith, and declared American Methodists free and independent of all Anglican hierarchal control. By the free expression of some sixty lay ministers in Baltimore in 1784 Wesley's actions were approved and the church was formally constituted. By means of the remarkably free ministry of the "circuit riders," permitting traveling preachers to hold revivals and establish new societies wherever they were "led by the Spirit," early Methodism spread more rapidly than any other religious movement in America.

When hierarchally-minded Francis Asbury and his like-minded successors began to impose arbitrary ecclesiastical controls over ministers and congregations there were various revolts on the part of the Republican Methodists, the Methodist Protestants, the United Brethren, the Evangelicals and the Negro Methodists. When the Civil War came, Southern Methodists withdrew and set up their own denomination.

GROWTH OF LIBERAL TYRANNY

Since 1939, however, Methodists in America have moved to become a unified church. Negotiations began which eventuated in the union of the Northern and Southern Methodists, the Methodist Protestants and the Evangelical United Brethren. Union overtures have been made to Negro Methodist bodies.

Along with these mergers have come greater restrictions on ministers and congregations so that an Episcopalian bishop remarked not long ago, "Only the Roman Catholic Church has a more autocratic church government than the Methodists." This control by a central ecclesiastical establishment has been responsible for much of the unrest that characterizes American Methodists today. It prevents any possibility of biblical reform within the churches and forces dissidents to leave its ranks to rectify the wrongs they would protest.

This central ecclesiastical establishment came under domination by Liberals beginning with a meeting of a small group of "modernists" in Boston early in the twentieth century. They agreed to work together for the liberalizing of the denomination. A four-point program was accepted: (1) place a rationalist in every chair of English Bible in the various church colleges; (2) liberalize the Book Concern; (3) liberalize the church rituals; (4) liberalize the approved Course of Study for the training of the ministry. Strongly evangelical Bishop Thomas B. Neeley said of this program:

> There is an anti-Methodist school of thought working through a few aggressive individuals to compel the Church to accept its views and, at the present time, to accomplish this without constitutionally changing the Articles of Religion or other standards of doctrine. The method is not that of frontal or open attack but of the sapper and the miner.

This strategy was overwhelmingly successful. In a generation the denomination was firmly in the control of liberals. Every Methodist college and university was in their hands. The Sunday School board had eliminated all its old evangelical leadership and was sending its emissaries to every conference in the land, spreading the new educational philosophy. Exerting its influence in the production of Sunday School literature in the Book Concern, liberalism was able to reach and mis-teach the many millions of children and youth in Methodist Sunday

Schools. Anti-Methodist doctrine soon began to appear in the books bearing the imprint of the official denominational publishing house. The Foreign Missions board was taken over and the evangelical missionary testimony of this great church was soon a thing of the past. Finally, through political manipulation, the Bishopric came under liberal domination and the whole episcopal framework of the Church down through district superintendents began to operate to the embarrassment of every evangelical minister. This was made possible through hand-picked Conference delegates chosen from graduates of liberal Methodist colleges. A large evangelical constituency remained in the denomination, especially among the rank-and-file of the membership, but they were the "unvoiced millions" helpless and hopeless when it came to dealing with the ecclesiastical machine.

No other American denomination supported the "social gospel" more wholeheartedly than the Methodist Church. It abandoned the idea of individual salvation from sin and turned toward the amelioration of the ills of society by means of legislation and ecclesiastical social action.

SOCIALISM AMONG THE METHODISTS

Dr. Harry F. Ward of Boston University sparked the organization of the Methodist Federation for Social Service—as it was originally called—an unofficial but powerful adjunct of the Methodist Church founded in 1907. Ward worked closely with the Communist party and its leaders for many years and wrote frequently for the party's official organ, the *Daily Worker*. He visited the Communist leaders in Russia and received advice from them as to the most effective methods of infiltrating American churches with Red propaganda. As an early chairman of the Civil Liberties Union he urged that Communists be seated on the ALCU Board of Directors. When he was voted down, he resigned to devote his time to the Civil Rights Congress, the legal defense arm of the Communist party in the USA. The Federation soon became the center of intense controversy in the Methodist Church. It became an official agency of Methodism in 1916, later changing its name to the Methodist Federation for Social Action. Bishops Francis J. McConnell and G. Bromley Oxnam (both with long records of support for left-wing organizations branded subversive of the United States government by the House Un-American Activities Committee) were the most active in their defense of Ward and his Federation. Oxnam in particular, who got his university training under Ward, called him "one of the greatest leaders in the new world industrial, social and economic planning movement." Ward and the Federation were finally so discredited in the minds of the American people as a whole that the Methodist Church had to disavow its relationship with them, although the present official Board of Christian Social Concerns of the Methodist Church continues to reflect their "party line."

It is interesting to note that Harry Ward's draft of a "Social Creed for Methodists" was adopted by the denomination in 1912 and later, through Bishop Oxnam's influence, formed the basis for the Social Creed of the Federal Council of Churches (now the National Council). It is said that when Ward on a visit to Soviet Russia showed the first draft of his Creed to Lenin the great Marxian Socialist approved it heartily as a first step toward Communist take-over of the USA. The Creed, as adopted by the Methodist Church, reads:

We stand for equal rights and complete justice for all men in all stations of life; for the principle of conciliation and arbitration in industrial dissensions; for the protection of the worker from dangerous machinery, occupational diseases, injuries and mortality; for the abolition of child labor; for such regulation of the conditions of labor for women as shall safeguard the physical and moral health of the community; for the suppression of the sweating system; for the gradual and reasonable reduction of the hours of labor to the lowest practical point, with work for all; and for that degree of leisure for all which is the condition of the highest human life; for a release from employment one day in seven; for a living wage in every industry; for the highest wage that each industry can afford and for the most reliable division of the products of industry that can ultimately be devised for the recognition of the Golden Rule and the mind of Christ as the supreme law of society and the sure remedy for all social ills.

The interpretations which accompanied the Creed called for a "co-operative society," condemned capitalism and the profit motive, and maintained that the reconstruction of the social order is the primary task of the church.

SUBVERSIVE PROPAGANDA

The Board of Christian Social Concerns is the center from which emanates all the left-wing socialist propaganda in Methodism. It has divisions of Human Relations and Economic Affairs, Peace and World Order, and Temperance and General Welfare. It has relations with a committee in each individual church through which its subversive literature is distributed. It influences the preparation of material for study in Sunday Schools, the Methodist Youth Fellowship, camps, assemblies, retreats, etc. The rising generation is being brainwashed regarding principles of human rights, personal freedom, social and political action, the American way of life, foreign policy and world peace.

The Board of Education is another arm of the Church which is responsible for disseminating subversive propaganda. It influences what is taught in Methodist colleges, universities and seminaries and also in the Sunday schools of all local churches. A study of their approved curricular materials shows that Methodists have officially rejected the Bible as God's special revelation to man. They condemn the idea of Bible authority because its books were written in eras of man's history which are totally passe in respect to modern life. The Bible message is held to be so limited in language, thought, characters and events that it is irrelevant in a space age. Approved materials are based on a humanistic-scientific philosophy of life and "seek fresh and more meaningful ways to teach the Christian faith," than the Bible affords. Liberated from biblical restraints, all sorts of new theologies and new moralities are foisted upon young students, destroying their faith and confusing their minds.

Most Negro Methodists are under the dominating influence of the Council-oriented Methodist Church. It has its own "Central Jurisdiction." Then there are the African Methodist Episcopal Church; the African M.E. Church Zion; and the Christian Methodist Episcopal Church which report a total membership of around 2,400,000—all in the National Council of Churches. They are participating in the negotiations for the creation of a united ecumenical church (COCU) and will bring to such a union a strong left-wing extremism in socio-political matters.

What the Methodist ecclesiastical establishment believes, teaches and practices coincides perfectly with what the National Council of Churches believes, teaches and practices. They both talk the same language and they are moving toward the accomplishment of the same goals. The Methodist Church is the largest constituent member of the National Council, makes the largest contribution to its budget, and exerts a tremendous influence in the formation of its policies and programs.

REVOLT AMONG METHODIST LAYMEN

But there is a growing revolt among Methodist laymen against these policies and programs. It is a common thing for disillusioned Methodist men to call meetings of their families in each others' homes to discuss the situation. They frequently invite critics of the Council to address them and provide information they cannot get from their pastors and church leaders. Sometimes they will draw up reports or circulate petitions calling for change but they seldom get any farther than that. In many instances these groups have been forbidden to hold further meetings on pain of excommunication of all members who persist in attending. Usually these edicts result in many families leaving the church altogether.

A good example of such protest occurred in First Methodist Church, Shreveport, Louisiana. Twenty Methodist laymen headed by Dalton Woods, prominent petroleum engineer, formed a panel to make a study of subversive influences in the Methodist Church and the National Council of Churches. After eighteen months of research and analysis they issued a 60-page brochure entitled *"Things You Should Know About Subversive Influences in Methodism."* It had chapters on the Board of Christian Social Concerns, Methodists and Socialism, World-wide Socialism, Methodism and Communism, Threat of Socialist Infiltration, Demoralizing and Destroying the Will to Resist, and other phases of the panel's findings. Its concluding chapter said:

"The threat of Socialist-Communist domination of our Church is an ever-present and ominous danger. The documented proof presented in this Report establishes the fact beyond doubt. Therefore, it is our problem, and our responsibility to prevent our Church from being trapped, controlled and dominated. We can prevent that from happening if we have the patience and faith, courage and determination to pursue the following program:

"(1) Withdraw local and national Methodist affiliation with the National Council of Churches.

"Every investigation of the dangerous, subversive influence in our Church reveals that the National Council of Churches is the originator and co-ordinator of much of the harmful, pro-

Socialist-Communist activities of our Church, and apparently of other Protestant Churches. Breaking this tie is an essential step in correcting the problem within our Church. This also will have the effect of severing the influence which some Methodist leaders have on other denominations through the National Council of Churches.

"(2) Dissolve the Board of Christian Social Concerns in the national Methodist Church with its organizational network.

"The subversive potential of this Board is far more obvious than its Christian potential. Furthermore, its existence violates a cardinal heritage of our Church . . . the principle of separation of Church and state.

"(3) We should remove anyone from our Church staff or ministry who, through lack of judgment or of Christian faith, knowingly conspires with the Communist Criminal Conspiracy in subversive organizations.

"(4) We should refuse to buy any Methodist literature which has a left-wing political theme. Also, we should refuse to allow such literature to be used in our Churches and, at the same time, we should work vigorously to remove the responsible editors and writers from our Church service.

"(5) We should select and allow only Christian professors, uncontaminated with Socialist-Communist philosophies, to teach in our Church universities, schools and seminaries.

"(6) We should withdraw financial support immediately from any branch or division of the Church at any level which is carrying on subversive or dangerous un-Christian activities until such time as these activities are effectively stopped and the responsble parties are removed from Church affiliation.

"(7) We should insist that our Church take up its rightful role as leader in the fight against the great criminal conspiracy

144

of Communism whose admitted objective is the destruction of all religious freedom in our Nation.

"(8) We should re-instill a spirit of national patriotism within our Church, emphasizing in our Church schools the great and bountiful blessings which we Americans have received as a result of our Christian spirit and our free enterprise system.

"(9) We should stress the responsibilities and blessings of the individual Christianity of Jesus and abandon the collectivism and mass conformity of Karl Marx."

Similar groups have been formed in North Hollywood and Sacramento, California; Lincoln, Nebraska; Cincinnati, Ohio and other centers too numerous to mention. They have broadcast their findings through reprints, tracts, news releases and booklets by the thousands.

Probably the greatest protest by Methodist laymen came in the organization of The Circuit Riders, Inc. Its original stated principles and purposes are as follows:

"(1) To promote and support the primary function of The Methodist Church to spread the gospel of Christ in the world.

"(2) To support those bishops and other leaders of the Methodist Church who oppose the spread of Socialistic and Communistic theories in our Church.

"(3) To oppose all efforts to propagate Socialism and Communism and all other anti-American teachings in the Methodist Church.

"(4) To assist in obtaining any action which may be necessary to require the Methodist Federation for Social Action to drop the word 'Methodist' from its name, vacate its office in the Methodist Headquarters Building in New York City, and remove its influence from our Church.

"These purposes are predicated upon the following facts and principles:

"The Methodist Church is engaged in the effort to spread the gospel of Christ in the world. Its passion is for the salvation of man. It conceives that Christ's primary concern is for the enrichment of the spiritual life of each individual person. He recognizes the sacred worth of the individual. Christ's spirit is that of love; men filled with His spirit are concerned for the welfare of their fellow men and seek to promote justice and mercy in the social, economic, and political order. The Methodist Church would enthrone Christ in the heart and life of the individual and thus infuse His Spirit into all segments of the social order.

"Socialism and Communism emphasize the class struggle, which is the antithesis of love; they are materialistic, not spiritual, in approach; Marxian Socialism and Russian Communism are admittedly atheistic and anti-Christ. They are basically contrary to Methodist thought and purpose.

"Notwithstanding the purpose and program of the Methodist Church, with which the great majority of its members are in accord, there is a minority segment thereof, including the organization known as the Methodist Federation for Social Action, which seeks to use the Church and its agencies to promote socialistic and communistic theories and anti-American activities. This is particularly evident in some phases of the youth program, in certain aspects of women's work, in some theological seminaries, and in the preparation of some of our Church and Church School literature.

"The Methodist Church should give dominant emphasis to its primary spiritual functions, oppose all insidious influences, repudiate the Methodist Federation for Social Action, and remove its influence from our Church."

Circuit Riders, Inc., opened its offices in Cincinnati, Ohio, and a dedicated Methodist business man by the name of

M. G. Lowman became its full-time executive director. Its services were soon sought by laymen not only in Methodist Churches but in all Protestant denominations. Its investigators uncovered startling and amazing facts about the Red network in American Protestantism. It publicized lists of prominent clergymen and educators with their subversive connections, according to the files of the U. S. House Un-American Activities Committee. The Liberal Establishment in the Councils and in the major Protestant denominations have done everything imaginable to smear and discredit Circuit Riders, Inc., but it still continues to carry on its work. The list of its accomplishments would fill a book. It is probably the most cordially hated organization in Methodism today. It is also one of the most effective deterrents of wholesale subversive advance within the denomination.

Ministers have less readily led in revolts against ecclesiastical tyranny and apostasy. When they have protested openly, adopted independent courses of action or failed to increase fiscal support of the unified budget, they have been demoted. Finally, finding themselves in small rural or village parishes, and without significant influence in the denomination, they have quietly acquiesced in the status quo and sorrowfully awaited retirement. But there have been exceptions. One was Bob Jones, southern Methodist evangelist, who once rivaled Billy Sunday in popular acceptance. Jones concluded that the best antidote for liberal poison in Methodism was to start a college committed to the old-time Wesleyan principles. Starting in Cleveland, Tennessee, Bob Jones College soon outgrew its quarters. Invited to Greensboro, South Carolina, the institution expanded into a University with a multi-million dollar complex of modern buildings on a large and beautiful campus. Here around a thousand young men are in training for the ministry and some three or four thousand youth are enrolled in a conservative biblically oriented educational program. Another was Bob Shuler of a large downtown Methodist Church in Los Angeles—one of the greatest preachers of his generation. He drew thousands to hear his thrilling evangelical sermons and to work energetically in the moral crusades he mounted. His magazine, *The Methodist Challenge*, with a wide national circulation, was long a gadfly to the liberal theological and sociological leadership of Methodism. All the forces of the Liberal Establishment and its bureaucracy were brought to bear against him. His church, which was faithful to him to the end, was finally eliminated through a series of devious legal actions, but his spirit went marching on. Bob Shuler was a free Methodist whose like will not be duplicated for years to come. His influence still inspires revolt against the forces of Liberalism in wide areas of Protestantism.

REVOLT IN THE CHURCHES

A serious threat to the growth of the Methodist Church is the vast deterioration of its small town and rural churches, once its source of spiritual strength as well as recruits for the ministry and mission field. The chief reason is the rejection by the people themselves of the liberal doctrines preached by the weaklings sent them from Methodist theological seminaries. Church rolls shrivel and offerings diminish. All liberal-minded denominations in these areas have the same problem. So finally, in view of the fact that ecumenical merger is in the immediate offing, the dying congregations are ordered to get together in support of one pastor between them. The surfeit of abandoned church buildings and parsonages persuades headquarters to dispose of their property, generally to some newly organized, rapidly growing evangelical church of Baptist, Wesleyan, or Pentecostal persuasion. Result: More losses and eventual extinction for the liberal churches and revival of the Protestant spirit in the community at large.

In the Southland there is growing revolt of considerable proportions against the leftism in Methodist pulpits, Sunday schools, and the socio-political projects and crusades mounted by the Councils of Churches. It is said that as a result of the "Delta Ministry" alone, more than ten thousand Mississippi Methodists left their churches in less than a year's time. This same situation is to be found in Louisiana, Alabama, Georgia and the Carolinas. The pastor of a large Methodist church in Mobile led hundreds of his members in the establishment of a new independent congregation and the construction of a commodious new building. His action so appealed to Methodists in a wide area that he is leading in the establishment of many new churches—some thirty had been organized at last report. A new Independent Methodist denomination is bound to result. This spontaneous action is matched by similar moves, a few of which will be noted: The organization of the Evangelical Methodist Church with 150 churches and some 10,000 members. The Fundamental Methodist Church with 12 churches and 1,000 members. The Congregational Methodist Church with 223 churches and 14,000 members. The Southern Methodist Church with 52 churches and 5,000 members. The Bible Protestant Church with 20 churches and 3,000 members. The Methodist Protestant Church with 15 churches and 2,500 members. Most of these groups arose in widely separated areas with no knowledge of the existence of the others, but with similar purposes. There is now developing an effort to bring them together in a strong denominational organization and to initiate an expansion program of large proportions.

There is nothing particularly new about this tendency of Methodists to take the "road to freedom" when they were fed up with what they considered to be the heretical and/or tyrannical policies of the hierarchy. Little is said about this ecclesiastical history of Methodism and little is known about the numerous denominations which have come into being as a result of such revolt. The only way the giant Methodist Church has been able to report gains in membership and growth in statistical status is through mergers. Mergers with the Southern Methodists, the Methodist Protestants, the Evangelical United Brethren and other smaller bodies have enabled them to report a membership in excess of ten million—the largest constituent body of the National Council of Churches. A review of the Wesleyan-oriented denominations which had their beginnings in defections from the Methodist Church will be enlightening. These churches have become veritable "cities of refuge" for Methodists who are seeking spiritual renewal and a haven of peace among Bible-believing brethren of like mind and heart.

CHURCH OF THE NAZARENE

Let us consider first, the Church of the Nazarene. Many people, concerned by the declining emphasis in the established churches of the doctrines of entire sanctification, by the encroachments of "worldliness," began to form independent congregations and fellowships specifically committed to the propagation of the doctrines espoused by John Wesley. As the years passed, these isolated "holiness groups" began to come together and loosely organized associations in various parts of the United States began to emerge. The principal ones were the Church of the Nazarene, chiefly centered in California; the Association of Pentecostal Churches, mainly in New England; and the Holiness Church of Christ, largely in Oklahoma, Texas, and Arkansas.

The first two of these united in 1907 at Chicago, Illinois, under the combined name of "Pentecostal Church of the Nazarene." The following year—October 13, 1908, to be exact—at Pilot Point, Texas, the Holiness Church of Christ also united to form what is now known as the Church of the Nazarene. In subsequent years other groups in the United

States, Canada, and Great Britain have united with the organization. In the union of 1908 there were 228 churches with about 10,000 total membership. Today there are about 5,000 churches with a world membership of over 400,000.

The Church of the Nazarene is distinctly evangelistic and missionary in spirit and program, which has resulted in phenomenal growth. Work is carried on in nearly fifty countries with the greatest concentration of membership being in the United States, Canada, Great Britain and South Africa.

From its earliest days the leaders of the Nazarene Church have stressed the importance of an educated as well as a Spirit-filled ministry. To prepare Christian leadership, both lay and ministerial, the church maintains six liberal arts colleges in the United States, a college in Canada, and Bible colleges in Great Britain, Central Europe, South Africa and Australia. Among them are: Bethany Nazarene College, Bethany, Oklahoma; Eastern Nazarene College, Wollaston, Massachusetts; Northwest Nazarene College, Nampa, Idaho; Olivet Nazarene College, Kankakee, Illinois; Pasadena College, Pasadena, California; Trevecca Nazarene College, Nashville, Tennessee; Canadian Nazarene College, Manchester, England; European Nazarene Bible College, Schaffhausen, Switzerland; South Africa Bible College, Unified, Transvaal; Nazarene Bible College, Sydney, Australia.

The church also operates a graduate school of theology in Kansas City—Nazarene Theological Seminary. Founded in 1945, it is one of the major institutions of its kind. It offers a three-year course leading to the degree of Bachelor of Divinity. Particularly significant is its strong department of missions, in which many outgoing missionaries received specialized training for their future work.

Two new junior colleges and a Bible college have been authorized by the General Assembly and these new institutions will be in operation by the end of the decade.

"Showers of Blessing," an international radio program sponsored by the Church of the Nazarene, can be heard weekly over 500 stations. Its "La Hora Nazarena" is the largest evangelical Spanish-language broadcast in the world. The Nazarene Publishing House, in Kansas City, Missouri, is one of the ten top denominational publishing houses in America. It produces 38 periodicals with 40 million copies printed annually, and 50 new titles or reprints in the book publishing field every year.

FREE METHODIST CHURCH

One of the most progressive denominations in the Wesleyan-Arminian tradition is the Free Methodist Church of North America. It has around 1,200 churches with a membership of 57,000 and a Sunday School enrollment of 140,000. It is affiliated with the National Association of Evangelicals.

The Free Methodists originated in the Genessee (New York) Conference of the Methodist Episcopal Church when a group of pastors protested apostasy from the Wesleyan doctrine of entire sanctification, membership in secret societies, approval of slavery, and the rented-pew system of church support. The revolt spread across the nation and resulted in the organization of the new denomination in Pekin, New York, in 1860.

Headquarters are maintained in Winona Lake, Indiana, where a large publishing house is also located. The denomination is intensely evangelistic not only in its local parishes but also in the world field. It maintains the Light and Life Hour, an international radio broadcast. It has missionary activities in many foreign lands and in underprivileged areas of North America.

Higher education is a major concern. Among Free Methodist colleges are: Roberts Wesleyan College, North Chili, N. Y.; Spring Arbor College, Spring Arbor, Mich.; Central College,

McPherson, Kan.; Wessington Springs College, Wessington Hills, S. D.; Seattle-Pacific College, Seattle, Wash.; Greenville College, Greenville, Ill.; and Los Angeles Pacific College, Los Angeles, Calif. It maintains affiliation with the Asbury Theological Seminary, Wilmore, Ky.

WESLEYAN METHODIST CHURCH

The Wesleyan Methodist Church was formed in Utica, N. Y., in 1843, during the agitation for the freeing of the slaves. The Methodist Episcopal Church was slow in taking a stand on the subject, but a group of courageous men refused to keep silent and broke with the denomination. After the Civil War Wesleyan Methodist emphasis veered to the doctrine of entire sanctification. Today there are around 1,100 churches with a membership of some 47,000 and a Sunday school enrollment of approximately 110,000. The Wesleyan Methodists are affiliated with the National Association of Evangelicals.

The high doctrinal and ethical standards, and exacting conditions of membership, have prevented phenomenal gains in numbers but its witness to Bible holiness has been maintained and strengthened. The Church's stewardship is remarkable; the average church member gives $228 per year to the support of its varied activities.

Wesleyan Methodist concern for higher education has led to the establishment and maintenance of Houghton College, Houghton, N. Y.; Central College, Central, S. C.; Miltonvale College, Miltonvale, Kan., and Marion College, Marion, Ind.

Negotiations are under way for merger with the Pilgrim Holiness Church, a denomination of similar doctrinal beliefs, which has about 1,100 churches, 34,000 members and an enrollment of nearly 100,000 in its Sunday schools. When this is fully accomplished a greatly enlarged program of Christian service will be initiated.

OTHER SEPARATIST BODIES

The Primitive Methodist Church is of English origin but owes its beginnings to Lorenzo Dow, an American Methodist evangelist, who visited the British Isles for a preaching mission. It has 90 churches with a membership of some 13,000 in the USA. Primitive Methodists are congregational in polity.

The Reformed Methodist Church grew and prospered in the northeastern states until 1952 when it merged with the Churches of Christ in Christian Union. The combined bodies now have 215 churches with 8,000 members and a Sunday school enrollment of around 15,000.

The Pillar of Fire is a holiness methodistic body organized by self-styled Bishop Alma White. It has 71 churches with over 5,000 members. It maintains Bible colleges at Zarephath, New Jersey, and Denver, Colorado.

Other small bodies too numerous to mention claim to be in the Wesleyan tradition; so also the Holiness Movement which includes nearly 100 Protestant groups. In full accord with John Wesley they teach that "regeneration removes love of sin, justification the guilt of sins already committed, and sanctification the inclination to sin in the future." Many of these people were formerly Methodists. The Methodist Church continues to be a major source for their numerical growth.

Almost without exception the churches in the pure Wesleyan and Methodist tradition which have separated from the original Methodist Church in America are strongly opposed to the National Council of Churches, its policies and programs, and thoroughly committed to the basic principles of American Protestantism. They represent an important sector of the growing movement to make it again a living and vital power in American life.

VIII

CONGREGATIONALISTS FOR FREEDOM

Congregationalists are proud of their free church heritage. Their American beginnings date from 1620 when the Pilgrim Fathers landed at Plymouth. The Pilgrim voyage to America was made necessary in order to re-establish a church on "the New Testament pattern"—a fellowship of those who had chosen to be followers of Christ, spiritually competent to direct its own life and work. They had pledged themselves to live and worship in freedom according to the dictates of conscience. One of the abiding effects of their costly plea for liberty is that true Congregationalists today will not submit to a conformity which their fathers resisted unto death.

ORIGIN OF CONGREGATIONALISM

A little historical background may be necessary to understand the genius of Congregationalism. The movement had its beginnings in England under the leadership of Robert Browne and others. Browne held that the Church is a congregation of believers in Christ in a specific locality and that the pattern of the Apostolic Church allows each local group of Christians to govern itself. It was not to be primarily responsible to the State, but to God according to the rules and regulations laid down by the Holy Scriptures. English Congregationalists were generally Calvinistic in their theology

though they had little interest in creeds and confessional standards as a means of uniting separate congregations. They
adopted the Savoy Declaration, which reads somewhat like
the Westminster Confession, but asserted their commitment
to the autonomy of the local church. The Pilgrims came out of
this heritage and were true to it.

After they set up their new community in Plymouth, the
Pilgrims were called to the aid of a neighboring Puritan settlement at Salem. Soon the two strains of English Separation
merged. In 1648 they jointly adopted the Cambridge Plat-
form which is sometimes called the charter of American Congregationalism. It was an echo of the Savoy Declaration with
somewhat greater emphasis on the freedom of the individual
and the local congregation. From that day to this the true
Congregationalism has grown and prospered in America within
the frame of reference of *Faith, Freedom and Fellowship*.

Until brought under the deadly influence of Liberalism American Congregationalists preserved their traditional integrity.
They never delivered up their freedom to ecclesiastical authorities of any kind, whether individuals, minorities or majorities;
nor have they submitted their conscience to the powers of State.

THE BLIGHT OF LIBERALISM

Their first experience with Liberalism came when a Unitarian
was appointed Hollis Professor of Divinity at Harvard College
in 1805. Loyal Congregationalists responded by founding
Andover Theological Seminary in 1808, as a place where their
ministers might be trained in the doctrines of their forefathers.
The Liberal movement grew stronger, and although most of the
churches bravely resisted this attack the split came in 1825 with
the departure of 125 influential congregations to form a separate
ecclesiastical body, the American Unitarian Association.

It was not until 1852 that Congregationalists made any significant retreat from their traditional church polity. In that year at Albany, New York, representatives of churches throughout the nation met and organized the National Council of Congregational Churches. Many felt that this move was insurance against Liberal encroachments, but it only created another extra-congregational institution which could be ravished and used as a medium through which the whole denomination might be delivered into the hands of the enemy. Every conceivable precaution was taken in the framing of the constitution to safeguard the freedom of the local churches, but this was not protection enough against the clever schemes the Liberal mind can devise for the achievement of its goals.

The next onslaught of Liberalism came in the introduction of theological heresies. German empiricism and destructive criticism, English transcendentalism and evolutionism, Austrian psychologism and American pragmatism took over the seminaries. Accompanying this development came Washington Gladden's crusade for "applied Christianity" which was akin to unalloyed socialism. He persuaded the National Council of Congregational Churches to appoint a Committee of Five on Capital and Labor and thus initiated the Liberal social action movement in Congregationalism. Gladden's disciples contended for the unification of society and turned to the State as the unifying agent. They held that the State was a high and God-like medium through which the Great Society could be achieved. It was Gladden who led Congregationalism into the Federal Council of Churches. He saw it as an organization through which Protestantism could unite for political action against capitalism and for the creation of a welfare state that would produce a modern utopia for the underprivileged.

PLANNING FOR A UNITED CHURCH

By this time Congregational Liberals had caught the vision

of One Church for One World. They began to collaborate with like-minded Liberals in other denominations and were the first to come up with a practical plan for a united church.

An overture of the National Council, supported by the International Convention of Disciples of Christ, invited all those denominations which "recognize one another's ministries and sacraments" to send official delegates to Greenwich, Connecticut, in December, 1949, for the purpose of creating a blueprint for this church. Here and in Cincinnati in 1951 was produced what was commonly called "The Greenwich Plan" for union under the name "United Church of Christ." The plan was never officially adopted but it became the first draft of guidelines that led to the destruction of Congregationalism and the creation of the present denomination called the United Church of Christ. Indeed, it visualized for Liberal ecumenists in all denominations a practical operative program for One Church for America. So important was this development in the history of church union that "The Greenwich Plan" bears reprinting:

The local church: The united Church would recognize and respect the freedom of each local church in the discharge of its local responsibilities. No fundamental changes in the structure or procedure of local churches would be required as a condition of entrance into the united Church.

Each local church would determine its mode of worship and of administering baptism and the Lord's Supper.

New Members would be received on profession of faith in Jesus Christ as divine Lord and Savior. Letters of transfer from other churches would be honored in accordance with the practice of the receiving local church.

Local churches which hold title to their own property would retain that title.

The ministry: Ministers would be ordained "to the ministry of the Church of Jesus Christ" and not to a single denomination. The act of ordination would be performed by the presbytery on recommendation of the local church and a presbytery examining committee. The bishop would preside at the ordination, "thus signifying that the one ordained is a minister of the whole Church." The presbytery also would be involved in the engagement or dismissal of a minister and would install him in the local church.

The united Church would accept "a reasonable and just share of responsibility" for the continuous employment of its worthy and qualified ministers during their active years and for the continued pastoral care of its local churches "without . . . infringing upon the freedom of the minister or of the local church."

The presbytery: To provide for the "fellowship of mutual counsel and co-operation," a presbytery would be constituted by 10 or more "contiguously located" churches of the united Church, including the minister and a lay representative from each.

Meeting annually, the presbytery would recruit, prepare and ordain ministers, have oversight and aid of ministers and churches, elect delegates to the conference and general council, and "set in order" and promote the spiritual welfare and co-operative work of the constituent churches.

The conference: This unit would embrace at least three presbyteries and would be comparable in function to a state convention, state association, synod, diocese or annual conference of existing denominations. It would be composed of both ministers and laymen and would meet at least once a year, with an elected presiding officer to be called a moderator. Each conference would elect a bishop who would serve as "a spiritual counselor and guide of its churches and minister and its administrative superintendent."

The conference would be responsible for the administration and promotion within its boundaries of the work of the Church as a whole. It would review the records and work of the presbyteries, constitute new presbyteries and divide old ones when deemed advisable and propose measures to the general council. Some 60 conferences, each with a bishop, might be required.

The general council: Responsibility of this unit would be to "foster and express the substantial unity of the united Church in faith, polity, purpose and work." Specifically, it would "do and promote the work of the whole Church in its national, international and ecumenical relations," and in general carry on the functions of the national convention, general assembly, general synod, general conference or general council of the uniting denominations.

It would be composed of approximately 1,200 delegates, with ministers and laymen in equal numbers. Newly elected bishops would be consecrated by the general council. The bishops would be ex-officio members with the right to speak but not to vote. Meeting regularly once in two years, the council would have a presiding officer known as a moderator.

Among work which the general council would co-ordinate and administer would be evangelism, home and foreign missions, ecumenical activity, Christian education, stewardship, publishing, pensions and social action. It would have power to create such corporations, boards, commissions and committees as are needed.

The great weakness of the Greenwich Plan, seen in the perspective of the current inter-church negotiations for union, is that it was too democratic!

AN ERA OF MERGER

Encouraged by the ease with which the waning Christian Church denomination (not the Disciples of Christ) was persuaded to merge with the Congregationalists, the new Liberal-controlled "General Council of the Congregational Christian

Churches" moved toward union with the International Convention of Disciples and the Evangelical and Reformed Church. The Disciples were not yet ripe for such a bold action, but the "E. and R." eagerly responded and negotiations for merger began. It mattered not that the Evangelical and Reformed Church had a polity which was contrary to the charter and spirit of Congregationalism and that any union would inevitably rob Congregational churches of their traditional freedoms. Liberals of both denominations were determined that they would get together and they did in 1957. Thereby hangs a tale of revolt against Liberal tyranny and the creation of a new free Congregational community, which is not generally known. It deserves extended space in this report.

Despite the fact that the General Council knew that thousands of Congregational churches opposed the merger and would fight to preserve their rights, the Liberal faction, under the leadership of Douglas Horton, moved with "all deliberate speed" to accomplish their purposes. In 1947 a "Basis of Union" was submitted to the Congregational Churches in full knowledge of the fact that the General Council had no legal authority to commit them to merger. The Council in an apologetic for its action said there would be a test vote on the "Basis of Union" and that it would not commit itself without approval of 75 per cent of the churches voting on January 1, 1948. It became apparent that such an affirmative vote could not be secured. In fact, 1,436 Congregational churches never even voted. The involved procedure which followed this quite evident rejection of merger is too complicated to recount here. Suffice to say that by "hook or crook" the "Executive Committee of the Congregational Church" was able to announce in 1954 that the General Council had approved the merger of the churches as provided in the Basis of Union (which it had never done and had no power to do) and proceeded to announce that the merger would take place June 25, 1957. Furthermore, the Executive Committee said it would "assume" that all Congregational churches and members would be included in the merger.

It became evident to all true Congregationalists that unless some protest should be made, this assumption of over-all authority over autonomous churches, if assented to, would mean the end of complete self-government in Congregational churches. So, in Detroit in 1955 there was a meeting in which an organization was formed for "Continuing Congregationalism." The Plymouth Church of the Pilgrims in Brooklyn, New York (where Henry Ward Beecher was once the famous pastor), sued to keep the General Council from taking all the financial assets of Congregationalism into the merger. The League to Uphold Congregational Principles, a group of prominent laymen headed by Frank Bean, then owner of the International Milling Company, made various and sundry protests. The Reverend Malcolm K. Burton, pastor of the First Congregational Church, Pontiac, Michigan, drafted a "Declaration of Rights of Churches and Ministers" and sought (unsuccessfully) to have it adopted by the General Council. From one end of the nation to the other revolt was in the air.

Finally, on June 25, 1957, at Cleveland, Ohio, the merger of the General Council of the Congregational Christian Churches and the Evangelical and Reformed Church was declared consummated under the nomen "United Church of Christ."

OPEN REVOLT BY FREE CHURCHES

Unrest had been apparent for some time. There had been decisions made in many quarters to repudiate the new denomination and to continue the traditional Congregational testimony and fellowship at any cost. After Cleveland came open revolt. It expressed itself in many ways. It has been conservatively estimated that 2,000 churches with over a half million members either had voted not to go into the merger or had loudly ignored

162

the merger appeal in the belief that independent, autonomous Congregational churches could not be forced to do anything against their will. But things were "different" after the merger.

Gradually the continuing Congregational churches began to get together in local Associations. In Michigan three local Associations of churches have been set up since the merger. All of them are functioning normally. Each has made provision for the "standing" of ministers and churches and each of them has set up the kind of associational organization which existed thirty-five or forty years ago throughout the nation. In Indiana several Associations already in existence simply voted to continue completely separate from the United Church of Christ.

Still other unreconstructed Congregationalists began to meet for fellowship in "Congregational Clubs." Ministers and laymen in a given area hold frequent meetings of a social nature at which papers on themes of interest are presented with discussions ensuing. Some are held in private homes, some in restaurants or hotel dining rooms. It is believed that this form of fellowship for concerted action will become increasingly popular among true Congregationalists who still hold membership in congregations related to the United Church of Christ. A large Congregational Club is located in the Los Angeles area. Mrs. James E. Solberg, an officer, tells how it came into being:

"The need became apparent to one person that some sort of fellowship for continuing Congregationalists for purposes of promoting Congregational principles (the Congregational Way) and the fellowship of kindred spirits was needed.

"Others were contacted by telephone to determine if this need were mutually felt. The answer was 'yes' from all.

"Pro-Congregational ministers were called to a small meeting to hear a statement of the need felt by so many. They concurred.

"A planning committee of like-minded people was set up, composed of pro-Congregationalists from both National Association and the United Church of Christ. Members were chosen to represent various geographical areas. An organizational meeting for the new Club was called.

"A list of known pro-Congregationalists was assembled and invitations to the organizational meeting were mailed. A notice of the meeting was placed in the newspapers.

"A temporary moderator conducted the meeting. There was a guest speaker. A dinner followed the meeting. Pro-Congregational literature was distributed. The temporary planning committee was authorized to nominate people for membership on a Planning Committee, this committee to be elected at the next meeting. Another committee was nominated from the floor to draw up a statement of purpose for the Club, the statement to be adopted at the next meeting. A collection was taken to underwrite printing and mailing expenses.

"At the next meeting the club was organized with a moderator, an assistant moderator, a secretary-treasurer and a planning committee. Members of the Club consisted of individuals and not churches. An honorary committee consisting of distinguished Congregationalists of the area was set up. Four regular meetings per year were scheduled. Special meetings are held as needed. Notices of all meetings are sent to all Pro-Congregationalists on a growing list. Announcements are made in the Los Angeles papers."

Already two couples from the Los Angeles Club have sponsored the organization in their community of a new Congregational Church true to Congregational principles. Others will follow.

NEW CONGREGATIONAL DENOMINATIONS

The most effective answer to merger has been the organization of the National Association of Congregational Christian Churches. It was formed in Detroit, Michigan, November 9 and 10, 1955, by delegates elected by called meetings of local churches and sent to this gathering for the express purpose of creating such a fellowship. Its founders believed that mere negative resistance would not preserve the traditional Congregational freedoms. It seemed to them all too clear that scattered churches, however staunch they might be in the

Congregational Way, would die of isolation and loneliness unless they found fellowship in a national association.

Functionally, the National Association has, of course, a more complex organization than a local association. Since it exists to deal with the large-scale, long-range concerns of the Churches, the National Association has assumed a functional structure. There is now a legal entity called the Corporation for the National Association, a Wisconsin corporation. The Missionary Society, The Building and Land Fund, The Congregational Foundation for Theological Studies and The Congregational Press are divisions of this parent corporation. There are also such Commissions as are necessary for carrying on the work of the Churches which lies beyond the local parish. These Commissions, together with the Executive Committee of the National Association, and the staff at the national headquarters, offer the local Churches the outreach which is the practical corollary of the principle of fellowship. The official journal of the Association is *The Congregationalist*. At Cheyenne, Wyoming, August 24, 1961, NACCC took the bold, but logical and necessary, step of declaring itself to be the successor of the former General Council of the Congregational Christian Churches. A carefully worded resolution asserted the readiness of the National Association to serve all Congregational Christian Churches not having become parts of the United Church of Christ, and stated that henceforth the denominational headquarters for the fellowship was 176 West Wisconsin Avenue, Milwaukee, Wisconsin. The National Association maintains the historic continuity of Congregationalism, not by paper statements in a setting of synodical authority, but by continuing the polity and usages of the churches as they were prior to the outbreak of the merger controversy.

Some of the largest Congregational Churches in the nation are members of the Association such as First Church, Los Angeles, and Park Street Church, Boston. New members are joining constantly.

The NACCC has no restrictions regarding theological beliefs, believing that this policy is inherent in the Congregational Way. This has not satisfied many conservative ministers and churches. They find their fellowship in the Conservative Congregational Christian Conference which was founded in Chicago, Illinois, in 1948. It maintains headquarters at Carlisle, Massachusetts. *The Congregational Christian,* its official journal, is published from West Mansfield, Massachusetts.

A CONTINUING CONGREGATIONALISM

The Committee for the Continuation of Congregational Christian Churches in the United States is endeavoring to keep in touch with all the churches that have not committed themselves to the merger. It sends out many carefully documented pages of printed matter and acts as a service medium for all who call upon it for help. It may be addressed at either Box 277, Marshalltown, Iowa, or at 97 Mary Day, Pontiac, Michigan.

Recently this Committee has felt an obligation to warn all Protestants in churches threatened with merger concerning the techniques which were used to mislead many Congregationalists and which may be used on them. In a flyer entitled, "The Ruthlessness of Church Union," the Committee says:

"The ruthlessness of modern church union is no different from that practiced in other centuries by powerful church leaders when they claimed Divine sanction for their acts in building one catholic church.

"Church union leaders lay their hands on all the church possessions and take these with them. They do not recognize the rights of any who disagree with them nor do they share properties with those who do not want to go along.

"The possessions seized by church union leaders are both denominational properties and the houses of worship of local congregations. In our Congregational Church merger all of the denominational properties have been taken by the merger people. There was never the slightest suggestion that these would be divided fairly or on a

166

proportionate basis with those not wishing to enter the United Church of Christ. In like manner a local church that voted by a fifty-five per cent majority to enter the United Church of Christ has taken its entire church property into the United Church of Christ and left nothing for the forty-five per cent of members who did not want to go along.

"At the time that the United Church of Canada was set up, an entirely different procedure was followed. In that instance a special act of the Canadian Parliament was passed to insure fairness to all concerned. Not only were the denominational properties divided on a pro rata basis, but even the local congregations were required to make provision for those who did not want to enter the United Church of Canada.

"In this country it was hoped that the courts would protect the rights of minority members. Instead they have given nothing but a run-around to the countless thousands of people who have been dispossessed, both in their national properties and in their local church properties, by this ruthless merger movement.

"Pressures are exerted upon ministers in the form of whispered threats. Even after the General Council had passed motions to the contrary, ministers have been told that they would lose their rights in the Annuity plan unless they took standing in the United Church of Christ. Likewise—even after the Church Building Society had adopted resolutions to the contrary—churches have been intimidated by whispered threats to the effect that their grant mortgages would become due and payable with back interest at six per cent from the time that they were issued if they took their standing out of the Associations connected with the United Church of Christ. In these cases the pressure tactics were absolutely unprincipled. Yet all of this has been part of the ecumenical mood and method.

"Ecumenists insist that they are fulfilling 'the will of Christ,' and they seem therefore to think that all the means which they employ are justified. The ruthlessness of the ecumenical movement stems from the oft-quoted claim that Christ, on the night that He was betrayed, prayed 'that they all may be one . . .' The quotation is more of a pious alibi than it is a genuine reason for pursuing the ecumenical movement. Because of their pious pretense, churchmen seem to think that they can take any ruthless course they desire . . .

"The same kind of unprincipled behavior as exhibited by national officials has been practiced by pro-merger ministers in local situations.

In almost countless instances these men have made all kinds of promises to get control and then brushed them aside as being unimportant afterward. Time and again, we have heard the unhappy story of a church which called a minister to its pastorate on the solemn promise that he would not advocate the merger. Then, after he was engaged, he turned around and spent his full energy ramming through a vote for the United Church of Christ. The same sanctimonious attitude that "the will of Christ" is being served has been used by these men as justification for the complete lack of integrity in their own actions.

"Pro-merger factions within local churches have never been willing to take 'No' for an answer. Even when a church votes repeatedly against a merger, the pro-merger element is continuously agitating for 'another vote.' In this they are aided and abetted by agitators from outside of the local congregations. Needless to say the agitators are connected with the United Church of Christ in its Associations, Conferences and other churches.

"The denominations engaged in the Blake-Pike plan for church union should see the unholy fruits of church union to date in Congregationalism. 'By their fruits shall ye know them.'"

There are still thousands of true Congregationalists trapped in churches which by "hook or crook" were persuaded to join the United Church of Christ. Many of these people are strongly opposed to the centralized authoritarian church government to which they are having to submit and also to its relationship to the National Council of Churches and the World Council of Churches.

LIBERALISM IN THE "UNITED CHURCH"

The United Church is much more closely related to the left-wing socio-political policies and programs of the Councils than was the Congregational Christian denomination. True Congregationalists are greatly distressed concerning the image the United Church presents to the world through its beatnik preachers and educators who now seem to have *carte blanche* to do as they please within a left-wing frame of reference.

In the so-called "Metropolitan Cathedral of Secular Issues" at the First Congregational Church of Chicago, on July 4, 1965 the following blasphemous litany was used to advance the new social revolution:

A Litany:

Leader: O God, the City, for people to live and work and to know one another.
Congregation: Help us to love the City.

Leader: O God, the Metropolis of all men's lives
Congregation: Help us to love the Metropolis.

Leader: O God who lives in tenements who goes to segregated schools who is beaten in precincts, who is unemployed
Congregation: Help us to know you.

Leader: O God, who hangs on street corners, who tastes the garce of cheap wine and the sting of the needle
Congregation: Help us to touch you.

Leader: O God, who is pregnant without husband, who is child without parent, who has no place to play
Congregation: Help us to know you.

Leader: O God, who can't read nor write, who is on welfare and who is treated like garbage
Congregation: Help us to know you.

Leader: O God who is black and who wishes he were white—NO! Not that he be white, but that he would not wish that he were white,
Congregation: Help us to see you.

Leader: O God who lives and no one knows his name and who knows that he is nobody,
Congregation: Help us to know you.

Leader: O God, whose name is spick, black nigger, bastard, guinea, and kike,
Congregation: Help us to know you.

Leader: O God, who pays too much rent for a lousy apartment because he speaks Spanish,
Congregation: Help us to know you.

Leader: O God, who is cold in the slums of winter, whose playmates

are rats—four-legged ones who live with you and two-legged ones who imprison you,
Congregation: Help us to touch you.

Leader: O God, whose church down the street closed and moved away,
Congregation: Help us to touch you.

Leader: O God, who is old and lives on forty dollars a month in one crummy room and can't get outside,
Congregation: Help us to know you.

Leader: O God, who is white and lives with Mr. Charlie, who is black and lives with Uncle Tom,
Congregation: Help us to see you.

Leader: O God, who lives in projects of Federal, State and City indifference,
Congregation: Help us to see you.

Leader: O God, who is fifteen in the sixth grade,
Congregation: Help us to touch you.

Leader: O God, who is three and whose belly aches in hunger,
Congregation: Help us to touch you.

Leader: O God, whose toys are broken bottles, tin cans, whose play yard is garbage and debris, and whose play house is the floors of the condemned buildings,
Congregation: Help us to touch you.

Leader: O God, who sleeps in the bed with his four brothers and sisters, and who cries and no one hears him,
Congregation: Help us to touch you.

Leader: O God, who holds tight to the hem of mother's dress, whose eyes are empty, whose tears are large and whose face is dirty,
Congregation: Help us to touch you.

Leader: O God, who is uneducated, unskilled, unwanted and unemployed,
Congregation: Help us to know you.

Leader: O God, who was laid off last week and can't pay the rent nor feed the kids,
Congregation: Help us to know you.

Leader: O God, who is a bum, a chiseler, who is lazy, because people say you are when you don't work and can't find a job,
Congregation: Help us to be with you.

170

Leader: O God, whose job at the factory is gone because the factory closed and left the city,
Congregation: Help us to know you.

The sponsors of this pantheistic worship service hold that the world is the only reality and that the only God men can know must be identified with that reality. The World, the City, the bum are the elements out of which we must construct a God relevant to the modern world. This is best done by developing the City of Man, the socialist world order.

A United Church of Christ pastor in Pittsburgh advised his brother ministers to subscribe to *Playboy* magazine. Said he, "The average minister's sermons would be more relevant if *Playboy* were required reading. . . . Its position is more authentically Christian than much that is heard from modern pulpits today. . . . Its founder, Hugh Hefner, is the hottest thing since Martin Luther."

Here and there groups of concerned laymen arise to protest this sort of social action leadership, only to discover that there is less and less opportunity to manifest the free spirit in the United Church of Christ. The National Council of Churches and the World Council of Churches set the course, the UCC Council for Christian Social Action follows "the party line" and the top leaders in the General Synod enforce acceptance of their left-wing social doctrines by the ministers and local church leaders.

For a long time opponents of merger and the creation of the new United Church of Christ have contended that the deepest and most significant aspects of the abandonment of traditional Congregationalism would be found in the realm of the spirit. Now they see its results in encroachments on the free spirit of man. These matters of the spirit are exceedingly personal and at the same time have a tremendous bearing upon the true meaning of "freedom." Nothing is more important to a genuine religious quest than the encouragement of free, honest, open, intellectual and spiritual inquiry. Whatever creates an atmosphere in which it is difficult or impossible for an individual to raise honest questions and to seek clear and balanced understanding, is an enemy of true freedom.

LIBERAL TYRANNY RAMPANT

The leaflets of the United Church of Christ and the National Council of Churches look upon questioning or probing into issues by conservatives as an act of defiance or criticism directed against the church. These leaders deliberately set the stage in such a fashion that individual ministers and lay leaders cannot honestly, openly and genuinely pursue the issues of truth and the deepest spiritual insights without running tremendous risks. They are immediately branded as trouble-makers and considered anathema to the leadership of the denomination.

A leading Congregationalist pastor has said:

"The areas in which the United Church of Christ has set a pre-arranged stage, on which only those who speak the right lines may comfortably appear, are numerous. At the Denver General Synod meeting in 1963 the moderator had sent out a preliminary letter practically demanding the position that the whole Synod should take on the race issue. The rest of officialdom fell into line. (This happened to deal with the racial question. It can, and does, happen in other fields as well.) One minister who attended as a delegate described his own feelings as he went out alone in the dark of the night after the first session, and sought to get his bearings. He knew that he was very much out of tune with what was being done and yet was absolutely helpless to make an effective protest.

"The very best of spiritual attainment is achieved by those who are not satisfied with one idea because they are aware of finer insights that need probing and bringing to the surface. The best of preaching is done by men who reject one possible idea after another in favor of better ideas. No movement, whether it be the Civil Rights movement of today or the ecumenical movement now or in the future, can afford to stifle the highest, most careful, and most honest criticisms. Yet this is precisely what is being done within the United Church of Christ because its leaders are among the most blatant and most crass when it comes to ignoring possible criticisms.

"The United Church of Christ has made cowards out of ministers. It doesn't pay to have ideas that go against the leaders. It is useless to raise questions. It would bring nothing but calumny and abuse upon the individual who would show such effrontery. The denomination is in the hands of a well-entrenched Liberal clique. The pretense of representation in the General Synod is so thin that it does not pretend to represent the thinking of the average person within the local churches. It is simply used as a sounding board by the national officials to tell the churches what they should think and how they should act, not vice versa. The Congregational free church spirit has departed from the United Church of Christ and 'Ichabod' has been written above its altars."

THE ROAD TO FREEDOM

American Congregationalism is choosing the Road to Freedom today and gives promise of being one of the most important factors in the rebirth of the Protestant spirit and Protestant advance. Henry David Gray, recently retired editor of *The Congregationalist*, in an inspired document entitled, "The Congregational Witness in the World Today," says:

"God will presently be asking . . . for those who will take their stand for the freedom wherewith Christ has made men free. Weaker brethren will flee, in times of uncertainty, to the authoritarian churches and states, but not so, please God, shall we. We have a witness to bear. We shall stand for a free faith—because we know, like our fathers, that it is 'hearts before God' that are important in time and eternity . . .

"In my mind's eye I see a new Congregationalism, purged of dross in the fires of controversy, cleansed of earthly reliance on man made 'ordinations,' 'institutions,' and 'organizations,' new-born on the foundation of the faith of the New Testament Churches, casting all its cares on Him who we are sure cares for His people and His Churches. Churches of free man will be centers of spiritual power! Centers of spiritual power will raise up a ministry of unusual competency, character, and consecration! Churches and ministers caring for the Spirit of the Living God will thrust branches into the ground to grow into new Churches, and will draw from from the depths of their love of God the financial sinews and dedicated lives needed to seek and to save men, women, children, and young people who today know not the Saviour, nor the liberty wherewith He alone can set men free!

"Make no mistake about it! This hour of history, pregnant with new nations waiting to be born, is our Divinely given opportunity. Our free fellowship has at its heart the essential needed by the nations and their peoples, the principle of adventure and of advance in the power of the Spirit, which does not depend on ecclesiastical machinery, or upon any other machinery.

"Our Congregational Witness depends on God; and therefore it cannot fail. We may fail God but He will never fail us. If we are devout and daring, we can 'do all things through Him Who strengthens us.' Unto Him be glory in the Church, world without end. Amen."

IX

"CHRISTIANS ONLY" FOR FREEDOM

"We are not the only Christians but we are Christians only," is the shibboleth of 5,000,000 people known at the local level as "Church of Christ," "Christian Church" or "Disciples of Christ." They constitute the largest complex of free congregational churches in America, of distinctly American origin. Four million of them have no connection with the National Council of Churches or the World Council of Churches and oppose the councils with vigor.

They had their origin in the early part of the Nineteenth Century on the Allegheny frontier. A document they venerate, as Americans venerate the Declaration of Independence, is the Declaration and Address in which they proclaimed their freedom from human creeds and denominational authority and proposed to "restore the New Testament Church in doctrine, ordinances and life" through an appeal to "the Bible and the Bible alone as the sole rule of faith and practice." They like to speak of their status in Christendom as that of a movement and not a denomination. Their "Restoration Movement" has grown from twenty people in Washington, Pensylvania, in 1809 to five million today—one of the most amazing religious developments in America.

Four million members acknowledge no extra-congregational authority whatever and adhere to their original and traditional commitment to the Free Church idea. They claim their "freedom in Christ" guarantees four practical freedoms—freedom of the individual, freedom of the local congregation, freedom of the ministry, and freedom of association. In one of their documents, *The Free Church*, their local churches are said to be—

"Free to constitute themselves communions with God through Christ, in the form of independent, autonomous units, without the permission of any human agency.

"Free to receive members according to the terms laid down by Christ and the apostles in the New Testament and to dismiss members who refuse to obey the rule of Christ.

"Free to choose and dismiss their own officers as provided in the New Testament without any outside authorization or approval.

"Free to call, ordain, retain and/or dismiss ministers without advice or approval from any extra-congregational body or ecclesiastical official. This right and privilege, however, must be exercised with deliberation, wisdom and caution while at the same time, by prayer and supplication, seeking the guidance of the Holy Spirit.

"Free to determine orders of worship and provide for the administration of the ordinances of Christ. Churches are not bound to accept liturgies, prayers, intercessions, observances of special days or any general method of conducting services provided by any extra-congregational agency. Indeed, to do so would tend to introduce a formalism into man's means of communication with God that could well destroy a spiritually meaningful and rewarding worship experience.

"Free to discipline their members in the 'nurture and admonition of the Lord' provided that such discipline is exercised with wisdom, love and forbearance, according to the instruction of Holy Scripture.

"Free to provide all necessary means of teaching and training in the Word of God and to encourage Christian education in all its varied aspects. No outside agency has a right to determine the standards, methods or literature to be used in this process. While advantage should be taken of every reputable provision for the improvement of the equality of instruction and administration, great discrimination should be exercised in choices and uses.

"Free to make their own provisions for the needy of church and/or community in ways that seem best suited to the local situation. Many churches are now erecting their own children's homes, rest homes, homes for the aged, welfare clinics and/or recreation centers. Where such substantial projects are impossible churches are free to support whatever good extra-congregational works they may choose.

"Free to send out their own missionaries and evangelists to seek and to save the lost in areas of their own choosing. They are at liberty to sponsor such workers and solicit aid in their support from other churches and individual Christians.

"Free to set up their own constitutions and by-laws and to make such rules of conduct or plans of work as may best serve their needs. Free exercise of initiative and creativity can assure maximum efficiency and progress. Offers of advisory assistance should be viewed with extreme caution lest they escalate into mandatory controls.

"Free to buy, build, maintain and dispose of property without the interference of any super-church or extra-congregational agency. They may and should reject all legal devices which would admit the rights of any district, state, area or national church body in such property.

"Free to manage their own finances. This involves the building of budgets, financial commitments from members, acceptance of stewardship goals, support of church agencies and foreign advice in all fiscal matters. Lists of 'approved' objects of support to the exclusion of others should be examined with extreme care in the light of their loyalty to the Word of God and the purposes to which the Church is committed.

"Free to associate with whatever churches of like mind and heart they may choose, in the support of whatever undertakings they believe are for the advancement of Christ's kingdom, praying for the good and prosperity of all churches in all places and for their peace, increase in love and mutual edification.

"Free to participate in councils, rallies, conventions, lectureships, clinics and conferences, seeking ways and means of improving the effectiveness of the local church in its God-given tasks. In all such instances it should be understood that the churches are not bound by any decisions reached in such gatherings.

"Free to refrain from association in any or all such gatherings without being disfellowshipped as brethren in a common cause. This freedom should also obtain in reverse, i.e., church should not refuse to fellowship those that prefer to attend and work in such assemblies.

"Free to reject all attempts to impose upon them creeds, covenants, ministerial orders, programs, standards, goals or ecclesiastical structures for the sake of a specious 'unity' or the achievement of 'the wholeness of the church.'

"Free to refuse any patronage or control by the State and to maintain strict separation of Church and State in all their activities.

"Free to maintain the highest possible standards in Church membership and in all relationships within and without their borders. Freedom is always justified by their ability to present the best possible image of the true Church of Jesus Christ as it is revealed in the Holy Scriptures. . . ."

For our purposes we shall consider this "Restoration Movement" in three categories—Rightist, Centrist and Leftist.

THE RIGHTISTS

The Rightists are generally known as Churches of Christ. They are extremely conservative in their interpretation of the Scriptures and in ecclesiastical practice. They number over 2,300,000 in the United States. A distinguishing mark is the fact that they will not use instrumental music in their worship services. About 80 per cent of their 17,000 churches are to be found in Texas, Arkansas, Louisiana, Tennessee, Mississippi, Alabama and Georgia. In Greater Nashville they have over 100 churches and a co-operative program of evangelism which often packs the city's largest auditoriums. The Central Church has a large and commodious edifice in the heart of the city with adequate equipment for educational and social work, a men's dormitory, a home for working girls, a day nursery, and a radio broadcasting studio. Its membership includes many of Nashville's leading business and professional men, and not infrequently governors and other leading statesmen. In Madison, a suburban community, is located the largest Church of Christ in America with nearly 10,000 members, a mammoth Bible school, a large auditorium that is packed twice every Sunday, a cottage-type Children's Home, a Home for the Aged and many other functional services which are provided in the name of Christ. In Texas there are a large number of great congregations such as Broadway Church of Christ, Lubbock, and Highland Church of Christ, Abilene. The former has over 8,000 members, maintains homes for children and the aged, conducts a complete Christian Day School with accredited elementary and secondary grades related to a Church of Christ accredited junior college (Lubbock Christian College). Highland Church has an amazing complex of activities the best known of which is the radio and television "Herald of Truth Hour" which is on some 800 stations in the United States. The local churches, through a well-trained and capable eldership, are responsible for all phases of educational, missionary, evangelistic and propaganda efforts that serve the brotherhood at large. Extra-congregational support of these enterprises is on a purely voluntary basis and is not made a test of fellowship.

Within the last generation, the Church of Christ has made a phenomenal growth. This is due to two things: (1) Its people have stood like the Rock of Gibraltar for "the faith which was once delivered unto the saints," amid the doubt and confusion superinduced by liberalism. They have challenged the spirit of compromise and worldliness and dared to be a "peculiar" people teaching and practicing what they believe is the Bible way of life. (2) They have come to realize that the silence of the Scriptures must be respected as well as the commandments of Scripture, but that obedience to its silence permits freedom of judgment and action. Old chasms of division are being replaced by ever-widening agreement and ground for fellowship.

To the educational leaders of the Church of Christ must go the praise for this encouraging development. Today there are a score of colleges operated by members of the Church of Christ. The colleges include Abilene Christian College, Abilene, Texas; Alabama Christian College, Montgomery, Alabama; Columbia Christian College, Portland, Oregon; Florida

Christian College, Tampa, Florida; Freed-Hardeman College, Henderson, Tennessee; Great Lakes Christian College, Beamsville, Ontario; Harding College, Searcy, Arkansas; Ibaraki Christian College, Ibaraki-Ken, Japan; David Lipscomb College, Nashville, Tennessee; Lubbock Christian College, Lubbock, Texas; Magic Valley Christian College, Albion, Idaho; North Central Christian College, Rochester, Michigan; Ohio Valley College, Parkersburg, West Virginia; Oklahoma Christian College, Oklahoma City; George Pepperdine College, Los Angeles, California; Southeastern Christian College, Winchester, Kentucky; Southwestern Christian College (Negro), Terrell, Texas; Western Christian College, Weyburn, Saskatchewan, and York College, York, Nebraska.

Only a few of these institutions can be described in the limited scope of this chapter. David Lipscomb College has an historic background of special significance to the brotherhood. It has spiritual ties to Tolbert Fanning's Franklin College (founded in 1842) and is the direct lineal descendant from the Nashville Bible School, established by David Lipscomb, William Lipscomb, and James A. Harding in 1901. In 1903 three large buildings were erected on David Lipscomb's farm on Granny White Road, Nashville, where more than twenty buildings of the modern David Lipscomb College now stand. Its history has been one of constant growth and expansion in physical and educational equipment. There is an enrollment of some two thousand in the liberal arts college, the high school, and the elementary school. D.L.C. is a senior college fully accredited by the Southern Association of Colleges and Secondary Schools. As in all Church of Christ colleges the chief feature of its program is its emphasis on the study of the Holy Scriptures and the building of Christian character. With assets of more than ten million dollars, it has a long-range development program to double its present status. The campus of D.L.C. is frequently the scene of ministerial meetings, elders conferences, evangelism clinics, study groups in Christian stewardship, youth problems,

180

Bible-school methods, and every phase of local church activity. It has become the cultural center of the Church of Christ community which is such a dominant factor in the life of Greater Nashville.

Abilene Christian College was founded in 1906 as a Bible-centered college of liberal arts. It has an enrollment of over three thousand. Its twelve-million-dollar equipment of modern, cream-colored brick buildings is a West Texas showplace, and its educational standing is fully accredited. The college was elected to the Southern Association of Colleges and Secondary Schools in 1951. The graduate school, which offers Master's degree in nine areas, was established in 1953. On its campus is held an annual Bible lecture series which features outstanding Church of Christ speakers and draws thousands of brethren. Other similar events in the fields of agriculture, and domestic arts, social science and education, journalism and English literature, music and art, make Abilene a religious, cultural, and educational center for Churches of Christ. A.C.C. has all the accoutrements of a modern institution of higher learning including top-rated football, basketball, and track teams, one of the largest college bands in Texas, a farm, etc.

Harding College has one of the best, well-equipped, air-conditioned small college plants in America. It has assets of more than ten million dollars, is fully accredited as a liberal arts institution and offers graduate study. It is nationally known for its contribution to the American way of life and offers a wide range of studies in this field. The students' religious life is a major concern.

Freed-Hardeman College is the fruit of the educational labors of A. G. Freed and N. B. Hardeman. It has a group of excellent buildings mostly constructed during Hardeman's twenty-six-year presidency. It operates as a junior college and is a member of the Tennessee Association of Colleges and the American Association of Junior Colleges.

Oklahoma Christian College had its beginnings as Central

Christian College at Bartlesville but later purchased a strategic location near the state capital, Oklahoma City. With eight modern buildings and an accredited liberal arts status it is destined to become one of the great Christian colleges of the Southwest.

In a beautiful location overlooking the Hillsborough River ten miles above the point where it empties into Tampa Bay, the Florida Christian College has five buildings and a big citrus farm. It is a fully accredited junior college in the Southern Association. It offers two years of advanced study in the Bible and religious education.

George Pepperdine College in Los Angeles rose almost overnight in 1937. It came into being because of the educational conscience of the man whose name it bears, one of America's outstanding businessmen, founder of the Western Auto Supply Company and other successful corporations. Through his munificent gifts completely modern buildings and equipment were provided on a spacious campus and a full corps of able educators were called to form its faculty. It is a fully accredited liberal arts institution with strong emphasis on Bible training and normally has an enrollment of one thousand students. Its graduate school has about seventy candidates for higher degrees.

Churches of Christ maintain "Bible Chairs" at the portals of state universities and colleges offering courses in Bible and counseling services. Many Day Schools have been organized in recent years and the number of such institutions continues to grow. A conservative, yet thoroughly accredited, education is offered.

There are scores of journals for circulation among the churches, most of which are small and may be short-lived. A new crop seems to develop each year. However, the *Gospel Advocate*, established by Tolbert Fanning and William Lipscomb in 1855 and carried on under the outstanding leadership of David Lipscomb and E. G. Sewell for many years, remains one of the most influential periodicals. The McQuiddy family, owners of a large printing establishment in Nashville, has given liberally to maintain the magazine and to develop a high-class Bible-school and book literature as a service to the churches. Under the forward-looking editorship of B. C. Goodpasture, the churches have been guided to adopt sensible practices, biblical in basic principles and essential to progress in the modern world. The *Advocate* has encouraged higher education, an educated ministry, missionary advance, effective education in the local church and a trained eldership and diaconate.

The *Firm Foundation*, of Austin, Texas, established in 1884 is a stalwart "defender of the faith." The Showalter family has largely sponsored its ministry. The monthly *Twentieth Century Christian* (1937) maintains high journalistic standards. The *Word and Work*, edited by R. H. Boll from 1915 until his death in 1956, serves the premillennial brethren. The appearance of two creditable quarterlies, *Restoration Quarterly* (1957) and *Restoration Review* (1959), marks scholarly attainment of encouraging stature. *The Minister's Monthly, Power for Today, World Vision, Christian Chronicle,* and *The Voice of Freedom* serve in the specialized fields. A listing of other journals would probably be obsolete in a few years. In 1960 there were an estimated forty-five Church of Christ publications in existence. *The Voice of Freedom* has a unique ministry in its advocacy of religious liberty and the doctrine of Separation of Church and State and has a circulation far beyond the borders of the Churches of Christ.

Churches of Christ are committed to an intensive and comprehensive program of missions both at home and abroad. They utilize all the traditional methods for extending their borders and some strange new ones. For instance, they have a project for establishing a strong testimony in the State of New Jersey, adjacent to New York City. They call it "Exodus: New Jersey." Over 300 individuals (125 families) have voluntarily sold their houses and lands, given up their business and professional occupations in Western and Southern states to "colonize" Somerset County, New Jersey. These people will set up new homes and means of employment in this area and at their own expense organize new churches, staff them with experienced elders, deacons and teachers and intensively canvass the area from door to door to win souls to Christ. A similar project is "Exodus Brazil" in which an entire ship was chartered and loaded with Church of Christ folk to establish "the cause" in Belo Horizonte.

There is strong resistance to any co-operative enterprise that might degenerate into a sect, institution, or denomination. Church of Christ brethren believe that if all believers in Christ remain simply Christians and keep the local church free and independent, denominationalism is utterly impossible. They say pure and unadulterated Christianity is undenominational. The spirit and letter of apostolic teaching is that Christians shall be of the same mind and the same judgment and that there be no divisions among them. The purpose of all true reformers through the centuries was to set people free from ecclesiastical bondage and bring them into the liberty of the sons of God. Only their successors who were smaller souls and inclined to seek prestige and authority were responsible for sect or denominational organization.

THE LEFTISTS

The Leftist sector of the Restoration Movement is completely under control of the Liberal Establishment of modern Protestantism. Its leadership has abandoned the Restoration idea, the full and final authority of the Holy Scriptures, and the complete autonomy of local congregations. Despite the fact that their following consists of not more than one million members and 4,500 churches they assume to represent all Christian Churches and Churches of Christ unrelated to the Rightist sector of the Movement. Leftists are completely in accord with the National and World Council programs and have contributed some of their outstanding leaders and officials.

As is true of most of the major denominations in American Protestantism, Liberals have infiltrated all their institutions most of which were created and developed to their present proud status by conservatives. They have virtually embezzled millions of dollars of permanent funds and vast holdings of property which they have turned to programs subversive of the Movement's original purposes. All this they are now engaged in delivering through the Consultation on Church Union into a merger with other denominations. (See pages 68, 69.) In another generation the distinctive testimony and the very existence of this sector of the Restoration Movement will be lost in the "One Church for One World" which the Liberal Establishment has envisioned.

The extent to which Leftists have gone in their support of the programs and purposes of the Liberal Establishment can be seen in the resolutions passed in the 1966 Dallas (Texas) Assembly of the International Convention of Christian Churches (Disciples of Christ). The Assembly, fully controlled by Liberals, endorsed (1) inter-racial marriage, (2) the controversial Delta Ministry and civil disobedience, (3) ecumenical relations with the Roman Catholic Church, (4) local church studies in the findings of the left-wing World Conference on Church and Society in order to prepare their members for participation in the new world social revolution, (5) revolutionary and reform political movements and, by implication, United States intervention in Santo Domingo, (6) left-wing labor and agricultural reforms, (7) changes in "archaic, contradictory and punitive" laws on marriages, divorce, homosexuality and other sexual perversions, (8) the right of public dissent and, by implication, marches, demonstrations, sit-ins and other anarchistic procedures, in order to advance left-wing social and political goals, (9) changes in historic practices of the churches in order to prepare them for ecumenical union, and (10) a proposed design to create a strong centralized ecclesiastical government with authority over the whole church.

THE CENTRISTS

The revolt of the Centrists from this program has been monolithic. One indication of its immensity is the development of what is called the North American Christian Convention. It has become one of the greatest annual religious assemblies in the nation, registering over 25,000 at Louisville, Kentucky in 1966, and continuing to grow by leaps and bounds. This Convention is a voluntary free assembly of interested individuals for the purpose of preaching, fellowship, and the dissemination of information. It has no official representative character. It even refuses to pass resolutions for fear such statements might be construed as representative of a point of view held by some sector or sectors of the Restoration Movement. The tone of the mammoth sessions is distinctly biblical, evangelical and conservative. Some 200 exhibits to be found in the convention halls depict and demonstrate the co-operative work being done by the brethren in the fields of education, world missions, evangelism, benevolence, publication, and other functional services.

Many special and regional assemblies are promoted by interested groups. The largest is probably what is known as "The Kiamichi Clinic" which draws between 3,000 and 4,000 men from all over the nation each year to Hanobia, Oklahoma, in the Kiamichi Mountains. It features preaching, fellowship and a strong testimony against the Communist conspiracy. About this same number of men and women come to Cincinnati, Ohio, each fall for the nationwide "Conference on Evangelism," sponsored by the Cincinnati Bible Seminary. As its name implies, it is concerned primarily with preaching and methods of implementing the Great Commission. The Southern

Christian Convention provides a meeting place for brethren in the southeastern states. The Midwest Christian Convention, the Pacific Christian Convention and an increasing number of State conventions draw great numbers of ministers, elders, deacons, teachers and their families who go home inspired to redouble their efforts in behalf of the Restoration. None of these gatherings claims any official character but they all make an important contribution to brotherhood life.

Strong local churches feature the work of the Centrists across the nation. Scores of churches with Sunday Schools of over one thousand and memberships even larger carry on active local programs. First Church, Canton, Ohio, has some 7,000 members and three other churches in the immediate area have around 1,000 members each. First Church, Columbus, Indiana, with over 2,000 members is housed in a magnificent Saarinen-designed edifice, with singing tower and mirror lake, occupying a whole city block. The Thousand Oaks, California, Church has a Frank Lloyd Wright building that is the marvel of the area and has plans for a colony of retirement homes and children's homes as adjuncts of an ever-enlarging ministry.

In the field of education a few schools of higher education had remained loyal to Restoration ideals, such as Milligan College, Johnson Bible College, Minnesota Bible College and Kentucky Christian College. But it soon became apparent that more institutions were necessary if the demands of the churches for trained leadership were to be met. Then ensued a "crash program" in which Centrists eventually established 32 new schools now enrolling over 4,000 students preparing for full-time Christian service.

The Cincinnati Bible Seminary, the largest of the newer schools, is located on a twenty-five-acre campus overlooking the city. Under the presidencies of Ralph L. Records and Woodrow W. Perry, the Seminary has taken a position of leadership in preparing youth for the ministry and the mission field. Many of the newer schools and direct-supported missions have been organized by its graduates. New buildings continue to rise to care for its growing enrollment. Currently more than seven hundred students are in residence. The Seminary has a Graduate School, of which Lewis Foster is dean.

In 1927, E. C. Sanderson purchased a site adjacent to the campus of what is now Kansas State University in Manhattan, and founded "Christian Workers University," now known as Manhattan Bible College. T. H. Johnson became head of the institution, guiding it during the formative years in which buildings were constructed, courses of study formulated, and faculty assembled. President Wilford F. Lown has carried on an effective moderate policy educating a leadership which will "speak the truth in love." Its graduates serve many churches in Kansas and its border states and are engaged in foreign missionary work

On the site of the historical Civil War Battle of Atlanta rise the new buildings of Atlanta Christian College. The campus was the gift of Judge and Mrs. T. O. Hathcock. First classes were held in 1928. James C. Redmon succeeded Orval Crowder as president in 1955. Their administrations were marked by great progress and the development of a strong Centrist constituency in the South.

Pacific Bible Seminary was organized in 1928 with first classes meeting in the Alvarado church, Los Angeles. George P. Rutledge, a former editor of the *Christian Standard*, was its first president. Under the presidency of James S. Hurst, a campus was purchased opposite the Long Beach municipal golf course, and buildings erected. President Kenneth A. Stewart has stabilized the work of the Seminary and greatly expanded its influence in this burgeoning metropolitan area in the West.

Ten years later (1939), E. C. Sanderson purchased property in San Jose, California, to establish San Jose Bible College, serving the vast middle Pacific coastal area of the brotherhood. It remained for President William L. Jessup to develop the strong institution which now occupies new buildings. The College's annual Conference on Evangelism spurs the establishment of new congregations and gives an evangelistic emphasis to the work of all the church. Alvan L. Tiffin is president.

In 1942, Ozark Bible College opened its doors in Bentonville, Arkansas. Two years later it moved to Joplin, Missouri, where it enrolls some five hundred students on a new campus. It serves the growing Ozark community of churches in the four-state area of Missouri, Kansas, Arkansas and Oklahoma, although it draws students from many other states. Under the leadership of President Don Earl Boatman and Dean Seth Wilson, great gains are being recorded. A School of Missions has been established.

Rivaling the Cincinnati Bible Seminary for numerical leadership of the new Centrist educational complex is Lincoln Christian College (formerly Lincoln Bible Institute), founded in 1944. President Earl C. Hargrove has been the moving spirit from the beginning. The institution seeks to grant the highest educational degrees. Lincoln has become the center of area rallies and conferences resulting in new churches, new missions, and more effective evangelistic and educational work in existing churches. An entire campus of new buildings has been erected. A significant graduate program is conducted in the Lincoln Christian Seminary. Enos E. Dowling is dean.

To this list may be added Midwest Christian College; Roanoke Bible College; Puget Sound College of the Bible; Eastern Christian College; Nebraska Christian College (1944); Boise Bible College (1945); Intermountain Bible College (1946); Southwest Christian Seminary (1947); Midwestern School of Evangelism (1947); Central Washington School of the Bible (1948); Great Lakes Bible College (1949); Louisville Bible College (1949); Dallas Christian College (1950); Platte Valley Bible College (1952); Church of Christ School of Evangelists (1952); Grundy Bible Institute (1956); Central Christian College of the Bible (1957); St. Louis Christian College

189

(1957); Memphis Christian College (1959); and Emmanuel School of Religion (1965).

Two colleges in the United States are serving Negro churches: College of the Scriptures at Louisville (1945) and Winston-Salem Bible College (1950). Colegio Biblico, at Eagle Pass, Texas (1945) and Mexican Bible Seminary, at Nogales, Arizona (1950) serve the Mexican missions.

Canada has three Bible colleges. Alberta Bible College began in 1932; Toronto Christian Seminary, in 1959; and Maritime Christian College, in 1960.

Each school in its own way is seeking to make a worthwhile contribution to Christian leadership training. More than four thousand students, most of whom are dedicated to full-time Christian service, are enrolled in these institutions.

Missionary activity, which had dwindled in size and spirit in the institutions controlled by Leftists, rose to new heights. Many missions on the world field split because of Liberal tyranny. Hundreds of volunteers went abroad to establish new missions. Today it is estimated that these so-called "independent" or "direct-support" missionaries of Christian Churches and Churches of Christ number over 800 serving in more than 30 foreign countries.

Centrist concern in the field of Christian benevolence is reflected in two hospitals, six homes for the aged, twelve children's homes with many other similar institutions projected in every area of the nation.

Standard Publishing, one of the largest and most modern printing establishments in the nation, produces annually millions of copies of publications serving Centrist churches. More than fifty capably staffed periodicals, including the 100-year-old *Christian Standard*, go out to an ever-expanding constituency in all sectors of the Restoration Movement and far beyond it to the evangelical Christian world at large.

An encouraging development in relations between Rightists and Centrists in this great Movement gives promise of better understanding and closer unity. There are those who opti- mistically predict that in another generation the 4,000,000 Christians they represent will be working together to achieve their common goals. It is said that these two groups are ex- panding so rapidly that a new Christian Church or Church of Christ is being opened every day some place in the world. It is characteristic of individual families that when they move to a community in which there is no congregation of their persuasion, they establish "a church in the house" and invite their neighbors to worship with them. In a short time property is purchased and a full-fledged new congregation is soon func- tioning. Thus the free church idea continues to demonstrate its effectiveness in advancing the Kingdom of God in a free America.

X

PRESBYTERIANS FOR FREEDOM

PRESBYTERIANISM has produced some of Christendom's most revolutionary leaders. Protestants owe Presbyterians a great debt for the part they played in deliverance from ecclesiastical despotism. For centuries Presbyterians have fought for the absolute authority of the Bible in all matters of faith and life and for the sovereignty of the individual conscience in its interpretation.

The names of John Calvin and John Knox are household words in the Protestant community. While these great men held views on the relationship of Church and State which are somewhat at variance with American political concepts, they made possible many new freedoms for the people of Switzerland and Scotland and planted the seeds of federalism which fructified, to a large degree, in the establishment of our American constitutional liberties.

There have been frequent cases of what might be called a "holy separatism" in Presbyterianism. The blessing of the faithful confession is still a very great reality. In this connection one thinks of the disruption in Scotland in 1843 when 470 out of 1500 ministers of the Church of Scotland left the General Assembly, left their churches, manses and stipends because their conscience did not allow them to sacrifice the divine right of the Church to the arbitrary law made by Parliament in London. Within one year 500 new churches were built, 500 new congregations of the Free Church of Scotland established, and the Reformed faith was saved for a hundred years. Even a separation can be a great service to true ecumenicity if it is separation from that which is bound to destroy the true church, the *Una Sancta Ecclesia.*

PRESBYTERIANS IN AMERICA

American Presbyterians are the direct descendants of their Calvinist forebears in England and Scotland. In England the establishment of Presbyterianism was deeply involved with the Puritan conflict. The Puritans were intensely Calvinistic in their theology and worship and opposed to the hierarchal form of church government. Under Oliver Cromwell they overthrew the Episcopal hierarchy, exiled royalist clergymen, deposed and executed the Archbishop and finally the King of England himself. Via Parliament and the "Scotch League and Covenant" came the Westminster Confession of Faith which has been the guiding light of Presbyterianism ever since. Indeed, it may be said that no other religious document has had so significant an effect on American church life and, incidentally, on many of America's political ideas. But it was in Scotland that Presbyterianism came to full flower. In its quest for freedom to practice its beliefs it took to the sword and fire. Any tourist can see today the massive ruins, which symbolize the wrack of ecclesiastical tyranny, left by the followers of John Knox. Modern Presbyterians who oppose similar tyrannies in their own churches and in the councils of churches come honestly by their crusading spirit.

The first presbytery in America was established in Philadelphia in 1706. By 1716 the presbytery had increased to such an extent that it was organized as a synod with four presbyteries. Presbyterianism went through long years of persecution, blood, sweat and tears until it became established as a respected and influential member of the American church family. Today in all its branches it numbers nearly five million communicants.

THE INTRODUCTION OF LIBERALISM

During the Civil War Southern Presbyterians withdrew fellowship with the Northern body. We shall consider them later. But Philadelphia has long been psychologically the center of American Presbyterianism. Because Presbyterians long insisted on thorough indoctrination in the Confessions, doctrinal innovations did not easily take root in the denomination. But the Liberal Establishment of American Protestantism finally infiltrated key positions. After the adoption by the General Assembly of the so-called "Declaratory Statement" in 1903, historic confessional standards were weakened. But even then with such stalwart theologians as B. B. Warfield and Robert Dick Wilson, missionary leaders like Robert E. Speer, lay leaders like William Jennings Bryan and John Wanamaker, and clergymen of the stature of Maitland Alexander and Clarence E. Macartney, it seemed that the descendants of John Calvin and John Knox might be impervious to a Liberal take-over. The General Assembly frequently warned the church to be on guard to preserve the Faith as set forth in the Holy Scriptures and the Westminster Confession.

Then the Union Theological Seminary of New York became the center of an activist Liberal onslaught. So strong were the evangelical forces, however, that Union's Presbyterian ties were severed. Despite this fact Union had so many pipelines to people and places of authority that by strangely devious means its Liberal theological and socio-political doctrines gained wide acceptance. Union's graduates began to show up in Presbyterian theological seminaries, prominent pulpits, and in key positions in Philadelphia, in the presbyteries and in the synods. In the ensuing battle for power liberals like George A. Buttrick and Henry Sloane Coffin became the administrative, theological and sociological leaders of the church. The conservative Philadelphia Presbytery demanded the ouster of liberal Harry Emerson Fosdick from the pulpit of the First Presbyterian Church, New York City. In 1923 the General Assembly condemned Liberalism in its "Five Essential Doctrines of the Word of God and Presbyterian Standards," but for all practical purposes it was meaningless. Liberalism had gained sufficient strength that hundreds of ministers were taking their ordination vows with "mental reservations" and "tongue in cheek." Indeed 1,292 ministers were bold enough to state their interpretations of the Westminster Confession in the noteworthy "Auburn Affirmation of 1923." It said in effect:

(1) We do not believe in the inerrancy of the Holy Scriptures or accept them as final authority in faith and practice; (2) we accept the Incarnation of Christ as a fact but deny the biblical doctrine of the Virgin Birth; (3) we deny that on the cross Christ "satisfied divine justice and reconciled mankind to God"; (4) we doubt that Christ rose from the dead "in the same body in which he suffered"; (5) we deny the supernatural element in Christ's miracles and (by inference) the supernatural element in his redemptive work.

The text of the Affirmation taken alone seemed comparatively harmless. It could only be fully understood in its true meaning when compared with the Westminster Confession itself and the historic Auburn Affirmation of 1837 which had let down the first bars to liberalism and was a portent of the "Confession of 1967" which gives promise of sounding the death knell for the Westminster Confession, as any longer the official expression of Presbyterian doctrine in the Northern church.

LIBERALISM IN CONTROL

Princeton, Presbyterianism's leading theological seminary, finally fell before the Liberal avalanche. Conservative scholars like J. Gresham Machen, Robert Dick Wilson, and J. Oswald Allis withdrew to set up Westminster Theological Seminary in Philadelphia. The Independent Presbyterian Board for Foreign Missions was organized. When the General Assembly repudiated the Board, and threatened to expel all churches and to excommunicate all pastors supporting it, it became apparent that Liberals sat on the seats of Presbyterian power. Under Eugene Carson Blake, Presbyterianism's highest office of Stated Clerk (deliberately so named to discourage ecclesiastical popery) became the seat of ruthless Liberal discipline exercised in all the pious, devious and sanctimonious ways that can be devised by clever religious strategists. The great theological seminaries had become centers of higher criticism, the Social Gospel and (in some classrooms) Marxist philosophies. Closer relationships were established with the National Council of Churches and the World Council so that the Presbyterian hierarchy became the medium through which the Liberal doctrines and programs of the councils were disseminated in the churches. The curriculum for Presbyterian church schools was revised for this purpose, and dire threats were made against all churches and ministers who failed to use its textbooks to the exclusion of all others. The make-up of the general division of publication guarantees that the Liberal point of view will determine the policies of all official periodicals and the type of books published. Independent journals like the old *Presbyterian Banner* and *The Presbyterian* were destroyed. In fact, all media of communication are now under Liberal control. Strengthened by merger with the old United Presbyterian Church (1958), the United Presbyterian Church in the USA has become a dominant factor in conciliar Protestantism.

While Liberals are in control of Northern Presbyterian institutions and denominational machinery, this does not mean that true Presbyterianism is dead or that the free spirit of American Protestantism has departed from this great communion. There are still within the United Presbyterian Church in the U.S.A. many individual churches that are veritable citadels of faith, possibly a few presbyteries and a whole host of ministers and laymen. They have chosen the Road to Freedom and they intend to travel it regardless of the cost.

CITADELS OF FAITH

Take the Philadelphia area as an example. Philadelphia Presbytery, despite the fact that it is the locus of the General Assembly and its ecclesiastical bureaucracy, is quite conservative. Many of its churches defy the Liberal "powers that be," using evangelical Sunday school literature in their church schools, co-operating in evangelical ministerial groups, and openly opposing the official socio-political views of headquarters. The influence of the late John Wanamaker still lingers. The voice of the elder statesman J. Howard Pew still speaks with authority. The spirit of the short-lived conservative Presbyterian periodical, *Christianity Today*, published in Philadelphia, and now revived in the great Protestant magazine which perpetuates its name, sways the thought and action of thousands of Presbyterians. The ministry of Donald Grey Barnhouse in Tenth Church lingers in his magazine, *Eternity*, his radio broadcast and the many agencies he initiated during his phenomenal career. His brilliant and powerful evangelical testimony still brings conviction and inspires to action. J. Gresham Machen was a Philadelphian. On the grounds of the beautiful Machen mansion now stands the Westminster Theological Seminary he founded—an institution dedicated to the training of a new leadership for a reborn Presbyterianism. Also on the magnificent estate of the Wilder family stands Faith Theological Seminary teaching a pure Calvinistic theology and graduating an ever-enlarging stream of committed pastors, teachers and leaders. Out of Philadelphia came two new Presbyterian denominations—the Orthodox Presbyterian

Church and the Bible Presbyterian Church—effective protests against Liberal dominance in the old Church and now dedicated to the dissemination of a constructive Presbyterian testimony throughout the nation.

First Presbyterian Church, Pittsburgh, stands like a Rock of Gibraltar for the old faith. Located in the heart of this great city in its magnificent cathedral-like edifice its testimony is heard and honored throughout the nation. Here Maitland Alexander and Clarence E. Macartney dignified the Presbyterian pulpit. Here for many years a thousand or more business and professional men of Pittsburgh gathered at a noon meal each week to be fed the Bread of Life by these masterful ministers. Robert Lamont carries on in this tradition. Many churches in the Pittsburgh Presbytery stand foursquare for the old faith. Calvary Church, Wilkinsburg, where Howard Tucker ministers, has taken a bold stand for the Gospel and vigorously opposes the liberal programs of both the National and World Councils of Churches. The Mount Lebanon Church, one of the largest in the nation, has a strong, clear testimony. So the number could be multiplied.

Seattle, Washington, where Mark Matthews carried on his unique ministry for many years in what he called "the largest Presbyterian church in the United States," is a citadel of faith in the Calvinistic tradition. Ralph G. Trumbull now leads the flock of First Church and exerts a tremendous influence in the many churches which call First Church their mother. In Tacoma stands Albert J. Lindsey in the great First Church shunning not to speak bravely and convincingly for the evangelical faith and for the social and political principles that have made America great. The Northwest also has Whitworth College which within the limits of its appointed ministry holds forth the Word of Life effectively.

In Los Angeles, California, the most rapidly growing complex in the nation, stands unswerving Florence Avenue Church with

William T. Strong as its pastor. On Wilshire Boulevard is the great Church where John Bunyan Smith stood for so many years battling for the right. Hollywood's First Presbyterian Church has been a tower of strength to thousands. Its laymen investigated and condemned the National Council of Churches. Here it was that the noted youth leader and educational expert, Henrietta Mears, built the largest Presbyterian Sunday School in America. When the "new curriculum" came out, she revolted at its liberal and theological and socio-political content and led in preparing a whole new biblical course of study. So widespread was the demand for this true-to-the-Bible literature that she established Gospel Light Publications to produce it. Today this company has grown to be one of the largest in the Sunday school publishers field with branches in many parts of the world.

In Duluth, Minnesota, First Church, under the leadership of Frederick Curtis Fowler, has become a lighthouse for the pure and unalloyed evangelical testimony. The Duluth Presbytery is one of the few in the nation that maintains its free and unencumbered autonomy as a center of Presbyterian integrity and strength. Dr. Fowler is active in many evangelical Protestant organizations and has served as president of the National Association of Evangelicals. He is in demand from coast to coast as a patriotic speaker calling for a rebirth of the righteousness that exalts a nation.

In the heartland of America there are many other strong citadels of faith such as Buena Memorial Church, Chicago, where William J. Larkin ministers; Covenant-First Church, Cincinnati, the mother church of Presbyterianism in southwestern Ohio, where Irvin Shortess Yeaworth leads; and the historic First Church, Schenectady, New York, under the inspired shepherding of Herbert S. Mekeel. Time would fail to tell of hundreds more that are keeping the eternal flame of the biblical and evangelical faith shining despite all the restraining influences that emanate from the Liberal Establishment.

THE NEW CONFESSION

A recent poll of conservative Presbyterian ministers in the Northern church asked the question, "What do you consider the most important issue confronting American Presbyterianism today?" It was the consensus of these men that it is the so-called "Confession'of 1967." In the context of the new Confession the supposedly evangelical statements it contains are quite meaningless. The Westminster Confession is "inspirational," built on the mighty acts of God as revealed in the inspired Word of God (the Holy Scriptures), and biblical defininitions of faith which are unchangingly true and essential for all men to believe. The new Confession is "revelational" presenting a wholly functional doctrine of the Church and its mission in the world. It is a Church reformed and always reforming to meet the needs of a changing world under the guidance of the Holy Spirit. The salvation it offers is purely social—"to be reconciled to God is to be sent into the world as his reconciling community." Every word, phrase, sentence and paragraph in the new document must be measured and interpreted by reference to this context which is the Liberal "social gospel" pure and simple. As John H. Gerstner has said, the new Confession is destined to become "an indelible blemish on the escutcheon of the Presbyterian Church."

Much is made of the fact that, even though the presbyteries and the General Assembly voted to approve the new creed, it will not become the sole and exclusive statement of faith for the denomination. It will only be placed in a *Book of Confessions* along with the Westminster Confession, the Apostles Creed, the Nicene Creed and several historic confessions of the Reformed tradition. Presbyterians can "pay their money and take their choice" of things to believe. This will, of course, have the effect of undermining and destroying the necessity of having any biblical faith at all, and of conditioning Presbyterians for inevitable participation in the Coming Great Ecumenical Church. The minister of a large midwestern church wrote, "The New Confession will remove us completely from the status of a Confessional Church and the Reformed doctrine and faith. I am opposed to it and my church is opposed to it. We may later find it necessary to withdraw from the denomination."

CONCERNED PRESBYTERIAN LAYMEN

Opposition to the New Confession was widespread among Presbyterian USA laymen. A Presbyterian Lay Committee was soon created which addressed itself to the task of informing Presbyterians about the dangers inherent in the document. The Committee consisted of such prominent lay leaders as: Roger Hull, Paul J. Cupp, Hugh F. MacMillan, John W. Humphrey, William C. Albertson, George Champion, Carlton G. Ketchum, Clayton Collyer, William B. Kiesewetter, Jasper Crane, Ronald C. Doll, Clarence McGuire, Fred Russell Esty, J. Howard Pew, Lem T. Jones, W. Robert Stover, Carl Trauernicht. Early in 1967 the Committee took large display space in all the leading metropolitan dailies in the United States setting forth "A Call to Every United Presbyterian." It read as follows:

The proposed "Confession of 1967," as approved by the 1966 General Assembly, confronts the United Presbyterian Church, U.S.A. with a serious challenge.

If this Confession is ratified by two-thirds of all the Presbyteries and approved by the next General Assembly in May of 1967, our church may well have undergone the most radical and revolutionary change in its entire history.

At the General Assembly, there was little opportunity for effective opposition, criticism or careful consideration of such an important change.

Therefore, anything that is to be done to stop this Confession from being adopted must be done by lay members and concerned ministers. As members of the Presbyterian Lay Committee, we are opposed to this new Confession. We firmly believe that, in its attempt to up-date the confessional position of the church, it undermines certain basics of our

Christian faith. It also lacks the clarity of our time honored West-minster Confession.

The purpose of this call is (1) to make sure that every Presbyterian is fully aware of the sweeping changes that have been proposed (2) to indicate what this may mean to the future of the Church and (3) what you still can do about it if you disagree with the changes being proposed.

*   *   *

Very few Presbyterians have read The Proposed Book of Confessions as it was approved by the 178th General Assembly in Boston on May 24, 1966. A surprising number of laymen are not even aware that such radical and revolutionary changes in the confessional position of the United Presbyterian Church are being proposed.

This proposed document is the result of some eight years of work of a Special Committee on a Brief Contemporary Statement of Faith. It was then reviewed and revised by a special Committee of Fifteen which considered suggestions submitted by Synods, Presbyteries, Ministers, Church Sessions and lay members.

As often happens with the written efforts of committees, the resulting product is so full of compromises, concessions, contradictions, and obscure sentences that it promotes serious disagreements in the way it is interpreted and applied.

Far more serious, however, is the radical nature of some of the proposals that shatter the very foundation of our faith.

All this has disturbed an increasing number of dedicated members. They are concerned over the direction our church is taking in its interpretation of the Bible and in its becoming more and more involved in secular matters at the expense of the true ecclesiastic mission of the church as defined in the Westminster Confession.

I. THE CHANGES

Let us illustrate with a few of the more radical changes found in the Confession of 1967.

Is the Bible "Words of Men" or the "Infallible Word of God"?

Did you realize that the Bible will no longer be considered as the inspired and infallible word of God? How far the authors would go

202

in humanizing the Bible can be realized in this excerpt from the new Confession:

"The Scriptures, given under the guidance of the Holy Spirit, are nevertheless the words of men, contained by the language, thought forms, and literary fashions of the places and times in which they were written. They reflect views of life, history and the cosmos which were then current. The church, therefore, has an obligation to approach the Scriptures with literary and historical understanding." (Part I, Sec. C, No. 2)

The Westminster Confession which is a part of our church constitution clearly states the truth that has guided us for twenty centuries:

"The authority of the Holy Scripture, for which it ought to be believed and obeyed, dependeth not upon the testimony of any man or church, but wholly upon God (who is truth itself) the author thereof; and therefore it is to be received because it is the word of God." (Chapter I, No. 4)

The Bible contains over 3,000 references to "the Word of God" as put into the mouths of the Prophets. Christ himself accepted the revelations of the Prophets as the true Word of God, and Christ, being Divine, could not have made a mistake.

Are you willing to give up your belief in the Bible as the true and infallible Word of God? Are the Scriptures a divine guide or is the Bible a human and, therefore, unreliable document?

The new Confession now attempts to answer these questions in a way that weakens the concept of the Bible as we have always accepted it. It claims to be a modern document necessary to challenge the modern age. But careful study reveals a close parallel between the criticism of atheists and extreme liberals down through history.

Involvement in Social, Political and Economic Issues

Here are three more illustrations of radical changes that are proposed by the new Confession:

"In each time and place there are particular problems and crises through which God calls the church to act. The following are particularly urgent at the present time:

(Part II, Sec. A, No. 4)

4a "The church is called to bring all men to receive and uphold one

203

another as persons in all relationships of life: in employment, housing, education, leisure, marriage, family, church, and the exercise of political rights. Therefore, the church labors for the abolition of all racial discrimination. Congregations, individuals, or groups of Christians who exclude, dominate, or patronize their fellow men, however subtly, resist the Spirit of God and bring contempt on the faith which they possess."

4b "The church, in its own life, is called to practice the forgiveness of its enemies and to commend to the nations as practical politics the search for cooperation and peace. This requires the pursuit of fresh and responsible relations across every line of conflict even at risk to national security, to reduce areas of strife and to broaden international understanding."

4c "A church that . . . evades responsibility in economic affairs . . . offers no acceptable worship to God."

Do you accept the belief that your church should take whatever position on any political, social, or economic issue the governing body of the church decides is the proper one? Who decides what issues are to be opposed, what are to be supported? On what basis are church leaders qualified to make a judgment on such secular problems of the day?

"Render therefore unto Caesar the things that are Caesar's; and unto God, the things that are God's" is the way Christ answered this whole question (Matthew 22:21). The Westminster Confession states it clearly:

"Synods and councils are to handle or conclude nothing but that which is ecclesiastical, and are not to intermeddle with civil affairs which concern the commonwealth." (Chapter XXXI, No. 4)

Protestant denominations generally have limited themselves in their jurisdiction to ecclesiastical and spiritual subjects. This fundamental was recognized by Christ, the Apostles, the Early Church, The Reformers, the Westminster Divines, and our own Church founders. However, all these have encouraged their members to become involved in economic, social, and political affairs wherever they possessed competence and knowledge as individuals, but not under the dictates of the Church.

II. WHAT THE CHANGES SIGNIFY

The 1967 Confession does not ring true. It is so filled with ambiguities, undefined statements, involved meanings, and obscure language that it becomes possible to rationalize almost any point of view the reader seeks to establish.

The Westminster Confession of Faith, on the other hand, is so clearly and succinctly stated that anyone who can read can understand its meaning. It does not require a group of intellectuals to explain it.

This greatest of all our church documents has been the safeguard of our Faith for centuries. As included in "The Proposed Book of Confessions" issued August 1966, the Westminster Confession of Faith remains as a part of our Church Constitution, although the Confession of 1967 makes only passing reference to it. Presumably it will have future recognition only from a literary, technical, and historical standpoint. Thus, its power to safeguard the Faith of our fathers will have been severely limited.

The drive was unable to stop a vote in the presbyteries favorable to the New Confession, but the Committee did not give up the fight. It carried it to the General Assembly. There it was defeated in its efforts. Some grave consequences can be expected for the Presbyterian Church in the U.S.A. as the result of the adoption of this Confession. Many churches have voted to reject it and ban all ministers who accept it. Many lay leaders are continuing their active opposition in divers ways.

Presbyterian laymen are as much concerned over the socio-political stance of the Liberal-controlled church as they are with its theological declension. J. Howard Pew in a trenchant article, "Should the Church 'Meddle' in Civil Affairs?" which appeared in *Christianity Today* and also in *Reader's Digest*, saw the "Confession of 1967" as weakening faith in the Holy Scriptures and thus creating a vacuum into which can pour all sorts of strange socio-political doctrines. He said that already Presbyterian preachers, educators and administrators are concerned not for the souls of men but for the world. Expressing this new concern are new-type evangelists, without any competence in either the field of statecraft or economics, who are attempting to pressure the churches into action on federal aid

205

to education, civil rights, urban renewal, the nation's foreign policy, and plugging for such controversial issues as the admission of Red China into the United Nations, disarmament, higher minimum wages, forcible union membership and a whole host of other distinctly civil affairs. Such strong protests seem to fall on deaf ears in Philadelphia where the Stated Clerk, chiefs of divisions and departments, officers of boards and commissions, and staff members galore have marched in civil rights demonstrations, participated in sit-ins, broken the law and courted jail sentences, lent their names to all sorts of subversive organizations, and invited Communist-oriented religious leaders into their councils and churches. Indeed, one Liberal pastor in Chicago said recently, "We may get into all sorts of trouble and even real schism if we press sociopolitical issues in the churches. Some congregations are going to be split right up the middle in the next ten years. So mote it be." Pew closed his article in *Reader's Digest* by saying, "If the church's social activists are to be halted from plunging the church again into areas where it has no jurisdiction, its concerned laymen and clergymen will have to make their voices heard in the high councils of their denominations." This is good advice, but one wonders at the effectiveness of protest at the highest denominational level where firmly entrenched Liberals are now taking their orders from New York and Geneva and not from the people who unwittingly placed them in their seats of authority. Many Presbyterian laymen are taking another course. They are withdrawing their financial support from the denominational hierarchy and the councils of churches which control its personnel. Indeed, these laymen are getting to the point where, if all else fails, they will withdraw from their denomination and cast their lot with other Christians who are truly concerned about the main business of the Church and are getting things done for Christ according to His will and way. Hundreds of prominent business men have already left the denomination.

MINISTERS IN REVOLT

It is not so easy for ministers to take the Road to Freedom. Their salaries and emoluments, their status and relationships are controlled by Philadelphia. Their congregations are cowed by the fact that their church properties are really not their own and can be padlocked against them or sold over their heads. Only a few pastors have had the courage or the temerity to take an open public stand for their convictions against the "powers that be." These men have paid dearly for their actions. Two or three examples:

Charles S. Poling, distinguished brother of Daniel A. Poling (long-time editor of *Christian Herald*), had held several of the larger churches of the denomination. At the time of his great decision he was pastor of the First Presbyterian Church, Phoenix, Arizona. For years he had sought to oppose trends toward liberalism and ecclesiastical power politics in his dearly-beloved communion. At the 175th General Assembly he saw the Church once again ally itself with godless forces in the nation in its official positions on moral, social and religious issues. He saw it moving away from its historic faith and toward absorption in a massive ecumenical ecclesiasticism. The atmosphere of the Assembly was, to him, so repulsive and hopeless that he returned to Phoenix determined to speak out boldly once and for all and take the consequences whatever they might be. He discovered that this meant being unfrocked as a Presbyterian clergyman, so February 17, 1964, he preached his famous sermon, "Choose You This Day," and withdrew membership from the United Presbyterian Church. His action was a sensation in the city and in the nation, insofar as the Liberal-controlled press would mention it. The denomination he had served so faithfully for many years turned against him. Its pulpits were closed to him. His character was assailed. Finally, answering to the pleadings of many disillusioned conservatives in a number of liberal Protestant churches in Phoenix, he consented to become the pastor of a new undenominational independent church true to the fundamentals of the Christian faith and the basic ethical and social principles of the American way of life.

Stuart H. Merriam, brilliant conservative minister of the historic Broadway Presbyterian Church, New York City, was ousted from the pulpit in May 1962 by action of the New York Presbytery. Merriam had opposed the socio-political program of the Board of Missions and the Commission on Ecumenical Mission and had dared to raise funds for the support of an independent mission in New Guinea. He had spoken repeatedly against the "alarming and inordinate" powers over the churches assumed by Liberals in the higher echelons of authority—presbyteries, synods and the Philadelphia bureaucracy. When he was placed under the "jurisdiction of presbytery" the church split. Those who supported Merriam were permitted for a time to meet in the church basement for services which he conducted but at the same time another minister approved by the presbytery held services in the sanctuary. Merriam appealed his case to the General Assembly. When it gave its expected decision upholding presbytery, Merriam's salary was ordered stopped and he was barred from the Broadway building. Presbytery announced that he had not been amenable to constituted authority and that his conservative theology and his actions had demonstrated his unfitness to serve a Presbyterian church in the neighborhood of Columbia University. Merriam withdrew from the Presbyterian church and buried his life in the jungles of New Guinea in an independent missionary ministry to the aborigines.

The most publicized case of a Presbyterian minister who dared openly and publicly to challenge the authority of the Liberal Establishment is that of Carl McIntire. He was pastor of the large and influential Collingwood (New Jersey) Church in the environs of Philadelphia. Under his ministry it had grown and a beautiful commodious church edifice had been erected. He made the "mistake" of supporting the revolt of J. Gresham Machen and others at Princeton and joining in the establishment of the Independent Presbyterian Board of Foreign Missions. Collingwood withdrew its support of denominational agencies and the Councils of Churches and took its stand for the creation of new media through which denominational and interdenominational work could be done without compromise of the fundamental and historic doctrines of the Christian Church. After a long and bitter feud with Presbyterian authorities the church building was padlocked against McIntire and the congregation which stood with him almost to a man. McIntire himself was unfrocked as a Presbyterian minister and smeared with every charge of malfeasance that could be devised by his persecutors. On the morning he and his people were denied entrance into the sanctuary they had toiled and sacrificed to build, a procession blocks long was formed and nearly a thousand people marched to a new temporary tabernacle that had been erected. Since that day a magnificent new colonial complex of church buildings has been erected to house the dissident congregation, now affiliated with the Bible Presbyterian Church.

Scores of Presbyterian ministers of smaller and unpublicized churches have left the fellowship of their denomination under similar circumstances. This trend is likely to continue.

PRESBYTERIAN CHURCH IN THE U. S.

The separation of the Southern Presbyterians from their Northern brethren is usually attributed to a division of views on the question of slavery. This was the most apparent reason for the division but it went deeper than that. It involved questions of theology, ethics and ecclesiastical procedure. The Southern presbyteries that withdrew constituted the Presbyterian Church in the United States which today has a membership approaching one million.

The Southern church has been marked by a greater theological conservatism than the Northern church and a strong antipathy for any sort of socio-political action. This latter position traces back to the original break when Southern churches insisted that according to Presbyterian church law the General Assembly had no right to introduce and decide a political question, still less to make its decision a test of fellowship.

Southern Presbyterians lived in comparative peace and prosperity until the issue of participation in the Councils of Churches was raised. At this time conservatives in theology and social action were in charge of most of the denomination's institutional life, although there were glimmerings of Liberalism in the press and the theological seminaries. The great mass of Southern Presbyterians did not want to affiliate with the Councils, but many denominational leaders sincerely felt that their Church should show its concern for inter-church co-operation and united action in matters which were for the welfare of church and state. So through the years the Church has been in and out and is now again in the National Council of Churches and the World Council. No General Assembly meets, however, without receiving official communications from many Presbyteries asking the Assembly to withdraw from the Councils. Presbyteries are flooded with such protests from their constituent churches. Southern Presbyterians are very unhappy in this relationship.

CHURCHES MAKE BOLD DECISIONS

As in the Northern church there are mighty citadels of faith in Southern Presbyterianism—local churches that stand foursquare for "the faith once for all delivered" and that have taken a strong stand against the National Council.

Among the large and influential churches that have withdrawn support from the Council and/or agencies which support the Council are: First Church, Tyler, Texas; First Church, Johnson City, Tennessee; First Church, Knoxville, Tenn.; Parkway Church, Metarie, La.; First Church, Baton Rouge, La.; First Church, Charleston, S. C.; Gentilly Church, New Orleans, La.; First Church, Columbus, Ga.; First Church, Nashville, Tenn.; Williamsburg Church, Kingstree, S. C.; Union Church, Salters, S. C.; Manning Church, Manning, S. C.; Westminster Church, Shreveport, La.; Westminster Church, Rome, Ga.; First Church, Osceola, Ark.; First Church, Lufkin, Tex.; Vine Street Church, Birmingham, Ala.; First Church, Bessemer, Ala.; Westminster Church, Jackson, Miss.; Eastern Heights Church, Savannah, Ga.; Midway Church, Powder Springs, Ga.; Chickamauga Church, Chickamauga, Ga.; and Westminster Church, Greenville, S. C.

Other churches have gone farther. They have adopted official resolutions against the Council for wider distribution, or for transmission to higher courts. Among these are: St. Johns Church, Jacksonville, Fla.; First Church, Alexandria, La.; Covenant Church, Augusta, Ga.; First Church, Sumter, S. C.; Government Street Church, Mobile Ala.; Westminster Church, Asheville, N. C.; North Avenue Church, Atlanta, Ga.; Hull Memorial Church, Savannah, Ga.; First Church, Macon, Ga.; St. Andrews-Covenant Church, Wilmington, N. C.; First Church, Chattanooga, Tenn.; McIlwain Church, Pensacola, Fla., and Hyde Park Church, Tampa, Fla.

PROPAGANDA FOR THE FAITH

Some years ago a group of conservative brethren launched a new periodical called *The Southern Presbyterian Journal* dedicated to the preservation of the Southern Presbyterian way of life. They had been denied space in the *Presbyterian Survey* and the *Presbyterian Outlook* for the expression of their views.

This proved to be an extremely wise course of action. Without the *Presbyterian Journal*, as it is now called, the conservative voice would not be heard and the facts about Liberal encroachment upon Southern Presbyterian institutions would not be known. Brilliantly edited by G. Aiken Taylor, the *Journal* keeps stressing in a constructive Christian spirit the things Southern Presbyterians most surely believe, but in contrast to the things Liberals believe and the policies and programs they propose. It counsels action through the accepted denominational structures in defense of the faith and in promotion of its God-given task. The *Journal* is feared by the Liberal Establishment which is now rather firmly planted in the colleges and seminaries, the communications media, the boards and commissions, the synods and presbyteries. The *Journal* reaches the grassroots and has a tremendous influence among those who furnish the "sinews of war." Sooner or later the "powers that be" know that they will have to confront the necessity of choice as to whether they will wreck the denomination to achieve their goals or whether they will decide to peaceably abide by Presbyterian principles and law.

Supplementing the work of the *Presbyterian Journal* is a new activist organization known as Concerned Presbyterians, Incorporated. It was inspired and launched under the capable leadership of Kenneth Keyes, the South's leading realtor and an elder in the Shenandoah Church, Miami, Florida. Few Southern Presbyterians were aware of the fact that for the past fifteen years a liberal organization known as the Fellowship of Saint James had been working secretly to gain control of the political machinery of the denomination. In recent years they have succeeded in electing enough men of their choosing to control many of the important committees of the various Church courts and to assure effective majorities on the governing bodies, agencies and other institutions of the Church. The Fellowship also exercises considerable influence in the selection of ministers to fill pulpits of many of the larger and more important churches. When the Fellowship of Saint James came out of hiding, changed its name to the Fellowship of Concern, and began to agitate for more vigorous participation in the National Council of Churches, greater support for the higher critical view of the Bible, and participation in the Consultation for Church Union, conservatives felt that the time had come to fight fire with fire. As a result—Concerned Presbyterians, Incorporated.

A monthly news letter, *The Concerned Presbyterian,* is being broadcast everywhere. In its first issue it stated its purpose to be the returning of the Presbyterian Church in the United States to its Primary Mission—the winning of the unsaved to Christ and nurturing all believers in the Faith. It said Concerned Presbyterians, Incorporated are concerned—

because the primary mission of the Church—winning people to Jesus Christ and nurturing them in the Faith—is being compromised today by over-emphasis on social, economic and political matters, forgetting the basic necessity for regeneration.

because the integrity and authority of the Word of God are being questioned by dubious theories of revelation in some of the literature of the Church.

because some presbyteries no longer require complete loyalty to the Westminster Confession of Faith and the Catechisms.

because continued membership in the National Council of Churches involves us in activities, pronouncements and programs of which we strongly disapprove and repeated protests to that body have been ignored.

because the plan to establish a Central Treasurer now approved by the General Assembly indicates a determination to regiment the benevolence giving of the Church's members by "equalizing" their gifts—in effect actually thwarting the wishes of many donors.

because another determined effort has been started to effect a union of the Presbyterian Church U.S. with the United Presbyterian Church U.S.A. and unite with denominations that do not adhere to the Reformed Faith.

The new organization offers a wide range of literature for use in study groups and for general distribution. It carries exposes of the National Council of Churches and the activities of the Fellowship of Concern. It alerts true Presbyterians to all Liberal movements, plans and programs inimical to the denomination. It urges people to write letters, distribute literature, get elected to office, give or withhold financial support, win converts and above all to pray for victory in their righteous cause. Concerned Presbyterians, Incorporated are having a hard time convincing some Presbyterian pastors and churches that they should not withdraw from the denomination immediately. As an example, in Savannah, Georgia, two churches—Eastern Heights and Hull Memorial—voted overwhelmingly to withdraw. There is no question but that hundreds of churches and pastors are about to reach this stage in thought and action.

CONCERN FOR THE FUTURE

This crucial situation caused the *Journal* to voice the growing feeling that something drastic is likely to happen if the denominational leaders do not abandon their liberal policies and program and get back to the primary mission of the Church. Said the editorial:

We are concerned because of the growing ecclesiasticism within our own Church. Believing with all our hearts in the Doctrine of the Church and her high and rightful place in the life of the Christian and in the world itself, nevertheless the Church is the *Bride* of Christ and not Christ, and we must at all times guard this relationship, never according the Church those attributes and prerogatives which belong to Him alone. We believe in the courts of the Church as the divinely-instituted avenues of debate and decision, but we are unwilling to admit the *infallibility* of Church courts, nor are we willing to equate the decisions of the Church courts with the words of the Holy Writ.

While it is true that free discussion and a majority decision of Church courts should usually lead to right conclusions, and these conclusions should be accorded full respect, it is also true that there is not always full discussion in such meetings, nor are all of the facts always presented to those assembled. It is within reason to believe that some propositions come before Church courts without due analysis, either as to their origins or as to their ultimate implications. For this reason our Confession of Faith recognizes God alone as the Lord of man's conscience and places man's ultimate responsibility to Him, not to any Church court. In Chapter XXXIII, Paragraph III, we read:

"All synods or councils since the apostles' times, whether general or particular, may err, and may have erred; therefore they are not to be made the rule of faith or practice, but to be used as a help to both."

Anticipating danger in the future, because of the experiences of the past, the Westminster divines also said:

"God alone is Lord of the conscience, and hath left it free from the doctrines and commandments of men which are in any thing contrary to His Word, or beside it in matters of faith and worship. So that to believe such doctrines, or to obey such commandments, is to betray true liberty of conscience; and the requiring of implicit faith, and an absolute blind obedience, is to destroy liberty of conscience, and reason also." Chapter XXII, Paragraph II.

Every effort is being made to preserve the unity and peace of the Church. Stress is being laid on an unqualified faith and witness based on the Holy Scriptures and on the need for spiritual awakening and revival. There is earnest prayer for the Church, its agencies and institutions, its pastors and people that all may be used under the mighty hand of God to do His will in His way. But there is also a growing disposition on the part of true Presbyterians to no longer tolerate heresy and left-wing socio-political action in the name of the Presbyterian Church in the United States.

OTHER PRESBYTERIANS

No treatment of Presbyterianism would be complete without a word about the smaller bodies in America adhering to its system. The largest is the Cumberland Presbyterian Church, a Southern body Arminian in theology and more democratic in its ecclesiastical structure than either the Northern or Southern Presbyterian Churches. It numbers around 900 churches with an inclusive membership of over 80,000. The Orthodox Presbyterian Church is the outgrowth of the defection of J. Gresham Machen and others from the Northern church. It reports some 50 churches with a membership of around 12,000. The Bible Presbyterian Church, the outgrowth of the defection of Carl McIntire and others from the Northern Church, numbers about 40 churches with 10,000 members. Then there are the Scottish Presbyterian groups, perpetuating in this country the peculiar convictions of their spiritual ancestors, such as The Synod of the Associate Presbyterian Church of North America, The General Synod of the Associate Reformed Presbyterian Church, The Synod of the Reformed Presbyterian Church of North America (Old School) and The Reformed Presbyterian Church in North America, General Synod; all together they number some 160 churches with a membership totaling not more than 20,000. None of these four bodies is a member of the National Council of Churches or the World Council. Some are active in opposing both organizations.

When American Protestantism again begins to march like a mighty army down the Road to Freedom, there will be millions of Presbyterians in line.

XI

LUTHERANS FOR FREEDOM

TRUE LUTHERANS still honor the spirit of their progenitor Martin Luther and are inspired by the thought of what happened at the Diet of Worms April 17, 1521. On trial for heresy and disobedience, this poor German monk, standing solitary and friendless on the truth of the Holy Scriptures, dared to face Emperor Charles V with all the princes of Germany, papal nuncios and a great array of dignitaries spiritual and temporal, and fearlessly pleaded his case. When called upon to recant, Luther spoke two hours trenchantly, respectfully, wisely, honestly and bravely for the views he had come to hold in opposition to ecclesiastical and theological popery. Then he said. "Confute me by proofs of Scripture or else by plain, just arguments: I cannot recant otherwise. For it is neither safe nor prudent to do aught against conscience. Here stand I. I can do no other. God assist me!"

Carlyle has said that this event "may be considered the greatest scene of modern European history; the point, indeed, from which the whole subsequent history of civilization takes its rise . . . English puritanism, England and its parliaments, the Americas, the French Revolution, Europe and its work everywhere: the germ of it all lay there: had Luther in that moment of decision done other, it had all been otherwise!"

Luther-at-Worms is an eternal symbol of Protestantism at its best. Likewise Luther-at-Wittenberg, when he nailed his "Ninety-five Theses" on the door of the Castle Church. It used to be that all American Protestants celebrated "Reformation Sunday" to commemorate what happened that day at Wittenberg, but not any more. The National Council of Churches and its conciliar appendages, deeply infested by the Liberal popery of our time, find Luther's ideas distasteful. Indeed, only a few American Lutherans keep up the traditional observance, and many of them act as though they were ashamed to remember.

What is the state of Lutheranism today? The majority of Lutheran churches in the world have associated themselves with the World Council of Churches. Most of them are European State Churches suffering the moral and spiritual blight inherent in the Church-State system. They are riddled with secularism, rationalism, humanism, idealism, existentialism and socialism. Most of the theological fads that plague American Protestantism have had their rise in European Lutheranism. This does not mean that the evangelical, biblical faith is without a witness in these churches. Such great bishops as Lilje, Bergraav, and Dibelius have stood for the "faith once delivered" against terrific odds. A remnant of Bible-believing and Christ-honoring laymen still carry on in the best tradition of Luther. But Luther would "turn over in his grave" if he knew of the present state of the European churches that bear his name.

LUTHERANS IN THE UNITED STATES

American Lutheranism owes its beginnings mainly to immigrants who came from Europe to escape the oppression of monarchistic and militaristic government and the rationalism which was rampant in the State Churches. They sought a land that would give them a chance to grow up in a free society and to practice the faith of their fathers in all good consience. These Lutherans came in national and language groups: first, the Dutch; then the Swedes, the Germans, the Danes, the Finns, and all the rest. While the early colonists were readily integrated into the social and political life of America, the later Lutheran immigrants retained their European cultural backgrounds and had little to do with one another. This provincialism proved to be not without some blessings for it encouraged confessional loyalty, a community of mutual interest, and a deep concern for the religious instruction of children and the youth.

It was many years before the nationalist synods would acknowledge their basic kinship with one another and begin to think in terms of a united Lutheranism in America. Indeed, it was not until after World War I that an era of rapprochement began. Commissions on Lutheran Fellowship were set up. The National Lutheran Council came into being. Finally mergers began to take place. To understand the ethnic composition and the doctrinal stance of the major Lutheran denominations today we need some basic information.

The largest modern Lutheran body (3,250,000 communicants) is the Lutheran Church in America, an active constituent member of the National Council of Churches. It is composed of the United Lutheran Church of America (German), the Augustana Evangelical Lutheran Church (Swedish), the American Evangelical Lutheran Church (Danish) and the Finnish Evangelical Lutheran Church. There is a strong strain of Liberalism and hierarchical authoritarianism manifest in this communion.

The second largest body is The Lutheran Church—Missouri Synod (the largest without benefit of mergers). It is German in origin but is said to be the most Lutheran, the most Protestant and the most American of all the major Lutheran denominations. "Missouri" is "pushing" 3,000,000 members and is growing more rapidly than any other Lutheran body. It steadfastly refuses to join either the National Council of Churches or the World Council.

The third largest Lutheran body (2,500,000 communicants) is the American Lutheran Church, which is a member of the World Council of Churches but not, at this writing, of the National Council of Churches. It is composed of the Evangelical Lutheran Church (Norwegian), the American Lutheran Church (German), the United Evangelical Lutheran Church (Danish) and the Lutheran Free Church (Norwegian and Danish). There are strong currents of orthodox biblical faith and congregational freedom is still evident in this denomination.

The rest of the Lutheran denominations in America are: The Wisconsin Evangelical Lutheran Synod with 400,000 members; the Synod of Evangelical Lutheran Churches, 20,000 members; the Evangelical Lutheran Synod, 15,000 members; the Church of the Lutheran Brethren, 7,000 members; the Eielsen Lutheran Synod, 4,500 members; the Protestant Lutheran Conference, 3,000; and the remnant of the Lutheran Free Church which would not consent to merger with the American Lutheran Church. None of these bodies, representing a total constituency of around a half million, is affiliated with the National Council of Churches.

WORLDWIDE LUTHERANISM

The great gulf that for 200 years existed between American and European Lutheranism may be attributed to the fact that American Lutherans enjoyed a greater freedom than their forebears. Americans believed in the separation of Church and State. They accepted the principle of congregational autonomy, holding that the Church is not an earthly monarchy under a visible head, but a communion of saints under Christ, whose highest law for faith and life is the Holy Scriptures.

Europe has never been able to quite rid itself of the blighting heritage of the Holy Roman Empire which claimed complete rule over the souls of man. The Lutheran churches of Europe have never been able to attain that freedom from secular powers which the confessions of the Reformation claimed for the Church of Christ. When king or parliament speaks the church obeys, whether it be on a bishop's denial of biblical doctrine, unscriptural terms of divorce, or pre-marital sex. European Lutheranism's "kept" clergy are by and large imbued with a dangerous rationalism and an incipient secularism.

But the desire for Lutheran fellowship the world around kept pressing on the hearts and consciences of church leaders until finally a world meeting was held in Eisenbach, Germany, in 1923, which eventuated in the creation of the Lutheran World Federation at Lund, Sweden, in 1947. Thus nearly 70,000,000 Lutherans (the largest denominational element in Protestantism) were brought together. The constitutional terms upon which this semblance of unity was achieved sound good, but the predominance of European influence has been marked. The LWF is related, as a confessional body, to the World Council of Churches and is being slowly but surely infected with its left-wing socio-political virus.

LUTHERAN CHURCH IN AMERICA

America's most enthusistic member of the LWF, the NCC and the WCC is the Lutheran Church in America. Partly because it represents a greater variety of Lutherans than any other Lutheran group, it allows for a greater divergence in doctrine and practice. It is weak on biblical matters and many of its pastors take the low view of revelation. The strong Swedish element in the LCA maintains close ties with its European mother church. This is reflected in its liturgy, in its encouragement of centralization of power vested in synodical organizations, in its ecumenical outlook and in its neglectful attitude toward the Lutheran confessions. Samuel Simon Schumacher, for forty years president of Gettysburg Theological Seminary, set the latitudinarian pattern for LCA's confessional stand. He developed a synthesis of the various Protestant confessions of faith, said all the churches could unite in a Federal union, simply drop their divisive names, and work together for the common good of humanity. Today Franklin Clark Fry, LCA's most prominent clergyman, holds much the same view and has become one of the most ardent apologists for and capable leaders of the councils of churches. Liberalism runs rampant in LCA's pulpits. The social gospel has taken the place of the biblical gospel. Fewer sermons speak of the atonement, the resurrection and final judgment; more on such earthly problems as race relations, civil disobedience, government and the good society. The yoke of tyranny, implicit in unlimited support of the councils of churches, is meekly accepted. G. E. Ruff's *The Lutheran* is one of the most openly Liberal official denominational journals in America. LCA offers little hope of revolt against the Councils.

AMERICAN LUTHERAN CHURCH

The situation in the American Lutheran Church is not quite so discouraging. The strong Norwegian biblical strain in its make-up keeps the denomination closer to its orthodox doctrinal commitments than the LCA's. Through assurance that the World Council really believes its doctrinal statement of faith, ALC has voted to be a member. It has not yet been persuaded that the National Council is worthy of its trust. However, a number of its boards have accepted consultative relationships with the Council's functional units. Many outstanding pastors have vigorously and openly opposed all connections with the NCC. Laymen's groups have been formed to counteract NCC socio-political propaganda. Several locally sponsored radio programs deal realistically with the dangers of One Church for One World. Many ALC pastors emphasize the independence and autonomy of the congregation and frown upon supine acceptance of all denominational programs. There is, however, growing disunity in the ranks of the American Church. Theologically speaking, there are devotees of existentialism, neo-orthodoxy, the theology of Bonhoeffer, the revivalistic theology that encourages participation in the Billy Graham crusades, and even the rationalistic theologies of European Lutheranism. But a great many see this divisiveness as a normal and permissive way of life among free churches. They reassure themselves with the thought that it is better to have a church with a sound confessional base to which 95 per cent of its members are nominally committed than to cause any trouble about the 5 per cent who may be in error. With one foot in and one foot out of the Councils they think everybody will be satisfied and peace will prevail. What will happen to ALC in the days ahead is problematical. Council leaders are practically unanimous in the belief that in due time the denomination will be a full-fledged member of both the Councils and completely committed to their Super-Church policies and programs.

THE MISSOURI SYNOD

The citadel of true American Protestantism among the Lutheran family of churches is the Lutheran Church—Missouri Synod. For more than a century it has stood courageously for the biblical and evangelical Christian faith and refused to compromise it in any shape or form. When the councils of churches came on the Protestant scene, Missouri would have none of them and has maintained this stance with but little change to the present day.

Missouri's forebears were Saxons who fled Germany because of the rationalism that was rampant in the State Church and in the homeland around the 1840's. They came to Missouri and settled in Perry County and Saint Louis. They were imbued with a double portion of the spirit of confessionalism. Their fiery zeal for the whole body of Lutheran doctrine was made even more intense by the ardor of their piety. They organized into a synod in 1848 under the powerful leadership of C.F.W. Walther and set up headquarters in Saint Louis. Their denominational conviction and their religious fervor gave them an extraordinary facility in education and evangelism. They have been for years and are today the most rapidly growing sector of American Lutheranism. Repudiating their former hierarchical ideas they emphasized the sovereignty of the local congregation. Within their denominational structure Missourians enjoy great freedom, possibly exceeding that of any other major Lutheran body.

Among the major factors contributing to Missouri's prosperity is its publishing interests. Concordia Press produces only the highest quality materials in the graphic arts—Bibles, churchbooks, schoolbooks, religious periodicals, brochures, papers and tracts for propaganda purposes. To date the virus of liberalism has not noticeably infiltrated its editorial offices.

Education is a mighty arm of the church. Early in Missouri's history it insisted on maintaining its own parochial schools. Thorough Bible-based catechetical instruction provides every child in every family a knowledge of why he is a Christian and a Lutheran Christian. Ask the average Missourian what he believes and he can tell you. Higher education developed with its secondary schools, colleges and seminaries—all distinctly Lutheran and unwilling to make compromises with secular educational philosophies and methods. It is interesting to note that Missouri's first venture in seminary training was in a so-called "practical seminary" at Springfield, Illinois, which prepared consecrated men quickly to minister to the rapid influx of immigrants. Today its standards of ministerial training are probably the highest of any Protestant denomination in America. Concordia, its graduate seminary in Saint Louis, is housed in magnificent buildings with every facility imaginable, including its own radio station, and is staffed by scholars of high and unquestioned attainments.

Until World War I worship services were largely in the German language. German was spoken in most Missouri homes and was given preference in the parochial schools. Growth and expansion was largely in German communities. This provincialism tended to make the denomination self-centered and unaware of the possibilities of co-operation with other Lutherans and other Protestants. After the War great changes came. One of the liberating factors was the adoption of the English language as the approved medium of church and school work.

Then came Walter Maier. Dr. Maier was a member of the faculty of Concordia Seminary and a brilliant public speaker. He conceived the idea of "The Lutheran Hour" through which the biblical and evangelical Christian faith might be broadcast by radio. His program was an immediate success. Protestants of every faith responded generously with their support. Liberals did not like this. A Saint Louis Liberal clergyman via the *Christian Century* led the attack upon Maier. He accused the Mutual Broadcasting Company of "tolerating" programs "like The Lutheran Hour" because of the revenue they brought to their treasury, when they must know that "programs of this stripe are distasteful to Liberal church leaders, to much of the listening public and to network officials." He intimated also that such programs were mere rackets and called upon Mutual to "ban paid religious broadcasts altogether" as the other networks had been persuaded to do. This outburst revealed the fact that the Federal Council of Churches (now the National Council) was seeking to eliminate all conservative, evangelical broadcasts and to control all Protestant broadcasting exclusively. The Mutual network was the only holdout against the Council. Finally, under tremendous pressure reminiscent of the Spanish Inquisition, Mutual succumbed to the Council's policy and notified Dr. Maier that his program would have to be eliminated. Charles C. MacFarland, then the Federal Council's secretary, made this widely publicized statement:

". . . Our ultimate plan will probably be for the local federations of churches to endorse and local stations to present national programs provided on Sunday by the Federal Council whereby all will have their choice of hearing . . . a few selected preachers who have received the full endorsement of the Federal Council. . . . The Federal Council is now surveying the entire field throughout the country and signing up all available stations to carry its programs. . . ."

Mr. Frank R. Goodman, later head of the FCCC's Department of National Religious Radio, made this survey and signed up fifty or more stations "with ironclad contracts obliging them to use the Federal Council religious programs and none other."

At the Atlantic City conference a reporter asked, "Did you mean, Dr. MacFarland, that it is the expectation of the Federal Council to control all religious broadcasting, making it impossible for denominational conventions to get on the air and for pastors to broadcast sermons without Federal Council sanction?" Dr. MacFarland replied, "Precisely. The Council feels this to be a wise policy."

In a land of boasted freedom of speech and freedom of religion it was difficult for the Federal Council to achieve its purpose openly by contractual relations. A much more subtle approach became necessary. It opposed the *sale* of broadcasting time to any religious organization. It favored *free*, or *sustaining*, religious programs which might be controlled, according to Dr. MacFarland's "ultimate plan," through "local federations of churches." With Mutual's action it appeared that the Council had finally achieved its original purpose.

But the Liberal Establishment and the Council had not realized the power of an aroused Protestantism. Mutual's action touched off nationwide resentment. Conservatives held mass meetings of protest in some of the greatest auditoriums in the land. Finally, the newly formed National Association of Evangelicals joined forces with the protesters and brought pressures to bear on the radio industry and government agencies in the name of freedom of speech and freedom of religion with the result that The Lutheran Hour went back on the air. At Dr. Maier's untimely death, it was the largest and most popular religious radio program in the nation. "Missouri stock" in American Protestantism went to an all-time high.

There are still some Missouri Synod Lutherans who remember what the Council tried to do to them and to their efforts to disseminate the biblical, evangelical Christian faith in America. Missourians of the new generation ought to know about this bit of history and realize that the leopard has not changed its spots, even though it can be exceedingly gracious in its present-day approaches.

Today Missouri Synod Lutherans have the largest, the most artistic and the most effective radio and television religious programs on the air. Missouri was the first religious body in America to broadcast nationally via television. Its program "This Is the Life" is seen and heard over hundreds of stations and is a mighty factor in making the true Christian faith relevant to modern youth and the rising generation of new home builders in the nation.

Missouri has abandoned its isolationism and is now participating in co-operative ventures wherever possible without compromising its convictions. This changed attitude is being greeted with mixed emotions in the denomination. An enlightened leader feels that there is —

"need for us to lift our sights above old non-biblical concepts, accept the valid discoveries and worth-while advances of modern life and think, plan, and act accordingly. Many say that Missouri needs to abandon its isolationisms, provincialisms and traditionalisms which are obsolete and which might keep the church from a realistic approach to the actual problems of men in our day and time.

227

"They see the Christian world in a state of flux. Many of the old lines which used to separate Christians have little meaning in a modern frame of reference. Men who were 'liberals' yesterday are not so sure of their ground today as they face an atomic world and the possibility of the utter destruction of civilization and the human race. Evangelicals who were anti-cultural, anti-scientific and anti-educational yesterday are realizing the necessity of living effectively in a bigger, wider world than they even knew existed. While the great eternal facts and truths of Christianity are unchanging, men and institutions and science are changing and the church must meet them, challenge them, and help them grow in the direction of God and the Gospel. Christians must not condemn sincere thinking and growing men or refuse to meet with them (because of some preconceived notions about them) and talk and pray with them and teach them. These leaders, at the same time, see the need for self-examination, not only to determine whether Missouri is still in the faith, but also, as one has put it, 'to see whether we are guilty of self-righteousness and pride.' We need to humble ourselves and pray and seek the face of God in new and vital spiritual experience. We need a new endowment of the Holy Spirit and a new willingness to follow His leading within the teachings of the Word which He has given."

THE NEW LUTHERAN COUNCIL

This attitude has caused Missouri's leaders to take the denomination into the new "Lutheran Council in the United States of America" which was formed in Cleveland, Ohio, in 1966. Four Lutheran denominations are partners in this co-operative adventure: The Lutheran Church in America, the American Lutheran Church, the Synod of Evangelical Lutheran Churches (Slovak) and the Missouri Synod. Here Missouri is distinctly outnumbered by Liberal-controlled bodies. The confessional basis is, however, considered so strong and the limitations of the Council's activities so agreeable that dangers of Liberal infiltration are minimal. Yet Liberals do not give up easily. Time will tell whether the move was wise.

THE FUTURE OF "MISSOURI"

Although fully ninety per cent of the constituency of The Lutheran Church—Missouri Synod is sound in the faith, the denomination has a nucleus of Liberals who are beginning to "throw their weight around." Men like the brilliant and vocal Martin E. Marty, a staffer on the *Christian Century*, are "tolerated," as officials say, in a few pulpits and college chairs. This is the way all the major Protestant denominations in the nation were taken over by the Liberals. All they need is a "toe hold." They take it from there and they never give up until by clever and devious strategies they are in control of the key positions of influence and power.

It is interesting to note that the arch-liberal editor of *The Lutheran* (LCA) greeted Missouri's advent in the new Lutheran Council with a prophetic editorial intimating that it would be only a matter of time until Missouri was purged of its conservative leadership and would be safely in the fold of the National and the World Councils of Churches, and the new Ecumenical Church. This pundit sees Missourians as more interested in "endless programs and activities for education, evangelism and stewardship hammered out by staff officers"— more interested in organization than in theology. When a few members become concerned about new teachings, trends or practices, their pastors tell them not to be worried, to just support the denominational program and everything will turn out all right. When the top positions are captured the rest will be easy. Said Dr. Ruff, "The Missourians are not quite ready, but they are not as far behind as one might think."

The traditional spirit of loyalty and freedom which has characterized Missouri Synod Lutherans from their beginnings is the best assurance that they will by and large remain true to their Christian heritage in these trying times. In never-to-be-forgotten words C.F.W. Walther, first president of Missouri

Synod, speaking at the first convention of the Synod's Iowa District in 1879, said:

". . . As soon as we look more to our Synod than to the invisible Kingdom of God, the kingdom of grace and salvation, we become a sect. For this is really the essence of sectarianism, that one has his eye on his little fellowship above all, even though the kingdom of God may suffer harm thereby. That preacher is no true preacher who merely seeks to fanaticize his congregation for the Lutheran Church, or for the Missouri Synod, or, worse still, only for the Iowa District. Such men are bad preachers. They must rather direct people to Christ and say: See, we preach the true Word of God, in which the everlasting Gospel of Christ is continued; that is why you should adhere to us. Therefore we also say: Leave us as soon as we no longer do this . . . ."

Liberals are leaving no doubt about their intention to bring about co-operation of all Lutheran bodies in the new Lutheran Council in America and the Lutheran World Federation and eventually in the World Ecumenical Church. Liberal Dean of the Divinity School of the University of Chicago, Jerald C. Brauer, speaking at a special banquet in the Grand Ball Room of the Statler Hilton Hotel in Minneapolis celebrating the organization of the Lutheran Council, made some enlightening references to this goal:

". . . Tonight marks a turning point in the history of Lutheranism in the United States. It is proper that a celebration be held to commemorate this event. For the first time in American history, major Lutheran groups have become joint partners in a new venture of co-operation and work together. The founding of the Lutheran Council in the United States of America will undoubtedly rank as one of the key points of our history. Many in this audience thought they would never see the day when this event would take place. At long last, 96% of all Lutherans in the United States belong to a single co-operative agency through which they can carry on their work much more effectively and above all make a clearer total witness to American culture and to the world scene. . . ."

The Dean of the Chicago Divinity School then continued:

". . . Just as it is incorrect to make more out of the council than it actually is, it is equally incorrect to assume that it is forever doomed to an inferior role in relation to the various denominations that brought it into being. Its presence in the American scene is both a challenge and a possibility for the Lutheran Church bodies that created it. It summons them to move beyond denominationalism into a fuller manifestation of Lutheranism in a new form of the church within the United States. . . ."

Dr. Brauer called upon his hearers to join in the consultations on Christian union which are going on today. He said:

". . . The deeply serious question of the divided body of Christ remains before all Christian groups in American life and before all of the Christian faith, and hope on the part of the various Christian communions throughout the world. The largest circle of dialogue embraces not only the relation of Christian groups one to another but also the relationship of the Christian Church to its sister religion Judaism, and even to other religions of the world. . . ."

Dr. Brauer continued:

". . . Make no mistake about it, millions of Lutherans faithfully seek a fuller embodiment of the oneness of the Church. They seek this both within Lutheranism and within the full Christian community. They will not be satisfied with fearful and half-hearted efforts. These Lutherans, both clergy and laity, have been caught up in the new spirit that is sweeping through the Christian church. It is the spirit of unity born of love and knowledge, of forbearance yet deep conviction, of faithfulness to the past yet openness to the future. Let us no longer be afraid of the word union or unionism as we work together and study together. A new vision is sweeping Lutheranism in America. It is responsible, it is realistic, yet it is visionary. The Lutheran Council is part of that new vision and new hope for unity of Lutheranism in America. Pray God that some of us in this room tonight may witness that event. . . ."

Throughout Lutheranism today there is a new alertness as to what is being done to their biblical and evangelical faith. Lutherans are beginning to suspect that the Liberal Establishment would not only substitute a socio-political faith for the Gospel but also lead them into a huge centralized power-conscious ecclesiasticism comparable to that which Luther gave his life to reform. For example, a new independent magazine, *Lutheran News*, has appeared to warn all Lutherans against impending danger. Its circulation is growing rapidly. It deals with facts about the new trends, the new practices, the new theology and the new morality being foisted upon Lutheranism by the Liberal Establishment, all in the high and holy name of "Christian union and brotherly love." Only through free-lance, yet responsible, media like this will Lutherans ever know the facts about what is going on behind the scenes. Facts, then, call for courageous action.

Martin Luther, who knew what it meant to stand for his convictions in the midst of error and ecclesiastical tyranny, said something that modern Lutherans may well take to heart: "One must delight in assertions if he is a Christian. By assertions, I mean staunchly holding your ground, stating your position, confessing it, defending it and persevering in it unvanquished. And I am talking about assertions of what has been delivered to us from above in the Sacred Scriptures. . . . Nothing is more familiar or characteristic among Christians than assertions. Take away assertions, and you take away Christianity!"

The time has come for American Lutheranism to assert or die.

XII

OTHER PROTESTANTS FOR FREEDOM

SPACE LIMITS forbid adequate coverage of the large number of denominations outside the aegis of the National Council of Churches. (See Appendix A.) They number 37,303,793 communicants, composing a potentially powerful factor in Protestantism's determination to be free from the yoke of Liberal tyranny and the ecclesiastical domination of a Super-Church. We have dealt with the major religious families. Now we shall consider those remaining groups which the Council considers to be of vital concern for its plans for future growth and development. (See pages 246, 247.)

THE PENTECOSTALISTS

The most rapidly growing complex of churches outside those previously considered is that known as the Pentecostal Movement. Pentecostalism in America rose rapidly because of the blight of worldliness, formalism, agnosticism and ecclesiasticism in the older Protestant denominations. The Baptism of the Holy Spirit as a special work of grace and evidenced by charismatic gifts is the basic doctrine of the Movement. Speaking with tongues receives prime emphasis and religious fervor marks most Pentecostal meetings. To the observer this ecstasy may appear as religious frenzy, sometimes bordering on the bizarre, or again as a more or less controlled ecstatic manifestation. Thousands of Christians who have never known a vital touch with God or a religious experience that changes and transforms life find immense satisfaction in Pentecostalism.

Until recently most observers have been inclined to regard Pentecostalism as a passing phenomenon, but now it is taking its place as a permanent and respected phase of Protestantism. Pentecostals themselves recognize the dangers of extremism and the more responsible bodies have organized what is called The Pentecostal Fellowship of North America. Membership includes the Assemblies of God, the Church of God (Cleveland, Tenn.), the International Church of the Foursquare Gospel, the Pentecostal Holiness Church, the Open Bible Standard Churches, the International Pentecostal Assemblies and the Zion Evangelistic Fellowship. Most of these bodies have become constituent members of the National Association of Evangelicals. If all bodies claiming to be Pentecostal are considered, there are some 1,750,000 members in the American Movement none of whom are related to the National Council of Churches.

In 1958 Henry P. Van Dusen, of liberal Union Theological Seminary and leader in the National Council of Churches, became convinced that the Council should do something to win such a large and rapidly growing Protestant communion. In that year he wrote an article for *Life* magazine in which he censured the traditional churches for their attitude toward the Pentecostals. Since that time books, magazine features and newspaper articles—Catholic and Protestant, secular and religious—have been written about Pentecostalism. Van Dusen and other Council leaders have advocated acceptance of what they call "the third force in Christendom" as full-fledged members of the Council. In many local and regional councils this has been done. Several foreign Pentecostal bodies have been received as members of the World Council of Churches.

The Assemblies of God is the largest of the Pentecostal denominations. It was organized in 1914 in Hot Springs, Arkansas, and in 1916 it established headquarters in Springfield, Missouri. It is composed of self-governing churches which constitute 44 districts and six foreign language branches. It reports over 8,500 churches and 600,000 members. Its emphasis on Sunday school work has resulted in an enrollment of far over a million in its Bible classes. Its foreign missionary endeavors cover 73 lands with an American and national leadership exceeding 2,000. Its publishing house at Springfield is one of the largest and best equipped in Protestantism and turns out millions of pages of educational material every year. Late in starting its program of higher education, the denomination now has nine colleges with an enrollment of 3,500.

The second largest Pentecostal body is the Church of God with headquarters at Cleveland, Tenn. It is not to be confused with other Pentecostal bodies bearing similar names. It was organized in 1886 in Monroe County, Tennessee, under the name Christian Union. It was reorganized in 1902 as the Holiness Church under the subject name of Church of God. It has a membership of over 200,000 in 3,500 churches. It has a Sunday school enrollment of over 300,000. Its large, well-equipped publishing house and Lee College, its leadership training school, are located in Cleveland.

The International Church of the Foursquare Gospel was founded by Aimee Semple McPherson who for many years was the pastor of the world-famed Angelus Temple in Los Angeles, California. From this center developed the present denomination which has 750 churches and 90,000 members.

The Pentecostal Holiness Church grew out of the holiness movement of the early 1900's and is strongest in the South and Middle West. It is premillennial in belief, emphasizes Christian perfection in the tradition of the Wesleys, and requires Pentecostal baptism of the Holy Spirit, accompanied by glossolalia. Its form of church government is patterned after that of the Methodist Church, with headquarters in Franklin

235

Springs, Georgia. It has some 60,000 members in 1,300 churches and a Sunday school enrollment of 125,000.

Open Bible Standard Churches represents a merger of two Pentecostal bodies effected in 1935. It has headquarters in Des Moines, Iowa, and numbers 27,000 communicants in 260 churches.

The Movement has through the years been marked by the development of groups adhering to the teachings and programs of outstanding evangelists. Currently the most popular is Oral Roberts who draws great assemblies in a healing ministry. At Tulsa, Oklahoma, he has built a multi-million-dollar complex of educational, publishing and propaganda agencies, the most notable of which is Oral Roberts University. Roberts reaches millions with his radio and television programs.

THE MENNONITES

Around 260,000 American Protestants are known as Mennonites. They owe their origin to the Anabaptist Movement in Europe. Their faith was introduced to America in the 1860's and has been marked by many different expressions in ecclesiastical organization. In general, it may be said—

The Anabaptists and Mennonites hold to the distinctively Protestant doctrines: salvation by grace through Christ, rejection of the papacy, the validity of marriage for all orders of clergy, the view that there are but two eternal destinies—heaven and hell.

The Anabaptists insisted on freedom of conscience, and the separation of church and state, stressed the voluntary character of church membership, deferred baptism until the subjects could consciously repent and believe, held that infants and children were saved without baptism, rejected force and violence in all human relations, including all forms of military service, and held to a rather literal interpretation which led them to reject the swearing of oaths. They stressed the brotherhood character of the church, rather than a hierarchy.

A word of caution must be sounded on the use of the term "Anabaptist." The Anabaptists from which the Mennonites are spiritually descended were remarkably, though not fully, homogeneous. But many sixteenth century writers, and others since then, often lumped all groups together which rejected the state church system, and called them all Anabaptists—whether Swiss Brethren, Melchiorites (followers of Melchior Hofmann), Obbenites, Anti-Trinitarians, or what. Due to various sources of origin, linguistic differences, and minor differences in practice and polity, the Mennonites today are not tightly united in one body. Almost all groups, however, are since 1948 united in the Mennonite World Conference; and most Mennonite groups are united since 1920 in a program of world-wide relief and humanitarian service "In the Name of Christ," in an organization known as the Mennonite Central Committee, commonly called the MCC in Mennonite circles. The three largest groups in America are (1) The Mennonite Church, sometimes called "Old Mennonites," around 100,000 baptized members; (2) the General Conference Mennonite Church with less than 60,000 members; and (3) the Mennonite Brethren Church with under 30,000 members. None is a member of the National Council of Churches.

THE BRETHREN CHURCHES

There are several distinct groups of Brethren of various origins in the United States. They number some 250,000 members. The doctrines they hold in common are those basic to Protestantism plus (1) opposition to written human creeds, (2) emphasis on the "good life" as revealed in the Sermon on the Mount, (3) brotherhood as a center of reconciliation with God, (4) peace, including non-resistance in the time of war and opposition to every form of religious oppression, and (5) avoidance of all luxury and advocacy of living the simple life.

The Church of the Brethren, with headquarters at Elgin, Illinois, is the largest of the groups with an inclusive membership of 200,000 in 1,100 churches. This body is, strangely enough, affiliated with the National Council of Churches, although this relationship is beginning to draw fire from a constantly increasing number of opponents. The denominational leaders were enticed into the NCC largely because of its position on peace, but now that its policies have become increasingly marked by Super-Church propensities and plans for church mergers which call for compromise of the fundamentals of the Christian faith, many leading men in the Church of the Brethren are having second thoughts about inter-church cooperation.

In 1882 the Brethren Church, with headquarters at Ashland, Ohio, withdrew from the Church of the Brethren. It numbers 116 churches with some 20,000 members.

A similar separation resulted in the organization of The National Fellowship of Brethren Churches, with its chief center of activities at Winona Lake, Indiana. They are sometimes called "The Grace Brethren." The Fellowship numbers 180 churches with 27,000 members.

The Brethren in Christ Church, which owes its origin to a religious awakening in the Susquehanna River valley of Pennsylvania, has 155 churches with about 8,000 members and a Sunday school enrollment of nearly 20,000.

The last named communion finds extra-congregational fellowship with the National Association of Evangelicals.

THE SOCIETIES OF FRIENDS

The Friends, commonly called Quakers, had their origin in England under the leadership of George Fox (1624-1690).

They occupy a unique position in Christendom inasmuch as they combine "enthusiasm" and mysticism as the cornerstone of their religious fellowship. In their concept of the Inner Light they hold that God is immanent in the world and in man and thus knowable directly and immediately.

Because of persecution by the Established Church, Quakers immigrated to America as early as 1660. With the advent of William Penn, an ardent Quaker, and the founding of Pennsylvania, they came in increasing numbers.

In the early 1800's American Friends were infiltrated by liberalism and unitarianism. Today the Philadelphia Yearly Meeting and the Religious Society of Friends (Hicksites) are riddled with Liberalism. The so-called Orthodox Quakers who compose the Five Years Meeting of Friends are supposed to be sound in the faith, but what that means in view of the theory of the Inner Light is a moot point.

The liberal-minded Quakers have joined the National Council of Churches and are prominent in its left-wing activities. There has been remarkable outreach on the part of Quakers, especially in the fields of education and humanitarianism. Their efforts to alleviate suffering in World War I and World War II and since in backward poverty-stricken lands have been outstanding. Unfortunately the activities of the American Friends Service Committee, aided and abetted by National Council leaders, have been strongly tinctured with extremely liberal philosophical and social views, bordering on Marxian communism.

Conservative Quakers have refused to go along with this kind of program. A number of State Yearly Meetings have withdrawn from the main bodies and from all association with the National Council of Churches. Among these are the Kansas Yearly Meeting, the Rocky Mountain Yearly Meeting, the Oregon Yearly Meeting, the Ohio Yearly Meeting and the Pacific Yearly Meeting. Several of these bodies now find their inter-church fellowship in the National Association of Evangelicals.

REFORMED BODIES

There are 125 separate Reformed and Presbyterian bodies in the world, following John Calvin's theological and ecclesiastical principles. The Pan-Presbyterian-Reformed alliance has 60,000,000 adherents at the world level. In America, however, several bodies of European origin have perpetuated their national social, cultural and political mores in separate Reformed denominations.

The Reformed Church in America is Dutch in origin and Presbyterian in polity. Rutgers University and Hope College are representative of its best thought and life. Its doctrinal standards are the Belgic Confession, the Heidelberg Confession and the Canons of Dort. It embraces many of the historic colonial churches of New York and New Jersey. There are 921 RCA churches in America with a membership of 228,924. Its eastern churches are active in the National Council of Churches; its western churches are in many cases noncooperative. Merger negotiations are being carried on with the Presbyterian Church in the United States.

The Christian Reformed Church was organized in 1857 by Dutch emigrants to Michigan and Iowa. It rejected fellowship with the RCA because of its liberalism. There are 597 churches in America with 262,088 members. Headquarters are located at Grand Rapids, Michigan, where Calvin College and Theological Seminary are maintained. At one time the CRC was a member of the National Association of Evangelicals, but now is related to no interdenominational body. Its Christian Day School system is one of the finest in the nation.

CHURCHES OF GOD

The oldest of these bodies is the Church of God (General Eldership) with headquarters at Harrisburg, Pennsylvania. It was founded in 1830 by John Winebrenner, a minister of the German Reformed Church, who withdrew from his church and embarked on a crusade to restore the Church of the New Testament. He and his followers held that it is inherently sinful to use non-biblical names to designate a church, any denominational creeds as tests of fellowship, and any man-made forms as aids to worship or church government. The body is presbyterian in form of government. There are today some 375 churches with a membership approaching 40,000.

The Church of God, with headquarters in Anderson, Indiana, was founded in 1880 by D. S. Warner, a minister of the Winebrennerian church, who claimed to have discovered a great spiritual principle which was the identification of the visible and invisible church in a spiritual congregation of Christians from which no Christian could be excluded by any man-made rules or corporate forms of organization. Related to this doctrine is the theological emphasis on "entire sanctification" and the practice of divine healing. Local congregations are free and independent in polity. They recognize "the Lord's people in all communions through an irresistible drawing of the Spirit." They reject all human ecclesiasticism and have established the ideal of a Spirit-filled and Spirit-directed Church. This branch of the Church of God has grown steadily until today it has some 2,300 churches with an inclusive membership of around 150,000 and a Sunday school enrollment of over 250,000. At Anderson, Indiana, it maintains a mammoth camp ground, where 20,000 members gather annually for inspiration and information. Anderson is also the seat of Anderson College, Warner Press and other activities essential to the life of the churches.

Both of these bodies steadfastly remain outside the membership of the National Council of Churches.

CHRISTIAN AND MISSIONARY ALLIANCE

The Christian and Missionary Alliance was organized as a missionary society in 1887, and thus is not a new denomination or group as some have thought in coming in contact with an Alliance church for the first time.

In many cities and towns, Alliance churches have been witnessing for Christ and demonstrating New Testament missionary principles for scores of years.

Looking back over the more than three-quarters of a century of growth, leaders in The Alliance can see that the work involving about 1,200 churches with 70,000 members in the homeland and 900 missionaries overseas has necessarily taken on some denominational aspects, although the founders had envisioned only the beginning of an evangelical missionary movement.

The revered founder of The Christian and Missionary Alliance was Dr. A. B. Simpson, a dignified Presbyterian minister who attracted to his side a scholarly Episcopalian, Henry Wilson; a militant Salvationist, Kelso Carter; a solid Mennonite, Albert Funk, and a jubilant, old-fashioned Methodist, Stephen Merritt; as well as strong Baptists, Congregationalists, Plymouth Brethren and other outstanding men and women of many different creeds and names.

Throughout the United States and Canada the Alliance operates in fourteen districts as the home base. In addition, the Home Department superintends the work in Puerto Rico and conducts missionary activities among Indians, mountain people, Mexicans, Negroes, Jews, Eskimos and others.

Abroad, its major mission fields include: Latin America—Argentina, Brazil, Chile, Colombia, Ecuador and Peru; in

Africa—Congo, Gabon, Guinea, Ivory Coast, and Mali-Upper Volta; in the Near East—Israel and Arab Lands; in the Island World—Indonesia, Japan, New Guinea, and the Philippines; on the Asiatic mainland—India's Gujarati Area and Marathi Area, Viet Nam, Cambodia, Laos, Thailand, and China-Hong Kong and Taiwan.

Recent world statistics for a year throughout the 23 fields show Alliance churches had 133,878 members, 93,715 Sunday school scholars and 33,566 inquirers under regular religious instruction, while the total Alliance forces of 3,899 missionaries and national workers operated 192 mission stations, ministered to 3,375 church groups, preached in 180 different languages and principal dialects, and baptized 9,969 new converts.

The Alliance finds its inter-church fellowship in the National Association of Evangelicals.

EVANGELICAL BODIES

There are quite a number of denominations which might be mentioned in this category. The National Council of Churches has manifested an interest in three.

The Evangelical Congregational Church is the remnant of the movement known as the Evangelical Association organized by Jacob Albright in the early nineteenth century. Known after 1922 as the United Evangelical Church, it sought union with the United Brethren Church. When it became apparent that a centralized rule by bishops was contemplated in the new denomination, the strongly congregational element withdrew and organized the Evangelical Congregational Church. It reports 165 churches with a membership of over 30,000. A publishing center, theological seminary and benevolent institutions are maintained at Myerstown, Pennsylvania.

The Evangelical Covenant Church of America had its roots in Sweden and was the outgrowth of biblical studies and spiritual awakenings in the State Church. Swedish immigrants founded the American body in 1885. According to its constitution its congregations accept the Holy Scripture as God's Word and as the only rule of faith, creed and conduct. They seek to perpetuate their evangelical freedom of thought and worship by avoiding both an unevangelical modernism and the rigidity of confessional fundamentalism. ECCA reports 520 churches with a membership of some 65,000. North Park College in Chicago is the center of its educational life.

The Evangelical Free Church of America, commonly called the "Free Church," represents a merger of several small Swedish and Norwegian churches in 1950. It allows greater liberty in doctrine than the Evangelical Covenant Church but is strongly biblical and evangelical in its Christian faith. It has 483 churches and a membership of about 40,000. Trinity College and Seminary train its continuing leadership.

All of these denominations are unrelated to the National Council of Churches. Two find their inter-church fellowship in the National Association of Evangelicals.

ADVENTIST BODIES

Adventists regard continuous struggle between the forces of good and evil, culminating in the second coming of Christ, as the basic cosmic principle of the universe and look for the establishment of His millennial reign as the only hope for the liberation of the disinherited and the final punishment of their oppressors. Adventists are not at all attracted by the social gospel and the efforts of National Council zealots to establish a world Utopia.

Two Adventist bodies are on the approved list of the National Council of Churches: The Advent Christian Church and the Seventh-day Adventist Church.

The Advent Christian Church is considered to be a traditionally orthodox Protestant body with the exception of its belief in conditional immortality and the extinction of the wicked after final judgment. It has 407 churches with an inclusive membership of 31,000. It maintains two colleges: Berkshire Christian College and Aurora College.

The Seventh-day Adventist Church, with headquarters in Takoma Park, Maryland, has 3,125 churches with about 350,000 members in the USA. Its world membership exceeds 1,000,000. The denomination stresses the imminence of the Second Coming of Christ. Taking the Bible as their sole rule of faith and practice, Seventh-day Adventists are fundamentally evangelical, holding to the full inspiration of the Scriptures and the deity of Christ. They accept prophetic teachings of Ellen White and insist on the observance of the seventh day of the week as the true Sabbath. They are intensely evangelistic and tithe their income. They have a complete system of education beginning with elementary day schools and culminating in colleges and universities with accredited graduate schools in theology and medicine. Their hospital ministry, regarded as one of the finest in America, represents an investment of many millions of dollars. Several publishing houses are maintained in various parts of the world which produce high-class literature. The radio program, Voice of Prophecy, is heard around the world. The doctrines of Separation of Church and State and Religious Liberty are vigorously promoted throughout the nation by means of an attractive magazine, *Liberty*, which has a large interdenominational circulation.

All Adventist churches are opposed to the National Council of Churches. Many claim prophetic grounds for their attitude.

THE NATIONAL COUNCIL'S "APPROVED LIST"

Now, as to the idea that many of the non-council churches are on "the approved list" of the National Council of Churches:

It is not generally known that the Council has for years been infiltrating many of the unaffiliated denominations and establishing bridgeheads in important areas of their functional life. The Council is embarrassed by the fact that it represents only a minority of American Protestants in full-fledged official denominational memberships. It is determined that this situation must be changed. It has prepared, therefore, a "List of Non-Member Communions Approved for Membership in Units." The most recent listing available contains the names of 34 denominations, as follows:

Advent Christian Church
American Lutheran Church
American Holy Orthodox Catholic Apostolic Eastern Church
Assemblies of God
Associate Reformed Presbyterian Church
Brethren Church (Ashland, Ohio)
Brethren in Christ
Church of Christ (Holiness) U.S.A.
Church of God (Anderson, Indiana)
Church of the Nazarene
Churches of God in North America (General Eldership)
Cumberland Presbyterian Church
Evangelical Congregational Church
Evangelical Covenant Church
Free Methodist Church of North America
Friends, Kansas Yearly Meeting
Friends, Ohio Yearly Meeting
General Baptists
General Conference of the Mennonite Church
Lutheran Brethren of America
Lutheran Church, Missouri Synod
Mennonite Brethren Church of North America
Mennonite Church
National Primitive Baptist Convention of the U.S.A.

North American Baptist General Conference
Pilgrim Holiness Church
Reformed Episcopal Church
Salvation Army
Schwenkfelder Church
Seventh-day Adventists
Southern Baptist Convention
United Brethren in Christ
United Missionary Church
Wesleyan Methodist Church of America

Most of the denominations listed above now actually have official relationships with one or more units of the National Council's organizational structure. In many cases the rank-and-file members of these churches know nothing about this relationship. If they knew, they would demand immediate severance. Very often the arrangement has been a matter of staff or bureau action, approved of course by the highest echelons of officialdom in the denomination.

The procedure that is generally followed for a denomination to get on the "Approved List" is to make application for membership in one of the units of the National Council of Churches as may be desired by that particular communion. That unit, then, would refer the matter to the General Constituent Membership Committee of the National Council. This committee would check into the beliefs and structure of the communion and would bring its recommendation to the General Board of the National Council for approval. The General Constituent Membership Committee would then check into the stability of the denomination as to whether they had been in existence long enough to have a stable base, whether they have indicated a spirit of co-operation with other churches, and whether they are prepared to participate in one or more of the units of the National Council. In the latter instance there is more attention given to evidences of co-operation with churches already in the

Council and to church structure. To all intents and purposes, if a denomination gets on the "Approved List" it is definitely in line to become a full-fledged member of the Council.

There is great appeal to membership in Council units. It gives its members the benefit of vast experience of experts in a given field of endeavor. It broadens the scope of authentic knowledge concerning methods of operation, achievements and future plans. It eliminates undue competition and makes co-operation possible in areas of common concern. Such a relationship does not call for the sacrifice of conviction or denominational distinctives.

Take one or two examples: The Broadcasting and Film Commission has valuable contacts with radio and television networks. It has know-how in program, promotion and station relations. It has experts in varied communications media. It can give valuable advice in finance, research, distribution and many other areas of concern. Take Christian Education at the local church level: The Department of Education Services can give expert advice in children's work, youth work, adult work, family life, administration and leadership, curriculum development, audio-visual education and relationships between the Church and the Public School.

DANGERS IN CONCILIAR CO-OPERATION

Evangelically and biblically oriented personnel from conservative Protestant denominations go into these relationships in the Council with "their eyes open" and feeling perfectly capable to distinguish "good from evil," to take what they want and leave the rest alone. Before long, however, after developing personal friendships with Liberals, and accepting offers of co-operation, they find themselves under obligation to the Council. Such relationships often result in job offers or exchanges of personnel in conference programs. So close is this camaraderie that conservatives may find themselves no longer able to bear a courageous testimony for the things they most truly believe or to be critical of the heresies and dangers implicit in the Liberal conciliar philosophy which impregnates all the programs of the Council. After a few years in this heady atmosphere they are ready to advocate full-fledged membership of their denomination, or at least not to oppose it.

Co-operation in the programs of regional, state and local Councils of Churches carries with it the same dangers. In this instance, many such councils insist that there is no relationship with the National Council, when they know this is not true. The programs provided at these levels follow the "party line" implicitly. If they did not the pastors and leaders of the churches whose denominations are official members of the Council would register effective protests. Even local ministerial fellowships are often deeply involved in the Council network of authority. Naive conservatives sacrifice a strong clear testimony for their convictions and contribute to Council prestige and power in their sentimental desire to promote unity, peace and good will through any form of Liberal conciliarism.

The present *status* of the National Council and its satrapies is by no means *quo*. It sees the whole of "responsible Protestantism" as its potential monopoly. It will neither slumber nor sleep until it has achieved this end.

The crying need of the hour in American Protestantism is a new birth of freedom in Christ and a new responsibility in Christian fellowship, far removed from all forms of structural collectivism and from a false ecclesiasticism, created though it may be for the purpose of achieving an effective communion of all Christians.

XIII

INTER-CHURCH ACTION

ALL PROTESTANTS, despite doctrinal separatism, are basically one in their recognition of Christ as sovereign of all life, in their acceptance of the full and final authority of the Holy Scriptures, in their love of religious liberty and in their desire to act unitedly and effectively in matters of common concern.

When it became apparent that the Councils of Churches had abandoned their distinctly Protestant heritage and embarked on a Liberal-controlled totalitarian socio-political power program, many Protestants began to seek some new medium through which they might continue their historic co-operative endeavors.

NATIONAL ASSOCIATION OF EVANGELICALS

Probably the largest, most responsible and most promising of these ventures resulted in the formation of the National Association of Evangelicals. It had its beginnings in the New England Fellowship in 1929. When a nationwide co-operative vision gripped NEF leaders a call went out for an exploratory meeting. It was held in 1942 in Saint Louis, Missouri, and was attended by hundreds of leaders from all parts of the land. It was the consensus of those present that a constitutional convention should be held in Chicago, Illinois, the following year to effect a permanent national organization. On May 3, 1943, more than a thousand evangelical Protestants converged on Chicago's Hotel LaSalle for the history-making convention. They represented some 50 denominations in one way or another. In an atmosphere akin to Pentecost the "National Association of Evangelicals" was born. It was composed of denominations, independent religious organizations, local churches, groups of churches, and individuals committed to a Statement of Faith expressing the least-common-denominator of Protestant Christian doctrine. A promotional headquarters was opened with related regional offices covering the nation. Functional units were created for service in many fields of inter-church co-operation. The new organization was in business!

Liberals immediately criticized the Association as "giving sectarianism a new lease on life" and as encouraging "the reactionary and dissident wings of the great Protestant denominations" in the Council. What they failed to see was that at least a remnant of American Protestantism (always strongly evangelical in character), had declared its freedom from the shackles which liberal leadership had forged. The Chicago meeting was a practical expression of the inherent characteristics of Protestantism. Here was no effort to build another organic ecclesiasticism. This was a thing of the Spirit and grew out of a common faith "once for all delivered to the saints." Chicago said again that American Protestantism is essentially democratic and free. It believed in a religious freedom that will not go along on any road that leads to Rome. It despised totalitarianism in any form and feared councils of churches which assumed to speak for the churches and carried within them the seeds of a coming super-church.

Liberals needed to mark well the events of Chicago. They were witnessing the beginning of an open, organized rift in American Protestantism which was bound to affect every Protestant denomination and institution in the land. If liberalism insisted on controlling the machinery of these bodies it would no longer find supine submission on the part of Protestants. Those who believed in the basic truths of the Christian faith were through trying to co-operate with those who had branded themselves as apostate. Evangelicals were saying, "As for me and my house, we will serve the Lord." They were not content to continue as suppressed minorities or in inarticulate and misrepresented majorities in the traditional organizational patterns. They were eager to burst their bonds and launch out in a great evangelical revival that would bring new light, life, and growth to the true body of Christ. Possibly several decades might elapse before their courageous action at Chicago should bear full fruitage but they were completely committed and had great confidence that they had chosen the high road and that all they had done was to the greater glory of God.

As the National Association of Evangelicals stands today (1967) it numbers in its membership forty complete denominations, individual churches from forty other denominations, and many Bible institutes, colleges and seminaries, ministerial fellowships, evangelistic organizations, youth groups, benevolent institutions, as well as individual Christians. The actual individual membership of the NAE proper exceeds 2,000,000. There is a service constituency through its commissions and affiliated agencies of more than 10,000,000.

The actual official membership of the NAE by denominations and associations is as follows:

Assemblies of God
Baptist General Conference
Bible Standard Churches
Brethren in Christ Church
Christian Church of North America, Inc.
Christian Union
Church of God (Cleveland, Tenn.)
Church of the United Brethren in Christ
Churches of Christ in Christian Union
Christian and Missionary Alliance

Conservative Congregational Christian Conference
Elim Missionary Assemblies
Evangelical Congregational Church
Evangelical Free Church of America
Evangelical Mennonite Brethren Church
Evangelical Mennonite Church of North America
Evangelical Methodist Church
Free Methodist Church of North America
Holiness Methodist Church
International Church of the Foursquare Gospel
International Pentecostal Assemblies
Mennonite Brethren Church of North America
Missionary Church Association
National Association of Free Will Baptists
Ohio Yearly Meeting of Friends
Oregon Yearly Meeting of Friends
Pentecostal Church of Christ
Pentecostal Church of God of America
Pentecostal Holiness Church
Pilgrim Holiness Church
Primitive Methodist Church of the USA
Reformed Presbyterian Church of North America
Rocky Mountain Yearly Meeting of Friends
United Fundamental Church
United Holy Church of America
United Missionary Church
Wesleyan Methodist Church of America

Conferences and Associations:

Advent Christian Church, Northern California Conference
Advent Christian Church, Massachusetts Conference
Advent Christian Church, New Hampshire Conference
Anchor Bay Evangelistic Association
Association of Fundamental Ministers and Churches
Baptist General Conference of New England

Church by the Side of the Road
Evangelical United Brethren Church, Pacific
   Northwest Conference
Evangelical United Brethren Church, Montana Conference
Evangel Church, Inc.
Full Gospel Church Association
Grace Gospel Evangelistic Association
National Holiness Association
National Negro Evangelical Association
New England Evangelical Baptist Fellowship
Railroad Evangelistic Association, Inc.

All major denominations in America (Baptist, Methodist, Presbyterian, Lutheran, Christian, Congregational, etc.) are represented by many individual ministerial or local church memberships in the National Association of Evangelicals. The 24,000,000 orthodox Protestants in the denominations outside the National Council of Churches find in the NAE their most effective instrument in time of need.

Among the denominations officially aided in the NAE's service constituency are The Lutheran Church (Missouri Synod), The Church of the Nazarene, The Conservative Baptist Association of America, Christian Churches, Churches of Christ and many others that might be mentioned.

The NAE is a voluntary association of evangelical churches, denominations, organizations, and individuals for united evangelical action. It is not a council of churches. It does not seek the union of churches. It has no means of exercising control over its constituent members. Essential services are rendered in every major field of Christian activity and its testimony for the fundamental doctrines of the evangelical Christian faith is increasingly effective.

Commissions and affiliated agencies operate in the following fields:

Evangelism and Spiritual Life—A constant nationwide evangelistic emphasis is being encouraged by the Commission. It does not promote evangelistic campaigns, believing that this is the distinctive task of the churches, but it inspires, encourages and educates for evangelism by all means at its command. The Commission provides programs for observance of the World Week of Prayer, the World Day of Prayer and special observances for the development of spiritual life in the churches.

Higher Education—This Commission has had a tremendous influence in building and perfecting the higher educational program of the evangelical cause. Accrediting, textbook needs, classroom techniques, administration, business management, public relations, etc., are some of the areas of service.

Sunday School—This work is carried on through the National Sunday School Association. Evangelical Sunday School teachers and leaders by the thousands participate in the Association's activities at national, state, and local levels.

Christian Day Schools—Evangelicals have aroused conscience on the necessity of Christian-based education for the boys and girls of this generation. The National Association of Christian Schools has aided hundreds of communities in setting up Christian Day Schools to meet growing needs, providing teacher training, placement, and other services.

Publications—United Evangelical Action, the official news magazine of the National Association of Evangelicals, is issued monthly and reaches evangelical leaders in all parts of the nation and throughout the world. It endeavors to promote the work of the National Association and its affiliated agencies and has often been the medium through which evangelical action has produced effective results in national life. Books and brochures are produced as needs arise.

Foreign Missions—Voluntary united action among evangelical mission boards and missionaries is expedited through the

Evangelical Foreign Missions Association. Its office in Washington promotes better public relations; deals with diplomats of all nations; arranges passports, visas, and other legal matters; etc. The purchasing office in New York City serves missionaries as well as churches and ministers in America.

Laymen's Council—Evangelical laymen are manifesting a growing interest in the development of the National Association of Evangelicals and its allied agencies. To channel this interest and make it most effective the Laymen's Council has been formed with chapters in a growing number of areas.

Women's Fellowship—Evangelical women are forming auxiliaries for co-operative effort in all sections of the nation where the NAE is organized. They hold regular meetings and support such projects as child evangelism; hospitals; homes for girls; work with shut-ins, the aged, cripples, and incurables; world relief; evangelism among unsaved women at all social levels; etc.

Evangelical Action—This Commission, through the Washington office of the NAE, keeps a finger on the pulse of the nation and when necessary makes vocal the evangelical view on governmental and social matters.

Radio-TV Broadcasting—The National Religious Broadcasters, Inc., has within its constituency most of the larger broadcasting interests in America. When the industry planned to eliminate "commercial" religious broadcasts it was NRB which "saved the day." Today it is having similar influence in holding the line for evangelical broadcasters in television.

Government Chaplaincies—This Commission represents the constituent denominations of NAE in providing evangelical chaplains for the armed services. It answers hundreds of inquiries each year and endeavors to see that evangelical bodies receive due recognition in all matters pertaining to governmental chaplaincies. Its standing with the office of the chief of chaplains is of the highest quality.

World Relief—Beginning with aid to Europe's needy millions following World War II, the World Relief Commission has sent food and clothing worth many millions of dollars to all parts of the world. Its New York office is constantly sending aid to orphan children and hospital cases; to the needy of Southern Europe, notably in Yugoslavia and Greece; to Korea and other Oriental lands where the need is so great.

International Relations—The Commission on International Relations was largely responsible for the organization of World Evangelical Fellowship in 1951. Through its office it maintains contacts with other evangelical organizations throughout the world and promotes projects of mutual benefit among the various autonomous evangelical organizations affiliated with the WEF.

Social Concerns—This Commission seeks to apply social teachings of the Holy Scripture in practical life situations. Evangelical welfare associations are being encouraged throughout the nation.

Stewardship—Various promotional activities serve to increase giving to the Lord's work. Annual reports indicate that member denominations rank in the topmost brackets in per capita giving among American Protestant bodies.

Theology—Studies and discussions are provided to keep abreast of current developments in this field and to assure vital relevance of the evangelical biblical faith to modern life.

The NAE is related to the World Evangelical Fellowship which was formed in Woudschoten (Zeist), The Netherlands, in 1951. This body which maintains headquarters in London, England, gives promise of providing those services for evangelicals which liberal Protestants receive through the World Council of Churches.

EVANGELICALS AND SOCIAL ISSUES

Evangelicals have no objection to social action. They know that Christianity is primarily a doctrine leading to newness of personal life in relation to God, but that it is also a better way of life in society. They have always stood for truth and righteousness in society as well as in the individual life but they hold that the primary concern of the church lies in the supernatural and spiritual realm and that social and political righteousness must forever rest on the meaning of the content of the biblical revelation.

Evangelicals stand ready to join in the formulation of a philosophy of social action, provided it is based on an orthodox theology. If such a philosophy can be produced once again the Church will become the mighty force for righteousness in the nation and a mighty testimony to the full orbed Gospel of Jesus Christ. Nothing less than such a testimony is adequate for the cultural crisis which has overtaken the western world. Christians will then have more biblical perspective of the needs of humanity and of the policies which our nation must follow if it is to remain true to its divine purposes and functions. They will see that there is Christian social justice for an industrial age and they will be able to speak with authority in such matters in a way in which the liberals can never speak because their concept of social justice is not based upon the revealed righteousness of a sovereign God.

Resolutions dealing with social issues are adopted in the national and regional conventions of the National Association of Evangelicals, but they are considered to be merely the expression of opinion of those who attend. They have no binding commitment upon its members or its related agencies. The contrast between its pronouncements and those of the National Council of Churches is striking. The following synthesis may be of interest:

258

The New Treason: Believing that the authority of the State is sanctioned by God, the NAE deplores the burning of draft cards, subversive movements and seditious utterances of all kinds, and prevalent disloyalty to the United States.

The New Morality: The NAE maintains the finality of the ethics of the Ten Commandments and the New Testament, condemns sin in public and private relations and the representation thereof in stage, screen, radio, television and in the press. It opposes gambling, lotteries and other games of chance which encourage private gain without honest toil. It believes that the breakdown of morality leads to the breakdown of society and the unwise increase of the power of the State.

Federal Aid to Education: It is essential that Christian educational institutions remain free and separate from State control. Federal laws authorizing various forms of subsidy carry with them the intimation (despite disclaimers) that government controls are inevitable. The dangers of Federal aid must be avoided at all costs.

War Against Communism: The NAE decries any action by our government that would favor communism under the leadership of Red China or Russia or that would weaken the security of non-communist nations of the world. Evangelicals declare their loyalty to the established constitutional government of our country and the accompanying requirements of civil obedience.

Right to Work: Every man has the right to work according to the dictates of his own conscience under God and in consonance with his rights under the U. S. Constitution. (Representatives of the NAE appeared at congressional hearings to protest the repeal of Section 14b of the Taft-Hartley labor law.)

Religion in the Public Schools: The NAE favors the enactment of suitable legislation by the Congress which will strengthen present provision for the free exercise of religion in our institutional life and allow reference to, or the invoking of the aid of God, in any public document, proceeding, activity, ceremony or institution on a voluntary basis. (NAE representatives appeared at Congressional hearings in favor of the so-called "Dirksen Amendment" to the Constitution.)

The Great Society: The NAE condemns any interpretation of the Gospel of Christ which denies the essentiality of conversion of lost and sinful persons: doubts the existence of moral absolutes; encourages a trend from God to man, from the individual to the group; and advocates the use of political methods to achieve "the will of God." The advocacy of radical social changes and of readjustment in human relations while the cleansing and renewal of the individual are neglected can only result in corruption and chaos. Those who treat crime as a disease and not as a sin; protect the rights of criminals and disregard the plight of their victims; destroy individual responsibility in favor of social consensus; and accept economic and political corruption as justifiable means for the achievement of good ends are contributing to social delinquency and not to a redeemed social order. The idea that all human beings (of whatever sort) need to do is fall into a faceless line and join in the prepaid, inevitable evolutionary ascent to Utopia can only lead to moral and social catastrophe.

AMERICAN COUNCIL OF CHRISTIAN CHURCHES

Growing out of similar backgrounds and the need for cooperative action in various areas of concern, another group of Protestants, alienated from the Councils of Churches, organized the American Council of Christian Churches in September, 1941. Originally it was composed of only two small denominations—the Bible Presbyterian Church and the Bible Protestant Church. It was different from the National Association of Evangelicals in three respects: It demanded immediate and complete separation from denominations, corporations, associations and councils in which apostasy existed. It sought to create an official "council of churches," in composition and structure similar to the apostate councils, rather than a loosely knit fellowship of evangelicals. And, finally, it adopted a polemical, negative program of propaganda against the apostate councils, rather than a constructive emphasis upon Christian faith and work.

According to the best available information, the present membership (1966) of the ACCC consists of the following denominations:

American Baptist Association
Bible Presbyterian Church
Bible Protestant Church
Congregational Methodist Church
Evangelical Methodist Church
Fundamental Methodist Church
General Association of Regular Baptist Churches
Independent Baptist Bible Mission
Independent Churches, Affiliated
Methodist Protestant Church
Militant Fundamental Bible Churches
Tioga River Christian Conference
United Christian Church
World Baptist Fellowship

The ACCC states that it represents "some 1,500,000 Christians throughout the United States."

The ACCC maintains services for its constituent members, similar to those provided by the National Association of Evangelicals, and is related to the International Council of Christian Churches at the world level. Prominent among the service agencies are: The Radio and Film Commission, International Christian Youth, and Associated Missions.

A number of widely publicized institutions related to the American Council and ardent in its support are: *Christian*

261

Beacon, edited by Carl McIntire; the "Twentieth Century Reformation Hour," a national radio program featuring Dr. McIntire; Faith Theological Seminary; Shelton College and the Christian Admiral Hotel located at Cape May, New Jersey.

Probably there is no more greatly feared and maligned antagonist of the Councils in the nation than Dr. McIntire. He publicizes every departure from traditional Protestant Christian doctrine and practice from one end of the nation to the other. His documentation is convincing and leaves no doubt in the minds of the masses as to the guilt of the Liberal Establishment and the Councils it controls.

THE FUTURE OF INTER-CHURCH ACTION

It is altogether possible that American Protestants have not yet seen ultimate achievement in inter-church co-operation outside the Councils. The whole Protestant world is in a state of flux. Many of the old lines which used to separate have little meaning in modern frames of reference. Men who were "liberals" yesterday are not so sure of their ground today as they face the atomic age and the possibility of the ultimate destruction of civilization and the human race. Protestants who were anti-cultural, anti-scientific and anti-educational yesterday are realizing the necessity of living effectively in a bigger, wider world than they knew existed. While the great eternal truths and facts of Christianity are unchanging, men and institutions and science itself are changing and we must meet them, challenge them, and help them grow in the direction of God and the Gospel. We must not condemn sincere thinking and growing men or refuse to meet them (because of our preconceived notions about them) and talk and teach and pray with them to discover common ground for co-operative endeavor.

Protestants today and tomorrow need to rise above all organizations of men in a bigger, broader fellowship, as big and as broad as the eternal Church of God. God has abundantly blessed those who yesterday took a stand for truth and right in the midst of apostasy and conciliar tyranny. These heroes of the faith have built great churches, Bible institutes, colleges and seminaries, and missionary enterprises that span the world, publishing houses, radio ministries and inter-church agencies that show every mark of the blessing of God. But if we allow these works of our hands to obscure the fact that a new generation, from within the old Protestant structures, is just beginning to get its eyes open and to seek co-operation and action, we shall miss a great opportunity to build larger and to act more effectively than ever before in our history.

True Protestant Christians in America need to mobilize all their forces, finances, endowments, and personnel in the local churches, in the faithful communions, in inter-church agencies, in education, in evangelism, in journalism, in radio and television, in missions—in all fields and spheres of Christian service—for a movement of such proportions that the God of our Fathers can take it and use it mightily for the accomplishment of His purposes in this New Age which is upon us.

XIV

GRASS-ROOTS REVOLT

IN EVERY SECTOR of American Protestant life there is revolt against the National Council of Churches and its satellite councils. Like the revolutions of history this revolt is not planned or forced by heavily financed and well-organized agencies. It is coming as naturally as the growth of an oak from an acorn. It is being increasingly provoked by the actions of the Liberal Establishment which controls the Councils.

The pastors in pulpits and the laymen in the pews who are leading in the revolt are reluctant to act. They have been disposed to suffer while evils were sufferable, rather than to right them by abolishing the forms to which they have been accustomed. But, after long years without any correction of abuses or the introduction of any improvements—indeed, with the increase of heretical and subversive efforts to destroy the very foundations of faith—these peaceful souls are erupting and acting with brave new spirit.

In this chapter are recorded only a few examples of hundreds that could be cited.

THE POLING POLL

The first has to do with ministerial revolt. On February 22, 1966, the General Board of the National Council of Churches, meeting in St. Louis, adopted a resolution calling for the admission of Communist China to the United Nations and the granting of United States diplomatic recognition to the Peiping regime.

This widely publicized resolution—and similar statements from other church bodies—had caused dismay in nations throughout the world who stand in firm opposition against Communist aggression and enslavement and who look to the United States as the leader in this crucial world struggle. Particularly tragic was the effect on the morale of young Americans battling Communism in Vietnam. If their own churches and church leaders favored accommodation with totalitarian, atheistic and predatory Communism, should they give their lives in resisting it?

In the belief that these resolutions and statements did not represent the American Protestant community—and that the great majority of Protestant clergymen are one with their fellow Americans in opposing any steps which would help strengthen Communist China—Daniel A. Poling, Chaplain of the Chapel of the Four Chaplains in Philadelphia, undertook to poll *individual* American Protestant clergymen on this historic question.

Three questions were put to over 65% of the Protestant clergymen, selected at random from every state in the Union: are you in favor of the admission of Communist China to the United Nations at this time? are you in favor of the expulsion of the Republic of China from the United Nations in order to satisfy Communist Chinese conditions for joining? are you in favor of the United States granting diplomatic recognition to Communist China at this time?

The "No's" were overwhelming. Of those responding, 72.9% were opposed to the admission of Communist China to the United Nations; 93.7% were opposed to meeting the basic Red Chinese conditions for joining the United Nations; 71.4% were opposed to diplomatic recognition of the Peiping regime. This great reaffirmation of support of present United States policy toward Communist China was made in spite of the tremendous

265

and continuing campaigns advocating appeasement of Red China which have been leveled at American clergymen.

The results of this poll should have set the record straight. Those church bodies or officials who took a differing point of view had every right to do so. But the Council of Churches had been "insulted" by this revolutionary act. It determined to smear Dr. Poling and the poll and force the churches to accept their subversive view.

Dr. Poling has been a friend of the Council and had a part in its beginnings. He was a member of the National Council's Commission for a Just and Durable Peace, under the chairmanship of John Foster Dulles. He was associated with the Broadcasting and Film Commission of the National Council. He served on the Commission on Evangelism of both the World Council and the National Council of Churches under Dr. Jesse Bader. He has supported and is supporting the Church World Service of the World Council. But he was now out of step with the Liberal Establishment and therefore had to be repudiated!

NCC officials insisted that the action of the Council had been misrepresented. The *Christian Century*, long an articulate spokesman for Council aims and programs, charged that the poll was a "contrived consensus."

The charges against Dr. Poling's poll were completely without foundation. Council leaders were upset by the fact that the monopoly the National Council had enjoyed in the area of seeming to speak for "40,000,000 Americans" had been broken. Dr. Poling might have reflected the opinions and convictions of even more than 40,000,000 Americans when he said in his widely published reply: "You cannot compromise with tyranny or win victories by appeasement." Or, when he said: "My Bible says, love your enemies. My Bible does not say, join your enemies, promote your enemies, strengthen their cause. Certainly we would promote our enemies, we would join them, and we would strengthen their cause, were we to admit them diplomatic recognition. Certainly, too, if their cause is evil, finally we would injure them as well as ourselves by promoting it. There is nothing soft about God's love as revealed in Jesus Christ. It took Him to a cross."

THE FREE CHURCH ASSOCIATION

In something of the same spirit of grass-roots revolt, a group of Los Angeles ministers from several denominations launched what is known as the Free Church Association in an effort to crystallize and activate opposition to the tyranny of the Liberal apparatus. Said their call to action:

"What's happening to the Church?

"A number of leading clergymen are repealing the separation of Church and State by acting to combine churches into a giant instrument of ecclesiastical and political power.

"When church leaders and religious bodies enter the area of political action, they speak as though all Christians were of one political mind. Yet Christians will always have legitimate differences on political, economic and religious questions. For these reasons, the move toward unity has proved divisive.

"Across the country, individual ministers, laymen and their local churches seek to separate themselves from political actions being taken in their names and preserve unity in their churches and in their denominations.

"They are opposed to any plan through which religion can be controlled by a few.

"They object to the erasing of sacred doctrines in preparation for mergers into One World Church.

"They object to the emphasis on materialism and secular interests of the religious bodies that claim to represent them.

"They deny the right of church leaders to make their political positions the stand of the entire Christian community.

"They deny the right of a few to assume the duty and conscience of

267

millions of laymen, who have never by any act of their own transferred their will, their resources or their responsibilities to the group, even if it were morally possible to do so.

"They seek instead to identify themselves with our religious heritage of freedom under God.

"The Free Church Association would establish a means for doing this.

"The Free Church Association is a free and open fellowship of ministers and laymen of all denominations, united in spirit, and seeking by educational means to strengthen and protect the traditional influence and importance of the local church in American life.

"Believing firmly that the blessing of individual differences requires freedom and diversity in religious expression, the Free Church Association will resist ecumenical monoliths and all totalitarian concepts in religion which tend to undermine the local church's primary concern of strengthening the relationship between man and God through emphasizing individual responsibility.

"The Free Church Association will gather and disseminate information, issue public statements, promote seminars and work co-operatively with other educational organizations concerned with preserving our religious heritage of freedom under God.

"It will endorse actions and pronouncements of churches, clergy and religious bodies in the area of social action when such activities reflect the Christian community and Christian beliefs by emphasizing individual morality and spiritual growth under the sovereignty of God— rather than substituting group morality and material goals under a governmental autocracy.

"Thus it will advance the cause of liberty for Christians and non-Christians alike."

The idea has yet to be implemented but it sets up a blueprint for action which should stimulate individual freedom and local church autonomy in many areas.

ACTION IN SAVANNAH

Christian laymen at the grass roots are also learning how to make organized attack upon the Liberal Establishment. Take the self-styled group, Committee of Christian Laymen, of Savannah, Georgia, as an example.

Frustrated by the limitations on their protest within their own churches the Committee set up meetings for Christian parents concerned about the welfare of their children who were being made targets for left-wing socialistic and subversive theological instruction in their Church Schools. Over 100 such gatherings were held at which films were shown, recordings were played, printed matter was distributed, and panel discussions were featured. Besides these meetings there were radio broadcasts that stirred up interest all over the city.

Then came action. Many individuals and groups were enlisted to appear before the County Grand Jury. Here they presented charges of subversion and propaganda hostile to the national interest against the Foreign Policy Association. The same was done about pornography in public school libraries. In the latter case, the Jury approached the Board of Education causing the removing of the filthy material. When the community had been thoroughly alerted to these evils, the Committee turned on the National Council of Churches with the same charges. The Vestry of an Episcopal Church in Savannah appointed a committee to study the charges, were convinced that they were valid, and led the church in framing a resolution against the National Council. In the next diocesan convention they called for withdrawal from the Council. When their motion was tabled and it became evident that nothing could be done to break Liberal controls, the Vestry recommended that the Church withdraw from the denomination. This was done by a strong majority vote. This widely publicized, almost-unprecedented action stirred the whole religious community in Savannah. A short time later two Presbyterian churches voted to withdraw from their denomination. The Methodists were aroused. When nothing could be done within their churches a large number of individual members withdrew and formed a new Southern Methodist Church which is growing rapidly.

269

Members of six Lutheran churches withdrew and formed an Independent Lutheran Church. All these withdrawals were for the same general reasons.

Chairman L. K. Roberts says the issues were becoming clearer and clearer to the committed American Protestants in Savannah. He says, "Only counter revolution will save the churches. We advocate such revolt within to begin with. If this fails, we unhesitatingly counsel withdrawal. We feel that every one who decides to act against the evils we face should anticipate the possibility that open schism may be necessary and be ready to act. We do not advocate violence in any form but we are determined that crooked church politicians must be ousted; unfaithful ministers must be turned out of pulpits; subversive Sunday school teaching material must be replaced, and church libraries purged of the subversive and pornographic literature recommended by the National Council of Churches. The 'wreckers' must be eliminated from all positions of leadership and control.

"The stark truth," says Mr. Roberts, "is that the people at the grass roots who fill the pews on Sunday morning, send their children and youth to Sunday school, and pay the bills have lost control of their churches, their conferences and conventions, and the educational and benevolent institutions they have sacrificed to build and endow. Too many of them have been swallowing piecemeal the socialistic, agnostic, unbiblical propaganda handed out from the pulpit and the classrooms, taking the poison a little at at time in what seemed to be less than fatal doses, not realizing that the Church is the target of evil forces intent on destroying our American Protestant way of life and the very foundations of our Western Christian civilization. Such people will not respond to the call to arms, but this must not deter us from action that goes all the way in purging the temple and reviving the 'faith once for all delivered.'

"The revolt has well begun in Savannah. We are seeing it started in communities all around us. We shall help to fan it to a flame that may well sweep America. Action at the local level, at the grass roots of American church life, is the only way to bring down the towering Super-Church which threatens all that American Protestants hold dear."

IN THE SAN FERNANDO VALLEY

As the Liberal Establishment and the top religious professionals move to effect denominational mergers and create a single uniform Super-Church, increasing pressures will be brought on local ministers and parishes. Ministers and laymen who stand for the Old Faith will find themselves attacked and maligned, as such free men in Christ have been persecuted throughout the history of the Christian Church.

This story is about a California Congregational Church which was forced into another denomination and the faithful remnant who would not "go along." Plans for merger were presented in three controlled congregational meetings and were accepted by a slim margin of votes. Then the "powers that be" placed a tough-minded socio-political Liberal in the pulpit pledged to drive out everyone who did not agree with him. When internecine war developed, the denominational authorities advised the leaders of revolt to leave peaceably. They said, "You can't win. We now control your church property. We will not permit you to dismiss your minister." When the faithful refused to acquiesce, a special meeting was called by extra-congregational officials in which "the trouble makers" were attacked, vilified, outvoted, and ousted. Among the group that left that meeting without a church home were those who had given thousands of dollars and years of devoted labor to build a church in which their children had been educated and from which their parents had been buried. Among them were three past moderators of the church, two church-school superintendents, six teachers, four choir members, a treasurer, two

271

financial secretaries, a building committee chairman, two church clerks, the church historian, a youth leader, several deacons and deaconesses, a trustee—some of the congregation's most faithful workers over the years.

Within a week fifteen of these people met in a home. There was no bitterness, no hatred—only sorrow. In the holy hours they spent together they were knit indissolubly into a fellowship with Christ and with one another that must have been akin to the upper-room experiences of Christ and His apostles.

These people rented a hall where they could hold Sunday services. They had no wealth, no standing, no professional leader, no denominational ties—absolutely nothing that most people consider essential to the founding of a church. They knew they were still Congregationalists, and in a very real sense in the tradition of their forebears who went through blood, sweat and tears to establish their churches.

The little band decided to take the same covenant the founders of the Plymouth church signed in 1620: "We covenant with the Lord and with one another; and doe bynde ourselves together in all His waies, according as He is pleased to reveale Himself to us in His blessed Word of Truth and in the majesty of His creation which surrounds us and of which we are an integral part."

They then formulated and accepted as their mission: To provide regular corporate worship services true to the Congregational tradition. To provide education for the individual who earnestly strives to know the will of God. To foster a Christian fellowship in which brethren might walk together in the ways of the Lord.

When it became known in the community that such a new church had been established, the meetings began to grow in attendance and interest. For eight months various members of the church occupied the pulpit as best they could, calling in an occasional guest minister. Then something wonderful happened. Among those who heard about their new venture was a professor in a nearby college. He had formerly been an accredited Presbyterian minister but had given up his charge because of Liberalism and ecclesiastical tyranny. When he visited the new congregation he was asked to preach. It was a case of "love at first sight" and he became their first pastor. They did their own installing and ordaining "under the guidance of the Holy Spirit." And everybody was happy.

Now the growing church is incorporated under the laws of the State of California as the "Congregational Church of the San Fernando Valley." They interpret their accomplishments since that time as strong evidence that God is smiling on their efforts. They take heart in the Scripture, "If God be for us, who can be against us?" The new moderators says, "We hope that our experience with the dictatorial practices of leaders in the merger movement will serve as a warning to other churches that are still free, and to the great denominations which are on the brink of ecumenical compromise and destruction."

"OPERATION FREEDOM"

As this book was being written a revolt of unusual proportions was being mounted in a great metropolitan church tightly in the grip of the Liberal Establishment and the National Council of Churches. For our purpose we shall call it Wesley Memorial Church although that is not its real name.

For ten years or more the local church leaders who were loyal to the biblical and evangelical Christian faith and the best traditions of American Protestantism had seen the gradual apostasy of their denominational hierarchy in matters of faith and action. They had recognized the fact that the pastors assigned to their pulpit and administrative staff were propagandizing the membership with left-wing socio-political doctrines. These faithful leaders sat under teaching which favored rejection of the authority of the Bible and the Church Discipline, approved U. S. recognition of Red China, admission of Red China to the United Nations, abolition of universal military training, suspension of atomic tests, compulsory unionism, federal aid to education, expanded government controls, and the new morality. They saw hundreds of thousands of pages of subversive literature being distributed to unsuspecting people. In every way they knew how, publicly and privately they tried to counteract the poison that was being disseminated but with little success. They knew that there were hundreds of people who resented and bitterly opposed what was being done to the church but they had no leadership, no right of assembly and could not speak with a united voice.

Finally, a group of about twenty capable men and women got together in a "council of war" and agreed on a plan of *sub rosa* action called "Operation Freedom." It was decided that study cells would be set up in all the areas or districts of church activity. A host and home were chosen in each. The host and a committee of his own appointment were to be responsible for inviting prospects in his area to meet in his home each week for a quarter. The invitation was to be for "home Bible study and discussion." This cell idea was not a new one. It had been used by the *Illuminati* before the French Revolution, by the Communists for infiltrating new nations, and by the underground during the siege of Paris in the last World War.

Actual operation was preceded by a training program for the teachers and directors of the cells. The program of Bible study follows this outline:

1. Christ Rejected by the Elders. John 14:16-30.
2. Christ and the Hebrew Hierarchy. Matthew 23.
3. Christ Our Hope. Acts 2.
4. Stephen and the Hierarchy. Acts 7.
5. Apostasy Foretold. II Timothy 3.
6. God Honors the Faithful. Hebrews 11.
7. An Exhortation to Faith. Hebrews 12.

8. Loyalty to the Faith. II Timothy 4:1-8.
9. False Teachers. Jude.
10. False Leaders. II Peter 2.
11. Watchmen on the Walls. Ezekiel 33.
12. Choose Ye! Joshua 24:14-24.
13. The Last Judgment. Matthew 25:31-46.

Each of these selections of Scripture lends itself to practical application to the local church situation and to the broader aspects of the problem of apostasy and subversion as presented by the councils of churches. The first meetings of these groups were successful far beyond the hopes of the planning committee.

The home-centered meetings capitalize on the informal neighborly atmosphere. The host and hostess make everybody comfortable and friendly. The teacher or director is not a church officer but just another seeker after truth. He meets the group on their level. Fortunately very capable men have been eager to lead in the study—a young insurance expert, a prominent neurosurgeon, a bank manager, a college professor, and the like. The class lasts for only one hour, but specially concerned persons may remain for another hour to ask questions and get further information if they so desire. Some really come to grips with the issues. It is not uncommon to get comments like this: "If what you are telling us is true, I think we are in a serious situation and something needs to be done about it. I want to get inside information so I can act intelligently." Relevant literature is distributed at each meeting, including books and tracts that can be distributed to other members of the church.

After the quarter's study, the cell groups will send out parties two by two to win new converts. Possibly a whole new set of study groups will be recruited while the original companies will carry on an intelligent propaganda effort against the Liberal apparatus.

The leaders are aware that quite likely the Liberals who are firmly entrenched in the church organization will move to stop these meetings. Failing this (they cannot keep the hosts from opening their private homes to any who wish to come) they will excommunicate everyone who dares to flout their orders. When this time comes there will undoubtedly be an open schism. A new church will then be established outside denominational boundaries with a very considerable membership made up of the nucleus recruited in Operation Freedom. Others are bound to follow their friends into this new group. The idea is to stay inside and work for the good of the church and the cause that hopefully through some providential change in leadership the church might return to its traditional posture and purpose. Failing in this, the alternative course will be followed.

The free spirit of Protestantism cannot be extinguished by any human agency. Daniel Webster, speaking of religious and civil liberty, once said: "Like the earth's central fire, it may be smothered for a time; the ocean may overwhelm it; mountains may press it down; but its inherent and unconquerable force will heave both the ocean and the land, and at some time or other in some place or other, the volcano will break out and flame up to heaven." This has happened before in the history of the Church and it will happen again and again and again!

XV

ADVICE FROM THE FIRING LINE

IN THE COURSE OF PLANNING this volume a survey of several hundred churches was made. All the churches were in denominations related to the National Council of Churches but in the process of freeing themselves from the tyranny of the Liberal Establishment. A Questionnaire was submitted (Appendix F) which pastors and church leaders filled out. Their observations and advice given out of their experience can be of tremendous value to those who have determined to journey on the Road to Freedom.

No names and places are given in order to protect the people and churches from the attacks and penalties they might suffer at the hands of Liberal hierarchies. Documentation is on file.

PREACH THE GOSPEL

Most pastors who replied stressed the importance of preaching the Gospel revealed in the Bible. They said if there was an uncertain message from the pulpit there was little hope of building a strong church loyal to Protestant principles. A Pennsylvania minister well expresses the view:

"The trouble with most people, even when they think they are sincere, is that they simply do not know, believe, and obey the Bible. If they did then false prophets could not lead them astray! John lays it right on the line when he tells believers in I John 4:1-6 to test everything that is presented to them to see if it really is of God and if those teaching such things are really of God.

"False prophets who reject the Bible and Christ have only the ideas of men to present to a lost world. The organized church today, as predicted in the Bible, is fast losing its real purpose. Becoming more apostate or unbelieving all the time it has no real message to present to a sinful soul to guarantee eternal salvation so seeks instead merely to change things in the world or society. The Bible teaches you can change the world only by changing the hearts of men and only the Gospel of Christ can do that.

"The true believer shares the Gospel of God's redeeming love with individual souls and true churches preach the Word of God, the Bible, in the power of the Holy Spirit and invite all to receive the Lord Jesus Christ as their personal Savior. Then He changes their lives and world. Usually those who are primarily seeking to change things in society are those who have no saving Gospel to offer to lost sinners."

LIVE THE GOSPEL

An Ohio pastor said:

"The preaching and teaching of the Gospel must be relevant to the time. The Word of God 'liveth and abideth forever.' Its great truths are as applicable to our day and time as they were to the period in which they were written. We must make them live in terms that will help our hearers be better men and women and provide them with the techniques of daily conduct that will bring them joy and satisfaction. Basic to this is the converted, changed and transformed life of the individual. The most radiant Christians in the world are those who have the Spirit-given power to live like Christ in every kind of life situation. There is no finer testimony to the value of the Church in the community than the lives of its members. When churches downgrade the Bible, the deity of Christ and the work of the Holy Spirit they become powerless to produce real Christians, because the churches themselves are lost."

APPLY THE GOSPEL

The pastor of a large Kansas church warned against Gospel preaching that is not applied to contemporary issues. Said he:

"I agree with the liberals that the pulpit must speak to contemporary issues. 'Religion unapplied is vacuous nonsense.' I do not believe the pulpit is to engage in practical politics. The duty of the pulpit is to state fundamental principles. The error of the liberals is to misstate the principles. For example, they are for the Negro because he is black and has been mistreated. I believe the Negro, like all people, is called to be a child of God. I have no interest in his color. The fact that the Negro has suffered means that we must help him to be a child of God even in suffering and that we should enlarge the compassion of evil white men. Christianity and force are incompatible. The turning of Christians to the State is to defeat the Gospel and deprive the Negro of the discipline he must achieve. In a similar way we may disagree with the liberals' endorsement of the welfare state. The error is not that they are speaking to contemporary issues but that they have misread the need. They forget the virtue of poverty. They believe man's salvation is in economics, in his stomach, rather than the grace of God. Liberals are utter materialists, hardly distinguishable from communists or fascists. My point is that the country, the world, and our churches are divided over a philosophic issue. We make a mistake in running away from the practical application of the Gospel."

All ministers polled agreed that the unalloyed Gospel of Christ must be central in all that is done to redeem American Protestantism.

INFORM THE PEOPLE

High on the list of essentials in the fight for freedom the respondees placed "an educated and well-informed people." They said, constructively speaking, first consideration should be given to the teaching of the Bible so that everyone in the church has a clear understanding of the fundamentals of the Christian faith. Of equal importance is instruction in the principles of American Protestantism. Then there must come an awareness of those economic, moral and political principles which have made America great. With this background people will be able to evaluate intelligently the programs that are presented to them by Church authorities and to make decisions in harmony with the will and purpose of God. But there is also what some call the negative approach to the problems the churches must face. The people need information concerning the dangers of communism, left-wing socialism, the councils of churches, the modern ecumenical drive, the new theology, the new morality and all the other evils that beset the churches.

THE PROTESTANT TRADITION

Throughout the replies runs the conviction that the future of civil and religious freedom and the political and social happiness that Americans now enjoy is dependent upon the influence of Christianity and Protestantism. They ask, "If the foundations are destroyed, what will the end be?"

A North Carolina church leader writes:

"History abounds with proof that the Protestant tradition will not flourish under an authoritarian church, or the American Dream under a collectivist system. The fruits of the Protestant Ethic are evident in the achievements of our citizens, and our country. This heritage has made the United States a land of opportunity for the aspirations of the individual. It has set an example of religious freedom, legal justice, human rights, economic attainment, educational opportunity, and individual self-fulfillment for the rest of the world. Where else on the face of the globe do a people enjoy such a legacy? This alone should give pause to reason; should make everyone think, before exchanging it, a glorious reality, for what could be a return to something not unlike the Dark Ages.

"Is it not strange that any thinking U. S. citizen should labor to destroy this legacy, be he Protestant or non-Protestant? What prudent individual would not prefer it to grandiose dreams which could turn into nightmares of barbarian despotism? If the American culture is to be replaced, what is to replace it? People who lack a culture have little to offer to any society. What adequate substitute has been devised, as yet, to take its place, either in religion or government? Admittedly, there is always change; but need it be for the worse? Change is not synonymous with progress, as some contend.

"What then prompts such a course in organized Protestantism? How much does the role of greed and self-interest play? Who benefits? What pressure groups stand to gain? Is memory so short, or knowledge of history so limited, that men of good will would voluntarily endanger these cherished principles? Is the clergy even now captive to coercion? Its voice is scarcely heard. There must be ominous forces at work.

"The Protestant tradition is all that stands between freedom of religion, the right to choose, and a monolithic authoritarian power structure, that by its very nature would subvert the Protestant way of life. Such a conclusion is not a matter of individual presumption. It has been affirmed by the leadership of many Protestant denominations affiliated with the National Council of Churches. This leadership has gone on record time and time again that it is committed to complete and total merger that will result in one church—one organizational structure.

"This leadership, through its role in politics, supports legislation that if implemented will destroy our National Sovereignty, debase our currency, invalidate our Constitution, do away with the free enterprise system, abolish the concept of separation of Church and State, eliminate individual freedom of choice, the right to own property, and the right to employ one's talents as one chooses.

"This leadership is committed to the abandonment of our Judaic-Christian teachings of morality, ethics, conduct, and spiritual salvation. It proposes to replace this with the new theology, the new psychology, the new sociology, the new political science, and the new economy, none of which has withstood either the test of science or the test of time.

"We must make our people aware of this situation in every way at our command."

THE WILL TO FREEDOM

Another top necessity, said most of the ministers and laymen polled, is the creation of a new obsession of freedom in the heart and conscience of the American churchman. A California layman writes:

"Too many of us are acting like slaves to the *status quo*. Every Protestant must be led to recapture the spirit of freedom which marked the life of Martin Luther. He came to the place where God and the Bible were his guiding light. He decided that he could no longer lay his liberties in Christ at the feet of popes or bishops, or trust them with powers which would enable them to subvert the church to their own purposes. The time has come to relight the flame of individual religious freedom that made possible the Protestant movement, created the Protestant ethic and made possible the realization of the American Dream. This is no time for silence or acquiescence. This is no time for quieting our disturbed consciences. Every Protestant and every Protestant church should bravely experience their own Reformation and begin making independent choices and decisions, and, if necessary, start new revolutions regardless of the cost."

WAYS OF WORKING

But enough of generalities. The answers to the questionnaires were filled with practical methods being used by aroused Protestants and Protestant churches to achieve desired ends. Out of the rich treasure of ideas the following are taken, arranged in alphabetical order for quick reference:

Action Groups: Kindred spirits that see eye to eye on the necessity for a given course of action hold meetings to plot strategies and actual confrontation of the enemy.

Advertising: Space can be taken in community papers for the presentation of the conservative point of view on crucial issues. When councils of churches may have adopted resolutions on controversial and/or political issues, state the opposite view in thoughtful and logical terms over the name of a committee such as "The Committee for Protestant Action" or "Christian Laymen, Incorporated."

Agitation: These groups should not let their opposition die but continuously stir up others to join them in their crusade for truth and right. Wherever opportunity offers in group conversations or in public gatherings, the issues are aired. This must be done without bitterness and bigotry, in a quietly positive and persuasive manner.

Answers: When heretical doctrines are advocated from the pulpit or in various church meetings and programs a group of intelligently informed brethren will publicly and openly give answers to the questions raised in the minds of the people.

Assemblies: Meetings can be called, in the church building if possible, but if not permitted, in hotel parlors or halls, at which given issues will be publicly discussed for the edification of all who may wish to attend.

Benevolence: Concern for the unfortunate and underprivileged in the name of Christ, co-operation with worthy charitable organizations and doing deeds of kindness to all regardless of race, nationality, religion help give the church a balanced and laudable image in the community.

Bible Classes: Very often in the most liberal churches there are adult Bible classes friendly to the preservation of the American Protestant Christian heritage. Active membership in such classes may result in opportunities to serve as officers, teachers or committee chairmen and to advance the cause of freedom. The open discussion periods may prove quite fruitful. There is no more effective antidote for error than the study of the Bible. The Bible is the greatest enemy of Liberalism.

Books: There are hundreds of good, sound books these days that deal with such issues as liberalism, the new theology, the new morality, socialism, communism, separation of Church and State, the free enterprise system, the Bill of Rights, the freedom of the local church, ecumenism, error in the councils of churches. An especially good example is *The Christian Alternative to Socialism* by Irving E. Howard (Crestwood). Read them. Digest them. Buy them by the dozens and distribute them everywhere.

Breakfasts: Hundreds of people eat their breakfasts in restaurants before they go to work. Arrange to meet prospects for the cause at breakfast. Have prayer. Talk about some current issue and, if the time seems right, seek commitments.

Campus Ministries: Churches located near colleges and universities contact students of their denomination, offer social services, moral and spiritual counseling, Bible studies, and discussion groups under capable leadership. This work results in contacts with other churches. It serves to acquaint young people with the "other side" of issues and doctrines advocated by liberal professors.

Cells: Form neighborhood groups to meet in homes for the study of the Bible and, later, books, tracts, and study outlines dealing with the issues confronting the church at local, area, national and world levels.

Clubs: A group of young adults in one church formed a "Freedom Club" meeting every Sunday evening for study and discussion. The theme of freedom is stressed in each meeting with application to the individual, the church, the community and the nation. Similar organizations with comparable purposes offer opportunities for enlistment and co-operation in specific projects.

Committees can be formed for the accomplishment of special aims. They can be given dignified and attractive names indicative of their purpose, such as "Committee of One Hundred for Christian Unity," "Committee for the Dissemination of Patriotic Information," "Committee for the Advancement of Christian Economics," "Committee for Spiritual Renewal," "Committee for Protestant Co-operation." Under such nomens meetings can be called, literature issued, propaganda disseminated, and special projects accomplished.

Common People should be given special consideration. The sophisticated liberals do not accept them as equals; consider them objects of charity and recipients of welfare grants. Lincoln said, "God loved the common people. That is the reason he made so many of them." The Gospel message, the biblical faith, the stand for Protestant ethics, the advocacy of the American way of life appeal to these people. As they make beds, hoe corn, drive trucks, sell groceries, drive taxis or clean windows they can give an effective testimony for the things they believe. When the time comes to vote they can assure majorities. Cultivate the common people humbly with love, understanding, and clemency and God will bless that relationship.

Co-operation with other like-minded churches has been found to enlarge fellowship and mutually strengthen their testimony in the community or area involved. Periodically joint meetings are held at which time they hear addresses and reports which advance the cause. United action in enterprises which do not involve compromise of convictions has brought encouraging results.

Core Groups: Ministers, who are ready to undertake the commitment of their church to their historic faith and the severance of relations with the councils of churches, have found it wise to bring together leaders in various phases and departments of church activity for study and discussion, and eventually to form a hard core of faithful helpers in the tasks that lie ahead. The group should not be too large but it should include some of the most influential and capable people in the church—persons who can be counted upon to be loyal through "thick or thin" in every conceivable situation and willing to take the consequences whatever they may be.

Crusades: Capitalizing on popular reaction for or against a given current issue, groups can be organized for effective action. For example, prayer in the public schools or proposed moves to approve interracial marriage. When the immediate purpose has been served continue the group in the fight for freedom in the churches.

Day Schools: There is a wave of concern for the children

of the rising generation because of the lack of respect in the public schools for God, the Bible, the Nation, the Flag and Authority, whether it be parental, religious or civil. Many conservative Protestant churches are encouraging the establishment of Parent-Community Christian Day Schools. It is becoming increasingly imperative that our children be trained up in the way they should go with belief in God, in the authority of the Scriptures and in the American nation "under God." One large church with a modern education building which was vacant six days a week turned its facilities over to a Christian Day School Board. Here hundreds of children are now being trained in a fully accredited curriculum to the glory of Christ and the Church. The future of the "faith once for all delivered" in this church is secure.

Dinners: Formal occasions at high class restaurants or hotel dining rooms can be staged with some outstanding conservative speaking on a live issue. Complimentary tickets can be provided for people of influence in the church and community. Carefully selected guests may be invited. There have been many important "conversions" at affairs of this kind.

Discussions: In efforts to give the people both sides of controversial issues, panel discussions can be set up in which well-known persons, noted for their advocacy of a particular position will speak, exchange views and answer questions. The choice of a fair-minded neutral moderator for such meetings is most essential. Even liberal ministers and lay leaders cannot with good grace deny the privilege of such high-level discussion.

Education: Beyond the Christian Day School there is necessity for a well-rounded, comprehensive program of Christian Education in every local church. In James DeForest Murch's book, *Teach or Perish*, the imperative necessity of such a program is set forth. The expansion he advocates in Adult Education would give opportunity to set up many new classes in Sunday evening hours, week-day groups and community schools offering courses in Doctrinal Distinctives, Christian Living, Sex, Courtship and Marriage, The Christian Home and Family, Separation of Church and State, Christian Economics, Personal Social Ethics, Christian Principles in Government, Christian Principles in Business, Christian Principles in Industrial Relations, Christian Principles in International Relations, Christian Unity and Modern Conciliar Developments. An intelligent well-informed church membership will stand for truth and not be the victim of liberal propaganda.

Elections: Conservatives should be alert when choices of leadership are made in the church and its various agencies. The names of sound men and women should be proposed. Support for them should be solicited. The full complement of conservatives in the membership should be on hand to cast their ballots for the right persons. Where control of this function of congregational life has been usurped by the Liberal Establishment, efforts should be made to bring about constitutional changes that will assure the democratic free choice of church leadership.

Evangelism: When a church is concerned about the souls of men and promotes an active program of door-to-door visitation to win men to Christ it is almost immune to the inroads of a social gospel. The church that has lost its sense of the necessity of obedience to Christ's Great Commission and its zeal to testify to others of the saving power of the Gospel has created a vacuum into which every form of error can easily flow.

Facts need to be disseminated. The record of events and the adoption of resolutions are sufficient in themselves to condemn the National Council of Churches to most loyal American Protestants. These facts should be published with suitable comments in church bulletins, news letters and in every other communication medium available.

Forums: Open meetings for public discussion should be

held as conditions warrant. It is the suppression of free speech that courts ignorance and error and that promotes disunity and strife.

Giving: It takes money, time and talent to mount a successful revolt against Liberal Establishment tyranny, whether it be in the local church or in broader religious areas. Usually there is enough conviction and commitment on the part of individuals to guarantee the necessary funds, but time and talent for effective leadership do not come so easily. Where the church budget includes many liberal causes, withdraw gifts and put them in a special independent emergency fund to finance the dissemination of conservative information.

Home Instruction and Discussion assure a solid base for operations. Where husband and wife spend time to inform themselves about the facts and the issues and to talk over plans and strategies they can constitute a valuable team. Children need to know what is going on and why. Homes can be valuable recruiting stations where neighbors and friends are invited in to tea or lunch and purposeful dialogue ensues.

Information: Regular news sheets should be issued at least once a month informing people of happenings in the councils and in the denomination which give evidence of Liberal control.

Information Material: A steady stream of information about the evils in denominational bureaucracy and conciliar circles should be placed in the hands of all the concerned of the church and community. Also information about what is being done to correct those evils.

Investigations: Church boards can be persuaded to appoint committees to investigate the nature and work of the councils of churches. In most cases the councils are in the budget and people have a right to know whether they are worthy of their support. See that conservatives have proper representation on committees. If the church will not consent to such a procedure, get some church organization to mount an investigation. See that wide publicity is given the project.

Lay Leadership should have increasing authority in the local church. Too often tight controls are exerted by the liberal professional clergy and staff, leaving little opportunity for the pew to express its views or determine policies or programs. Classes in Leadership Training may be organized to develop capable personnel.

Laymen's Groups: Where there is a laymen's fellowship or club in the church see that "the issues" are presented periodically for discussion and action. If there is no such group, organize one and see that the leadership is of the very best. If there is a United Men's Fellowship in your city or community be aware that it is altogether likely it is being used as a part of the national apparatus to achieve liberal goals.

Lectures: A week of lectures by an outstanding conservative minister, educator, editor or lay leader can be staged. Themes such as "The Ecumenical Movement," "Freedom and the American Churches," "Modern Theological Fads vs. The Word of God," "Science and the Bible," and "Protestantism in a Changing World" can be presented. Open discussion may follow.

Letters: Write complimentary letters to church leaders when they say or do something worthwhile. Write informative letters when erroneous statements are made. Write critical letters when high-handed actions are taken to force the church into liberal conciliar relationships. Write letters to the local newspapers and denominational journals promoting or defending the American Protestant way of life. Keep the letters going even though they are unacknowledged or unpublished. A constructive Christian spirit should characterize everything that is written.

Libraries: The church library should be provided with multiple copies of important books, brochures and tracts which give the facts about the conservative position. Publicize the fact that the literature is available.

Luncheons: Men's, women's or mixed luncheons can be sounding boards for information on the issues facing Protestantism. They may be free but limited to ticket holders, or they can pay for themselves. Outstanding speakers should be secured. Most churches will be closed to such affairs but they may be held in private dining rooms in restaurants or hotels.

Mass Meetings: Usually they should be avoided. They generate more heat than light and often lead to precipitate and unwise action. But there may be occasions where they may serve a worthy purpose.

Ministers' Fellowships: Sound ministers should seek the friendship of like-minded clergy in the community or region. Many such men have quit attending the ministers' meetings sponsored and controlled by the council of churches. They are hungry for fellowship with men who have common convictions, common aims and common problems. Join such a body if there is already one in existence. *The Remnant* is a good example. If not, organize one.

Neighborhood Groups: (See "Bible Classes," "Cells" and "Clubs.")

New Churches: There are many communities without adequate church coverage. People who are unhappy with their liberal church relationship can become "moving spirits" in organizing Sunday schools in these communities which will become nuclei for new churches. If the denomination opposes the move, go ahead independently. This is still a free country. Often churches started in this way have become havens of refuge for conservatives who have been frozen out of their traditional church homes. Their whole religious life has been reborn and revived by an experience of this kind.

News: When something worthwhile occurs in the process of promoting the conservative cause in the local church or community, see that a news story gets in the newspapers. Cultivate the church editors or reporters who are fair and objective in their attitude toward all. Give them background information for their files so they can deal intelligently with your stories.

Periodicals: Subscribe for and send to prospective readers the best weekly, monthly or quarterly conservative magazines. Trial subscriptions do not cost much and they may serve to win converts to the cause.

Petitions: When conditions are such that a united testimony will advance the cause, petitions may be signed and presented to proper authorities in the church, in the community and in the state and nation.

Prayer: "More things are wrought by prayer than this world dreams of," said Alfred Lord Tennyson. The whole revolutionary effort to restore American Protestantism and the Christian Faith of the New Testament should be bathed in prayer. Those who take the leadership in this crusade must have the sustaining power that alone can come from the Giver of all Good Things through personal daily and hourly prayer. Prayer in homes, in groups "wherever two or three are gathered together" and in assemblies is essential for guidance and strength.

Preaching: Biblical, evangelical Gospel preaching will do more to inspire loyalty and action than anything else. When the pulpit is closed to such preaching the "going is rough" for the faithful. The conservative minister will not fail to relate his Gospel message to the needs of the hour in his denomination and in American Protestantism.

Protests: The local church should let its voice be heard in protest against radical liberal policies and programs in its denomination or in the councils of churches. Such protests should be accompanied by constructive suggestions for change.

Radio: Sound ministers who have proper qualifications should be provided a regular radio program in which they can present Gospel messages relevant to the issues of the times. Lay groups can purchase time periodically to broadcast the truth about what is going on in American Protestantism. Such programs should receive a great deal of thought and be staged by experts. Something second-rate or without foundation in validated facts can do more harm than good.

Rallies: (See "Assemblies.")

Reading Lists: The councils of churches provide reading lists for libraries of all sorts and for individual consumption. While they suggest some good books and other literature, most of it is propaganda for the conciliar point of view. Some of it is subversive and pornographic. Secure the best possible expert advice to provide a "Protestant American" reading list for local church and communiy libraries which can counter the evil effects of the other lists.

Recruiting of volunteers for active participation in the crusade should go on constantly.

Seminars: (See "Lectures.")

Social Studies: In liberal-controlled churches there are bound to be several classes and clubs involved in left-wing socio-political studies. See that students receive books and pamphlets by men like Russell Kirk, Irving Babbitt, Christopher Dawson, Howard Kershner, Irving Howard, Gregg Singer, David L. Hoggan, Rousas J. Rushdoony and other conservatives who have written intelligently in this field.

Speak Up in meetings quietly and intelligently so that your views may be made known. Too often in gatherings controlled by liberals the impression is given that everybody is in favor of their ideas and programs.

Student Aid: Be on the alert to discover bright young men and women with a potential for leadership in various fields of Christian endeavor. See that they go to sound Christian colleges or Bible seminaries for their training. Raise the necessary funds to underwrite their expenses. Keep in touch with them. Encourage their efforts to attain success.

Sunday School curricula and the free literature distributed by the various departments and classes should be studied to determine whether it may contain liberal propaganda for socio-political programs and for modern ecumenical schemes. If it does, call for the appointment of an investigating committee to review the material and report back to the proper church authorities. See that the committee includes a fair representation of conservatives. If the report reveals dangerous doctrines, move for a change of literature. The survey indicated that many churches had switched to materials produced by Gospel Light Publications, Standard Publishing, Scripture Press, Moody Press and other evangelical houses.

Telephones should be in constant use in behalf of the cause. Personal contacts are of great value.

Television: (See "Radio.")

Training Classes: Carefully screen the textbooks used in Leadership Training Classes, especially if the church is committed to co-operation in Community Training Schools sponsored and controlled by the council of churches. Urge training of prospective leaders in all phases of church life, in local-church classes using sound texts.

Vacations offer opportunity to get acquainted with Protestants from many churches. Make it a policy to get them in conversations about conditions in their home communities. Have literature on hand to give them if they are interested.

Withdraw membership from the church if it appears that liberal denominational and conciliar policies and controls can never be overcome. Find fellowship with some other church which is sound in the faith and favorable to the American Protestant way of life.

Withhold all contributions which might be used to support

the councils of churches and liberal programs under the auspices of the denomination. If it appears that a "leveling-up" policy of fund distribution frustrates your purpose, withdraw all but token support of the local church. Find other objects of support in line with your convictions and aims and give as generously as ever.

Women's Groups: Where there is a women's fellowship or club in the church see that "the issues" are presented periodically for discussion and action. If there is no such group free of liberal control, organize one and see that the leadership is of the very best. If you are a member of the United Church Women of your city or community be aware that it is controlled by the council of churches and is being used as a part of the national apparatus to achieve liberal aims.

Youth Groups: In liberal-controlled churches youth groups are usually hot-beds of radical left-wing teaching and social action. Their program books should be carefully scrutinized. The agencies, conferences, schools and projects with which they have fellowship should be investigated. If necessary, protests should be made to church officials. Every effort should be made to discover individual young people who are amenable to exploration and study in conservative areas of thought and action. "Make friends" with them and "teach them the way of the Lord more perfectly." If feasible, encourage the organization of sound youth groups in the church or community. If such community groups already exist, inform your church youth about them and support them in every way possible.

All of these methods have been used with success in certain churches and communities. In others, they might not have been effective. Every situation needs to be studied carefully and thoughtfully before a particular approach or a particular method is employed.

It is thrilling to know that at this very moment there are

legions of loyal American Protestants throughout the nation using all these techniques to advance the cause of truth and right. Multiplied thousands are traveling down the Freedom Road toward the City of God.

EPILOGUE

A FAMOUS EVANGELIST whom God used to cleanse and empower untold thousands of lives used to tell his great audiences, "Start by drawing a circle around yourself and then, standing in the center of it, offer this prayer: 'Lord, bring Thy renewal to all the world, and begin the change by changing me. Amen.'"

This is the way American Protestantism is going to be reborn—through millions of individuals changed and transformed and dedicated to the task. The job will be accomplished beginning in YOU.

The individual is not supposed to amount to much according to modern standards. William H. Whyte in his trenchant book, *The Organization Man*, contends that there is no place in our modern collective society for individual freedom and individualistic beliefs. This is an age of the masses; the age of centralized organizational controls. This theory is accepted by the Liberal Establishment. That is one reason they see One Church for One World an absolute necessity in a Space Age. They say, "The individual Christian must be lost in the Church." They, accordingly, propose to restructure the Church in such a way as to make Christians the creatures of a powerful institution; faceless people to be moved about on a world chessboard by the top men of a great hierarchy for the achievement of liberal ecclesiastical, social and political goals.

But—did you ever study the parables of Jesus to see how

highly He valued the individual? They are mostly organized about "a certain man," "a certain king," "a certain house-holder," "a certain rich man." He did not tell parables about races, nations, or institutions. In them He focused our minds on the individual, and, incidentally, upon ourselves. His teachings have a personal thrust that inspires personal commitment and action. It is thus He expects to accomplish His ultimate purposes. Christ's own life is the supreme example of the premium God puts on the individual—He sent one person, His only begotten Son, and announced that belief in one God-man would give eternal life to all who would accept and obey Him. It is the message of the Christian religion that all problems which vex, perplex, and enslave humanity can be solved through the one, the only Jesus Christ.

Furthermore, man made in the image of God is the means by which God expects to accomplish His purposes in the Church and in the world. This belief is not *passe*, despite all the Liberals have done and are doing to destroy it. Take this example from modern science: The development of atomic energy has given new significance to the infinitesimal. The physics of a generation ago had much to say about potential and kinetic energy; the force exerted was calculated in terms of mass times velocity. One ton-weight hoisted to the height of ten feet and dropped had great kinetic energy; but if you dropped a tiny portion of that weight, a pound, say, little energy was involved. But now with our knowledge of atomic energy, we have learned to concentrate on the tiniest possible component of that one ton mass, the atom (so small that it cannot be seen), and release it to create astounding power. We now know that there is far more energy locked up in the individual atom than in the totality of atoms comprising the one ton weight dealt with *en masse*. The individual may be discarded today by the sociologists and the statesmen, the theologians and the ecclesiastics, as a negligible force in power planning and is often condemned as an obstruction to the achievement of their purposes. But God's evaluation of the individual eminently qualifies him to do the work He wants done. God and one man can constitute a majority in the battle for the right.

The problems of the American churches are piled up mountain high. One is prone to ask rather helplessly, "What can I do about them?" Indeed, one can be almost deluged and drowned with question marks, unless he can see that wrapped up within his own skin is the chief problem. Always the main problem is YOU. What are YOU going to do?

As we said in the beginning—

American Protestantism is going to be reborn through millions of individuals changed and transformed and dedicated to the task.

Decide today: "God helping me, this task will be accomplished, beginning in me!"

Then find someone to join you in your commitment and in your venture.

ACT TODAY FOR CHRIST AND THE CHURCH!

ACT TODAY FOR GOD AND COUNTRY!

APPENDICES

RELATIONSHIP OF PROTESTANT CHURCHES TO THE NATIONAL COUNCIL

(Based on Statistics given in *Year Book of American Churches*, 1965)

	Council Churches	*Non-Council Churches*
Advent Bodies		
Advent Christian Church		31,046
Church of God (Abrahamic Faith)		5,700
Life and Advent Union		235
Primitive Advent Christian Church		597
Seventh-day Adventists		346,286
African Orthodox Church		6,000
Amana Church Society		741
American Evangelical Christian Church		1,500 e
American Rescue Workers		3,210
Apostolic Faith, The		4,764
Apostolic Overcoming Church of God		75,000
Assemblies of God		543,003
Associated Gospel Churches		1,500 e
Baptist Bodies		
American Baptist Association		655,200
American Baptist Convention	1,559,103	
Baptist General Conference		82,309
Bethel Baptist Assembly		6,430
Christian Unity Baptist Assn.		657
Conservative Baptist Assn.		300,000
Duck River Associations		3,201
Evangelical Baptist Church, Inc.		2,200
Free Will Baptists		168,706
Gen. Assn. of Regular Baptist Churches		154,767
General Baptists		60,736
General Six-Principle Baptists		129
Independent Baptist Churches		1,500,000 e

	Council Churches	Non-Council Churches
National Baptist Convention	2,668,799	
National Baptist Convention, USA	5,500,000	
National Baptist ELSS Assembly		57,674
National Primitive Baptist Convention		85,983
North American Baptist Assn.		174,000
North American Baptist Gen. Conf.		52,625
Primitive Baptists		72,000
Progressive National Baptist Conv.	500,000†	
Regular Baptists		17,186
Separate Baptists in Christ		7,496
7th-Day Baptists, General Conf.	5,760	
7th-Day Baptists (German)		150
Southern Baptist Convention		10,393,039
Two-Seed-in-the-Spirit Baptists		201
United Baptists		63,641
United Free Will Baptist Church		100,000
Berean Fundamental Church		1,450
Bible Protestant Church		2,634
Bible Way Churches		35,000
Brethren Churches (German Baptists)		
Brethren Church (Ashland)		18,445
Brethren Church (Winona)		26,402
Church of the Brethren	201,958	
Old German Baptist Brethren		4,105
Plymouth Brethren		33,250
Brethren (River)		
Brethren in Christ		7,578
Old Order River Brethren		291
United Zion Church		865
Catholic Apostolic Church		500 e
Christadelphians		15,000
Christian and Missionary Alliance		62,355
Christian Catholic Church		7,000
Christian Churches (Disciples)	1,834,206	
Christian Nation Church		425
Christian Union		7,300
Christ's Sanctified Holy Church		600
Church of Christ (Holiness), USA		7,621
Church of Christ (Scientist)		800,000 e
Church of Eternal Life		113
Churches of God		
Church of God (Cleveland, Tenn.)		197,464
Church of God (Anderson, Ind.)		144,145
Church of God (Greenville, Tenn.)		30
Church of God (Seventh Day)		2,000
Original Church of God, Inc.		6,000
The Church of God		74,511
The Church of God (Denver, Colo.)		4,000
The Church of God by Faith		2,380

	Council Churches	Non-Council Churches
The Church of God of Prophecy		39,154
Churches of God (General Eldership)		36,995
Church of God and Saints in Christ		38,127
Independent Assemblies of God, Int.		5,000 e
Church of God in Christ		413,000
Church of Illumination		9,000
Church of Our Lord Jesus Christ (AF)		45,000
Church of the Gospel		42
Church of the Nazarene		342,032
The Church of Revelation		950
Churches of Christ		2,250,000
Churches of Christ in Christian Union		7,040
Churches of God (Holiness)		25,600
Churches of the Living God		
Church of the Living God		43,572
House of God		2,350
Churches of the New Jerusalem		
Gen. Conv. of the New Jerusalem, USA		3,758
General Church of the New Jurusalem	1,970†	
Evangelical Congregational Church		30,172
Evangelical Covenant Church of America		62,389
Evangelical Free Church of America		36,705
Evangelical United Brethren Church	757,719	
Evangelistic Associations:		
Apostolic Christian Church (Nazarean)		2,347
Apostolic Christian Church of America		8,535
The Christian Congregation		40,790
Church of Daniel's Band		200
Church of God (Apostolic)		600
Church of God as Organized by Christ		2,192
Metropolitan Church Association		443
Pillar of Fire		5,100
Federated Churches		88,411
Fire-Baptized Holiness Church		988
Fire-Baptized Holiness Church (Wesleyan)		1,007
Free Christian Zion Church of Christ		19,826
Friends (Quakers):		
Central Yearly Meeting of Friends		534
Five Years Meeting of Friends	71,552	
Kansas Yearly Meeting of Friends		8,302
Ohio Yearly Meeting of Friends		6,784
Oregon Yearly Meeting of Friends		5,944
Pacific Yearly Meeting of Friends		1,939
Philadelphia Yearly Meeting	17,313	
Religious Society of Friends (Cons.)		1,696
Religious Society of Friends (Gen. Conf.)		14,566
Holiness Church of God, Inc.		661
Independent Churches		40,276
Independent Fundamental Churches of America		56,456

	Council Churches	Non-Council Churches
Independent Negro Churches		12,337
Int. Church of Foursquare Gospel		89,215
Italian Church of North America		20,000
Latter-Day Saints:		
Church of Christ		3,000
Church of Jesus Christ (Bickertonites)		2,405
Church of Jesus Christ (Cutlerites)		22
Church of Jesus Christ, Latter Day Saints		1,787,869
Reorganized Church of Jesus Christ, LDS		162,027
Liberal Catholic Church		4,000
Lutherans:		
American Lutheran Church		2,468,407
Lutheran Church—Missouri Synod		2,591,762
Synod of Evangelical Lutheran Churches		19,184
Lutheran Church in America	3,227,157	
Apostolic Lutheran Church		6,994
Church of the Lutheran Brethren		6,947
Evangelical Lutheran Church (Eielsen)		4,220
Evangelical Lutheran Synod		14,608
Protestant Conference (Lutheran)		3,000
Evangelical Lutheran Synod (Wisconsin)		354,840
Mennonites:		
Beachy Amish Mennonite Churches		2,773
Church of God in Christ		5,000
Evangelical Mennonite Church		2,484
Evangelical Mennonite Brethren		2,536
General Conference, Mennonite Church		39,450
Hutterian Brethren		2,488
Mennonite Brethren Church of N.A.		13,000
Mennonite Church		77,285
Old Order Amish Mennonite Church		19,456
Old Order (Wisler) Mennonite Church		4,992
Reformed Mennonite Church		550
Unaffiliated Conservative Amish		1,414
Methodists:		
African Methodist Episcopal Church	1,166,301	
African M.E. Church (Zion)	770,000	
African Union Methodist Protestant		5,000
Christian Methodist Episcopal Church	444,493	
Congregational Methodist Church		14,274
Congregational Methodist Church, USA		7,500
Cumberland Methodist Church		65
Evangelical Methodist Church		6,088
Free Methodist Church of N.A.		56,826
Fundamental Methodist Church, Inc.		725
Holiness Methodist Church		1,000
Independent A.M.E. Denomination		1,000
Lumber River Holiness Methodist Church		360
The Methodist Church	10,234,986	

	Council Churches	Non-Council Churches
New Congregational Methodist Church		518
Primitive Methodist Church, USA		12,805
Reformed Methodist Episcopal Church		11,000
Reformed Zion Union Apostolic Church		12,000
Southern Methodist Church		4,025
Union American M.E. Church		27,560
Wesleyan Methodist Church of America		46,873
Moravians:		
Moravian Church in America	62,402	
Unity of the Brethren	6,030	
David Spiritual Temple of Christ, USA		40,816
New Apostolic Church of N.A., Inc.		15,703
Open Bible Standard Churches, Inc.		27,000
Pentecostals:		
Calvary Pentecostal Church, Inc.		8,000
Elim Missionary Assemblies		4,000
Emmanuel Holiness Church		1,200
International Pentecostal Assemblies		15,000
Pentecostal Assemblies of the World		45,000
Pentecostal Church of Christ		1,243
Pentecostal Church of God		115,000
Pentecostal Evangelical Church of God		229
Pentecostal Fire Baptized Holiness Church		574
Pentecost Free Will Baptist Church		10,000
Pentecostal Holiness Church		58,802
United Pentecostal Church, Inc.,		282,411
Pilgrim Holiness Church		33,270
Presbyterians:		
Associate Presbyterian Church		760
Associate Reformed Presbyterian Church		27,114
Bible Presbyterian Church, Inc.		10,000 e
Cumberland Presbyterian Church		80,455
Evangelical Presbyterian Church		6,769
Orthodox Presbyterian Church		11,994
Presbyterian Church in the U.S.	937,558	
United Presbyterian Church, USA	3,279,240	
Reformed Presbyterian Church (GS)		2,403
Reformed Presbyterian Church (OS)		5,985
2nd Cumberland Presbyterian Church		30,000
Protestant Episcopal Church	3,336,728	
Reformed Bodies:		
Christian Reformed Church		262,088
Hungarian Reformed Church	11,110	
Netherlands Reformed Congregations		2,500
Protestant Reformed Churches of America		2,798
Reformed Church in America	228,924	
Reformed Church in the United States		2,519
Reformed Episcopal Church		7,007
Salvation Army		261,014

	Council Churches	Non-Council Churches
The Schwenkfelder Church		2,300
Social Brethren		1,622
United Brethren in Christ		21,684
United Christian Church		530
United Church of Christ	2,023,611	
United Holy Church of America, Inc.		28,980
Volunteers of America		29,140
*Total Protestants in NCC	38,846,920	
Total Protestants Outside NCC		29,534,409
‡Deduct 20 per cent disaffected Church members who oppose NCC	7,769,384	
Add 20 percent disaffected Church members who oppose NCC		7,769,384
Actual Total Protestants in NCC	**31,077,536**	
Actual Total Protestants outside NCC		**37,303,793**

*This total does not include the Eastern Orthodox Catholic churches which are members of NCC.

‡This estimate is very conservative. For example: Out of the Christian Churches (Disciples) listed for 1,834,206, more than 1,000,000 are definitely opposed to the NCC.

e Estimate

†Added to NCC since 1965

APPENDIX B

NON-COUNCIL MISSION AGENCIES

1. EVANGELICAL FOREIGN MISSIONS ASSOCIATION

American Advent Mission Society
Assemblies of God, Foreign Missions Department
Baptist General Conference, Board of Foreign Missions
Bible and Medical Missionary Fellowship
Brethren in Christ World Missions
The Brethren Church, Foreign Missionary Society
The Brethren Church, Missionary Board
Child Evangelism Fellowship International
Christian Literature Crusade
Christian and Missionary Alliance
Christian Reformed Board of Foreign Missions
Church of God World Missions

Conservative Baptist Foreign Mission Society
Conservative Baptist Home Mission Society
Eastern European Mission
Evangelical Free Church of America
Evangelical Mennonite Church
Evangelistic Faith Missions, Inc.
*Far East Broadcasting Co.
*Far Eastern Gospel Crusade
Free Methodist Church of North America
Free Will Baptist Foreign Mission Board
Friends Church, California Yearly Meeting
Friends, Kansas Yearly Meeting
Friends, Ohio Yearly Meeting
Friends, Oregon Yearly Meeting
Grace Mission
International Church of the Foursquare Gospel
International Fellowship of Evangelical Students
*Latin America Mission
Mahon Mission
Mennonite Brethren Church of North America
Mexican Militant Mission
Missionary Church Association
Nazarene Department of Foreign Missions
Open Bible Standard Missions
Oriental Missionary Society
Overseas Crusades, Inc.
Pentecostal Assemblies of Canada
Pentecostal Holiness Church
Pilgrim Holiness Church World Missions
*Pocket Testament League
Primitive Methodist Foreign Mission Board
Reformed Presbyterian Church of America
*Trans World Radio
United Brethren in Christ
United Missionary Society
United World Mission
Wesleyan Methodist Church of North America
Woman's Union Missionary Society
World Gospel Mission
*World Radio Missionary Fellowship
Worldwide Evangelization Crusade
Youth for Christ International
American Leprosy Missions, Inc.
Bethel Mission of China
Bible Meditation League
Christian Nationals Evangelism Commission
*Evangelical Literature Overseas
Gospel Films, Inc.
Spanish-World Gospel Broadcasting, Inc.
World Gospel Crusades
World Vision

2. INTERDENOMINATIONAL FOREIGN MISSION ASSOCIATION

Africa Evangelical Fellowship
Africa Inland Mission
Andes Evangelical Mission
Arctic Missions, Inc.
Belgian Gospel Mission
Berean Mission, Inc.
Bible Christian Union
Bible Club Movement
Central Alaskan Missions, Inc.
Central American Mission, The
Ceylon and India General Mission
*Evangelical Literature Overseas
Evangelical Union of South Africa
*Far East Broadcasting Company
*Far Eastern Gospel Crusade
Global Gospel Broadcasts
Gospel Furthering Fellowship
Gospel Missionary Union
Gospel Mission of South America
Gospel Recordings, Inc.
Greater Europe Mission
Home of Onesiphorus
International Missions, Inc.
Japan Evangelistic Band
*Latin America Mission
Mexican Indian Mission
Missionary Aviation Fellowship
North Africa Missions
Orinoco River Mission, The
Overseas Missionary Fellowship
*Pocket Testament League
Ramabai Mukti Mission
Regions Beyond Missionary Union
Slavic Gospel Association
South America Indian Mission
Sudan Interior Mission
Sudan United Mission
The Evangelical Alliance Mission (TEAM)
*Trans World Radio
Unevangelized Fields Mission
United Faith Mission
West Indies Mission
Woman's Union Missionary Society
*World Radio Missionary Fellowship
Worldwide European Fellowship

---

* Belong to both E F M A and I F M A

3. ASSOCIATED MISSION BOARDS

Association of Baptists for World Evangelism
Baptist Mid-Missions
Bible Methodist Missions
Bible Protestant Missions
Board of Missions of the Christian Reformed Churches, Netherlands
Evangelical Baptist Missions
Fellowship of Baptists for Home Missions
Hiawatha Baptist Missions
Independent Bible Baptist Missions
Independent Board for Presbyterian Foreign Missions
Independent Board for Presbyterian Home Missions
Independent Faith Mission
International Christian Mission
Navajo Bible School and Mission
Northeastern Gospel Crusade
Northern Gospel Mission
World Baptist Fellowship
Bible Missionary Language School
Board of Missions, Methodist Protestant Church
Bristol and Clifton Protestant League
Christian Crusade
Christian Evangelical Mission
Christian Literature and Bible Center
The Evangelical Protestant Society
Fundamental World Wide Mission
Gospelaires Missionary Association
Livingstone Pioneer Mission
The Malaysia Christian Pioneer Mission
Philippine Association of Baptists for World Evangelism
Rural Gospel and Medical Missions of India (USA)
South Arizona & Sonora Mexico Mission
The Sovereign Grace Advent Testimony
Spanish Pioneer Mission
World Missionary Christians' Fellowship

4. UNAFFILIATED MISSIONS

Afghan Border Crusade
Africa Faith Mission
Afro-American Missionary Crusade
Air Mail from God Mission, Inc.
Algiers Mission Band
Alliance of the Reformed Baptist Church
Amazon Mission
Ambassadors for Christ Mission
American Baptist Home Mission Society
American Board of Missions to the Jews, Inc.
American European Bethel Mission, Inc.
American-European Mission

American Leprosy Missions
American Messianic Fellowship
Anglican Church of Canada
Anglican Church of Canada, Woman's Auxiliary
Associate Reformed Presbyterian Church
Back-Country Evangelism, Inc.
Baptist Bible Fellowship
Baptist General Conference, Board of Home Missions
Bethany Home, Inc.
Bethesda Mission
Bible Methodist Missions
Brazil Christian Mission
Brazil Gospel Fellowship Mission
Brazil Inland Mission
Calvary Baptist Mission of Puerto Rico
Canadian Baptist Foreign Mission Board
Carver Foreign Mission
Chinese Foreign Missionary Union
Christ for Greece, Inc.
Christian Mission for Deaf Africans
Christian Mission to South Korea
Christian Missionary Fellowship
Christian Missions in Many Lands, Ltd.
Church of God
Church of God in Christ, Inc.
Church of God of Prophecy
Churches of God (Holiness), Missionary Board
Churches of Christ Missions
Cleveland Hebrew Mission
Congo Inland Missions
Congregational Methodist Church, General Missions
Cumberland Presbyterian Church
Denbigh Missionary Fellowship
Door to Life Foreign Missions
Eastern Mennonite Board of Missions and Charities
Elim Missionary Assemblies
European Evangelistic Crusade
Evangelical Bible Mission
Evangelical Covenant Church of America
Evangelical Deaf Mission, Inc.
Evangelical Enterprises
Far East Apostolic Mission
Fellowship of Independent Missions
Fiji Missionary Fellowship
Friends, Central Yearly Meeting
Friends of Israel Missionary and Relief Society, Inc.
General Baptist Foreign Mission Society
German Missionary Fellowship, Inc.
Good Shepherd Agricultural Mission
Gospel Fellowship, Inc.
Greater Mexican Mission, Inc.

Haiti Inland Mission
Harvesters International
Highland Christian Mission
Holy Cross Liberian Mission
Independent Gospel Mission of Puerto Rico, Inc.
International Christian Leprosy Mission
Island Missionary Society
Jamaica Evangelistic Mission
Japan Gospel Fellowship Association
Japanese Evangelical Missionary Society
Japan Regular Baptist Mission
Korea Gospel Mission
Latin American Lutheran Mission
Lebanon Evangelical Mission
Latin American Orphanage and Broadcasting Corp.
Liebenzell Mission of U.S.A., Inc.
Lutheran Brethren Mission
Lutheran Church, Missouri Synod, Board of Missions
Lutheran Orient Mission Society
Lutheran Synodical Conference, Missionary Board
Marine Medical Missions, Inc.
Middle East General Mission
Mino Mission
Mission to Europe's Millions
Missionary Dentists, Inc.
Missionary Prayer & Literature Fellowship, Inc.
Missionary & Soul Winning Fellowship
Tommy Moss Evangelistic Assoc.
Mustard Seed, Inc.
Mennonite Church General Conference
The Navigators
Near East and Arabian Mission
New Life League
New Testament Missionary Union
New Tribes Mission
North American Baptist Missionary Society
Orthodox Presbyterian Church Comm. of Foreign Missions
Overseas Christian Servicemen's Centers
Pan American Missionary Society
Parana Valley Mission
Pentecostal Assemblies of the World, Inc.
Pentecostal Church of God of America
Peruvian Fellowship
Pioneer Bible Mission, Inc.
Red Sea Mission Team
Reformed Baptist Church, Alliance of
Reformed Episcopal Church, Board of Foreign Missions
Regular Baptist Missionary Fund, Inc.
Salvation Army
Seventh-day Adventist Church
Slavic and Oriental Mission

Source of Light Mission
Southern Baptist Convention, Foreign Mission Board
Southern Methodist Church, Board of Missions
Spanish America Inland Mission
Spanish Crusades, Inc.
The Mennonite Church
Things to Come Mission
United Church of Canada, Board of World Missions
United Pentecostal Church
Voice of China and Asia, Inc.
World Evangelical Mission, Inc.
World Mission Prayer League (Lutheran)
World Missions to Children
World Missions, Inc.
World Presbyterian Missions, Inc.
World Grace Testimony
World-Wide Missions
Wycliffe Bible Translators

APPENDIX C

HIGHER EDUCATIONAL INSTITUTIONS

1. COLLEGES AND UNIVERSITIES

Abilene Christian College	Church of Christ	Abilene, Tex.
Alabama Christian College	Church of Christ	Montgomery, Ala.
Alderson-Broaddus College	Southern Baptist	Philippi, W. Va.
Anderson College	Church of God	Anderson, Ind.
Andrews University	Adventist	Wilmore, Ky.
Asbury College	Wesleyan	Ashland, Ohio
Ashland College	Ch. of Brethren	Berrien Springs, Mich.
Atlantic Union College	Adventist	S. Lancaster, Mass.
Aurora College	Advent Christian	Aurora, Ill.
Azusa Pacific College	Undenom.	Azusa, Calif.
Barrington College	Undenom.	Barrington, R. I.
Baylor University	Southern Baptist	Waco, Tex.
Belhaven College	Presbyterian	Jackson, Miss.
Belmont College	Southern Baptist	Nashville, Tenn.
Bethany-Nazarene College	Nazarene	Bethany, Okla.
Bethel College	Cumberland Pres.	McKenzie, Tenn.
Bethel College	Mennonite	Newton, Kansas
Bethel College	Baptist	St. Paul, Minn.
Biola College	Undenom.	La Mirada, Calif.
Blue Mountain College	Southern Baptist	Blue Mountain, Miss.
Bluffton College	Mennonite	Bluffton, Ohio
Bob Jones University	Undenom.	Greenville, S. C.

310

California Baptist College	Southern Baptist	Riverside, Calif.
Calvin College	Chr. Reformed	Grand Rapids, Mich.
Carson-Newman College	Southern Baptist	Jefferson City, Tenn.
Columbia Christian College	Church of Christ	Portland, Ore.
Columbia Union College	Adventist	Takoma Park, Md.
Concordia College	Lutheran	Ft. Wayne, Ind.
Cumberland College	Southern Baptist	Williamsburg, Ky.
David Lipscomb College	Church of Christ	Nashville, Tenn.
East Texas Baptist College	Southern Baptist	Marshall, Tex.
Eastern Baptist College	Baptist	St. Davids, Pa.
Eastern Mennonite College	Mennonite	Harrisonburg, Va.
Eastern Nazarene College	Nazarene	Wollaston, Mass.
Erskine College	Asso. Ref. Pres.	Due West, S. C.
Findlay College	Church of God	Findlay, Ohio
Ft. Worth Christian College	Church of Christ	Ft. Worth, Tex.
Freed-Hardeman College	Church of Christ	Henderson, Tenn.
Friends University	Friends	Wichita, Kan.
Furman University	Southern Baptist	Greenville, S. C.
Geneva College	Reformed Pres.	Beaver Falls, Pa.
George Fox College	Friends	Newberg, Ore.
Georgetown College	Southern Baptist	Georgetown, Ky.
Gordon College	Undenom.	Wenham, Mass.
Goshen College	Mennonite	Goshen, Ind.
Grove City College	Undenom.	Grove City, Pa.
Hardin-Simmons Univ.	Southern Baptist	Abilene, Tex.
Harding College	Church of Christ	Searcy, Ark.
Houghton College	Wesleyan Methodist	Houghton, N. Y.
Howard College	Southern Baptist	Birmingham, Ala.
Howard Payne College	Southern Baptist	Brownwood, Tex.
Huntington College	United Brethren	Huntington, Ind.
John Brown University	Undenom.	Siloam Springs, Ark.
Judson College	Southern Baptist	Marion, Ala.
King's College	Undenom.	Briarcliff Manor, N. Y.
Louisiana College	Southern Baptist	Pineville, La.
Lubbock Christian College	Church of Christ	Lubbock, Tex.
Malone College	Friends	Canton, Ohio
Mary Hardin-Baylor College	Southern Baptist	Belton, Tex.
McPherson College	Brethren	McPherson, Kan.
Mercer University	Southern Baptist	Macon, Ga.
Meredith College	Southern Baptist	Raleigh, N. C.
Messiah College	Brethren in Christ	Grantham, Pa.
Milligan College	Church of Christ	Milligan College, Tenn.
Mississippi College	Southern Baptist	Clinton, Miss.
Northwest Christian College	Church of Christ	Eugene, Ore.
Northwest Nazarene College	Nazarene	Nampa, Ida.
North Park College	Evang. Covenant	Chicago, Ill.
Oklahoma Baptist Univ.	Southern Baptist	Okla. City, Okla.
Olivet Nazarene College	Nazarene	Kankakee, Ill.
Ouachita Baptist College	Southern Baptist	Arkadelphia, Ark.
Pasadena College	Nazarene	Pasadena, Calif.
Pepperdine College	Church of Christ	Los Angeles, Calif.

311

Pillsbury Baptist College	Baptist	Owatonna, Minn.
Roberts Wesleyan College	Free Methodist	North Chili, N. Y.
Seattle Pacific College	Free Methodist	Seattle, Wash.
Shelton College	Undenom.	Cape May, N. J.
Shorter College	Southern Baptist	Rome, Ga.
Sterling College	Presbyterian	Sterling, Kan.
Stetson University	Southern Baptist	De Land, Fla.
Union University	Southern Baptist	Jackson, Tenn.
University of Richmond	Southern Baptist	Richmond, Va.
Wayland Baptist College	Southern Baptist	Plainview, Tex.
Westmont College	Undenom.	Santa Barbara, Calif.
Wheaton College	Undenom.	Wheaton, Ill.
York College	Church of Christ	York, Neb.

2. BIBLE COLLEGES AND SEMINARIES

Anderson Theological Seminary	Church of God	Anderson, Ind.
Asbury Theological Seminary	Wesleyan	Wilmore, Ky.
Ashland Theological Seminary	Brethren Church	Ashland, Ohio
Atlanta Christian College	Church of Christ	Atlanta, Ga.
Aurora College	Advent Christian	Aurora, Ill.
Barrington College	Undenom.	Barrington, R. I.
Berkshire Christian College	Advent Christian	Lenox, Mass.
Bethany Bible College	Pentecostal	Santa Cruz, Calif.
Bethel College and Seminary	Baptist	St. Paul, Minn.
Biblical Seminary of New York	Undenom.	New York City
Calvary Bible College	Undenom.	Kansas City, Mo.
Calvin Theological Seminary	Chr. Reformed	Grand Rapids, Mich.
Central Bible Institute	Pentecostal	Springfield, Mo.
Central Christian College	Church of Christ	Moberly, Mo.
Central Wesleyan College	Wesleyan Methodist	Central, S. C.
Christian College of the Southwest	Church of Christ	Dallas, Tex.
Cincinnati Bible Seminary	Church of Christ	Cincinnati, Ohio
Columbia Bible College	Undenom.	Columbia, S. C.
Concordia Seminary	Lutheran	St. Louis, Mo.
Concordia Theological Seminary	Lutheran	Springfield, Ill.
Conservative Baptist Theological Seminary	Baptist	Denver, Colo.
Covenant College and Seminary	Evang. Presbyterian	St. Louis, Mo.
Crowley's Ridge College	Church of Christ	Paragould, Ark.
Cumberland Presbyterian Theological Seminary	Cumb. Presb.	McKenzie, Tenn.

312

Dallas Christian College	Church of Christ	Dallas, Tex.
Dallas Theological Seminary	Undenom.	Dallas, Tex.
Dayton Bible Institute	Open Bible Standard	Dayton, Ohio
Detroit Bible College	Undenom.	Detroit, Mich.
Eastern Baptist Theological Seminary	Baptist	Philadelphia, Pa.
Eastern Mennonite College	Mennonite	Harrisonburg, Va.
Eastern Pilgrim College	Pilgrim Holiness	Allentown, Pa.
Emmanuel School of Religion	Church of Christ	Milligan College, Tenn.
Erskine Theological Seminary	Asso. Ref. Presby	Due West, S. C.
Evangelical Congregational School of Theology	Ev. Cong.	Myerstown, Pa.
Florida Christian College	Church of Christ	Tampa, Fla.
Fort Wayne Bible College	Miss. Church Asso.	Ft. Wayne, Ind.
Free Will Baptist Bible College	Free Will Baptist	Nashville, Tenn.
Friends Bible College	Friends	Haviland, Kan.
Fuller Theological Seminary	Undenom.	Pasadena, Calif.
Golden Gate Baptist Theological Seminary	Southern Baptist	Mill Valley, Calif.
Gordon Divinity School	Undenom.	Wenham, Mass.
Goshen College Biblical Seminary	Mennonite	Goshen, Ind.
Grace Bible Institute	Mennonite	Omaha, Neb.
Grace Theological Seminary	Brethren Church	Winona Lake, Ind.
Greenville College	Free Methodist	Greenville, Ill.
Houghton College	Wesleyan Methodist	Houghton, N. Y.
Huntington College	United Brethren	Huntington, Ind.
Johnson Bible College	Church of Christ	Knoxville, Tenn.
Kentucky Christian College	Church of Christ	Grayson, Ky.
Lancaster School of the Bible	Undenom.	Lancaster, Pa.
Lee College	Church of God	Cleveland, Tenn.
Lincoln Christian College	Church of Christ	Lincoln, Ill.
Lutheran Bible Institute	Indep. Lutheran	Minneapolis, Minn.
Lutheran Bible Institute	Indep. Lutheran	Seattle, Wash.
Lutheran Bible Institute	Indep. Lutheran	Teaneck, N. J.
Lutheran Brethren Schools	Lutheran Brethren	Fergus Falls, Minn.
Malone College	Friends	Canton, Ohio
Manhattan Bible College	Church of Christ	Manhattan, Kan.
Marion College	Wesleyan Methodist	Marion, Ind.
Mennonite Biblical Seminary	Mennonite	Elkhart, Ind.
Mennonite Brethren Seminary	Mennonite	Fresno, Calif.
Midwest Christian College	Church of Christ	Oklahoma City, Okla.

313

Midwestern Baptist Theological Seminary	Southern Baptist	Kansas City, Mo.
Minnesota Bible College	Church of Christ	Minneapolis, Minn.
Moody Bible Institute	Undenom.	Chicago, Ill.
Multnomah School of the Bible	Undenom.	Portland, Ore.
Nazarene Theological Seminary	Nazarene	Kansas City, Mo.
Nebraska Christian College	Church of Christ	Norfolk, Neb.
North American Baptist Seminary	Baptist	Sioux Falls, S. D.
North American Theological Seminary	Baptist	Jacksonville, Tex.
North Park Theological Seminary	Evang. Covenant	Chicago, Ill.
North Central Bible College	Pentecostal	Minneapolis, Minn.
Northeastern Bible Institute	Undenom.	Essex Fells, N. J.
Northern Baptist Theological Seminary	Baptist	Chicago, Ill.
Northeastern Christian College	Church of Christ	Villanova, Pa.
Northwest Bible College	Pentecostal	Kirkland, Wash.
Northwest College	Pentecostal	Kirkland, Wash.
Northwest Nazarene College	Nazarene	Nampa, Ida.
Northwestern College	Undenom.	Minneapolis, Minn.
Nyack Missionary College	C & M Alliance	Nyack, N. Y.
Oakland City College	Baptist	Oakland City, Ind.
Ohio Valley College	Church of Christ	Parkersburg, W.Va.
Olivet Nazarene College	Nazarene	Kankakee, Ill.
Owosso College	Pilgrim Holiness	Owosso, Mich.
Ozark Bible College	Church of Christ	Joplin, Mo.
Pacific Christian College	Church of Christ	Long Beach, Calif.
Pacific College	Mennonite	Fresno, Calif.
Philadelphia School of the Bible	Undenom.	Philadelphia, Pa.
Piedmont Bible College	Undenom.	Winston-Salem, N. C.
Pinecrest Bible Institute	Pentecostal	Salisbury Center, N. Y.
Platte Valley Bible College	Church of Christ	Scottsbluff, Neb.
Powellhurst Bible College	Baptist	Portland, Ore.
Puget Sound College of the Bible	Church of Christ	Seattle, Wash.
Reformed Bible Institute	Chr. Reformed	Grand Rapids, Mich.
Reformed Presbyterian Theological Seminary	Ref. Pres.	Pittsburgh, Pa.
Rockmont College	Undenom.	Longmont, Colo.
St. Louis Christian College	Church of Christ	Florisant, Mo.
St. Paul Bible College	C & M Alliance	St. Paul, Minn.
San Jose Bible College	Church of Christ	San Jose, Calif.
Simpson Bible College	C & M Alliance	San Francisco, Calif.
Southeastern Bible College	Pentecostal	Lakeland, Fla.

314

Southeastern Christian College	Church of Christ	Winchester, Ky.
Southern Baptist Theological Seminary	Baptist	Louisville, Ky.
Southern California College	Pentecostal	Costa Mesa, Calif.
Southwestern Baptist Theological Seminary	Baptist	Ft. Worth, Tex.
Southern Pilgrim College	Pilgrim Holiness	Kernersville, N. C.
Southwestern Assemblies of God College	Pentecostal	Waxahachie, Tex.
Southwestern Christian College	Church of Christ	Terrell, Tex.
Toccoa Falls Bible Institute	C & M Alliance	Toccoa Falls, Ga.
Trevecca Nazarene College	Nazarene	Nashville, Tenn.
Trinity Evangelical Divinity School	Evan. Free Church	Deerfield, Ill.
Union Bible Seminary	Friends	Westfield, Ind.
Vennard College	Undenom.	University Park, Iowa
Washington Bible College	Undenom.	Washington, D. C.
Warner Pacific College	Church of God	Portland, Ore.
Western Baptist Bible College	Baptist	El Cerrito, Calif.
Wessington Springs College	Free Methodist	Wessington Spgs., S.D.
Western Conservative Baptist Theological Seminary	Baptist	Portland, Ore.
Westminster Theological Seminary	Presbyterian	Philadelphia, Pa.
Winebrenner Theological Seminary	Church of God	Findlay, Ohio
Wisconsin Lutheran Seminary	Lutheran	Mequon, Wisc.

3. BIBLE SCHOOLS AND INSTITUTES

Aenon Bible School	Pentecostal	Columbus, Ohio
Appalachian Bible Inst.	Undenom.	Bradley, W. Va.
Arizona Bible Institute	Undenom.	Phoenix, Ariz.
Asbury Bible College	Undenom.	Moline, Ill.
Atlanta Southern Bible College	Undenom.	Atlanta, Ga.
Baltimore Bible College	Undenom.	Baltimore, Md.
Baptist Bible College	Baptist	Denver, Colo.
Baptist Bible College	Baptist	Springfield, Mo.
Baptist Bible Institute	Southern Baptist	Graceville, Fla.
Baptist Bible Institute	Southern Baptist	Mayfield, Ky.
Baptist Bible Institute	Baptist	Okla. City, Okla.
Baptist School of the Bible	Baptist	Cleveland, Ohio
Berean Bible School	Bible Fellowship	Allentown, Pa.
Bethany Bible Training School	Undenom.	Chicago, Ill.

315

Bethany Fellowship Bible Institute	Undenom.	Minneapolis, Minn.
Beulah Hts. Bible Inst.	Pentecostal	Atlanta, Ga.
Baptist Bible Seminary	Baptist	Arlington, Tex.
Bible Christian Training Institute	Undenom.	Brooklyn, N. Y.
Bible Inst. of New England	Undenom.	Hartford, Vt.
Bible Standard College	Open Bible Standard	Eugene, Ore.
Bible Training Institute	United Holy Church	Goldsboro, N. C.
Boise Bible College	Church of Christ	Boise, Ida.
Buffalo Bible Institute	Undenom.	Buffalo, N. Y.
California Bible Institute	Free Will Baptist	El Sobrante, Calif.
Calvary Bible College	Undenom.	Sunnyvale, Calif.
Carver Bible Institute	Undenom.	Atlanta, Ga.
Central Baptist College	Missionary Baptist	Conway, Ark.
Central Pilgrim College	Pilgrim Holiness	Bartlesville, Okla.
Central Washington School of the Bible	Undenom.	Selah, Wash.
Chicago Bible College	Undenom.	Chicago, Ill.
Circleville Bible College	Church of Christ in Christian Union	Circleville, Ohio
College of the Rockies	Undenom.	Golden, Colo.
College of the Scriptures	Church of Christ	Louisville, Ky.
Dakota Bible College	Church of Christ	Huron, S. D.
Dallas Bible Institute	Undenom.	Dallas, Tex.
Decatur Bible Institute	Undenom.	Decatur, Ill.
Eastern Christian College	Church of Christ	Bel Air, Md.
Elim Bible Institute	Pentecostal	Lima, N. Y.
Emmaus Bible School	Plymouth Brethren	Oak Park, Ill.
Frankfort Pilgrim College	Pilgrim Holiness	Frankfort, Ind.
Fruitland Baptist Bible Inst.	Baptist	Hendersonville, N. C.
Fundamental Bible Institute	Undenom.	Los Angeles, Calif.
Glen Cove Bible School	Undenom.	Glen Cove, Me.
God's Bible School and College	Undenom.	Cincinnati, Ohio
Grace Bible College	Undenom.	Grand Rapids, Mich.
Grand Rapids School of the Bible	Undenom.	Grand Rapids, Mich.
Grand Rapids Baptist Theological Seminary	GARBC	Grand Rapids, Mich.
Great Lakes Bible College	Church of Christ	Lansing, Mich.
Gulf Coast Bible College	Church of God	Houston, Tex.
Immanuel College	Baptist	Atlanta, Ga.
Intermountain Bible College	Church of Christ	Grand Junction, Colo.
International Bible College	Undenom.	San Antonio, Tex.
John Wesley College	Independent	Greensboro, N. C.
King's Missionary Training Institute	Undenom.	Seattle, Wash.
Lexington Baptist College	Baptist	Lexington, Ky.
L.I.F.E. Bible College	Foursquare Gospel	Los Angeles, Calif.
Linda Vista Bible College	Baptist	San Diego, Calif.

316

Louisville Bible College	Church of Christ	Louisville, Ky.
Lutheran Lay Training Inst.	Lutheran	Milwaukee, Wisc.
Manahath Educational Center	Evangelical Methodist	Altoona, Pa.
Memphis Christian College	Church of Christ	Memphis, Tenn.
Miami Bible Institute	Undenom.	Miami, Fla.
Michigan Bible Institute	Baptist	Flint, Mich.
Mid-South Bible College	Undenom.	Memphis, Tenn.
Midwest Baptist College	Baptist	Danville, Ill.
Midwestern Baptist Schools	Baptist	Pontiac, Mich.
Midwestern School of Evangelism	Church of Christ	Ottumwa, Ia.
Montana Inst. of the Bible	Undenom.	Billings, Mont.
Mount Echo Bible Institute	Undenom.	Great Valley, N. Y.
Mount Vernon Bible College	Foursquare Gospel	Mt. Vernon, Ohio
New Tribes Bible Institute	Undenom.	Milwaukee, Wisc.
Nogales Bible School	Free Methodist	Nogales, Ariz.
Northwest Bible College	Church of God	Minot, N. D.
Oak Hills Bible Institute	Undenom.	Bemidji, Minn.
Omaha Baptist Bible College	Baptist	Omaha, Neb.
Open Bible College	Pentecostal	Des Moines, Ia.
Oregon Bible College	Church of God	Oregon, Ill.
Orthodox Baptist Institute	Baptist	Ardmore, Okla.
Ozark Bible Institute	Undenom.	Ozark, Ark.
Pentecostal Bible College	Pentecostal	Sacramento, Calif.
Pentecostal Bible Institute	Pentecostal	Tupelo, Miss.
Piedmont Bible Institute	Baptist	Cramerton, N. C.
Pinecrest Bible Institute	Pentecostal	Salisbury Center, N. Y.
Practical Bible Training School	Undenom.	Bible School Park, N. Y.
Reed College of Religion	Undenom.	Los Angeles, Calif.
Rio Grande Bible Institue	Undenom.	Edinburg, Tex.
Roanoke Bible College	Church of Christ	Elizabeth City, N. C.
St. Petersburg Bible Inst.	Pentecostal	St. Petersburg, Fla.
Salem Bible College	Undenom.	Salem, Ohio
Shenandoah Christian College	Undenom.	Roanoke, Va.
Southwestern Baptist School	Baptist	Phoenix, Ariz.
Southeastern Bible College	Undenom.	Birmingham, Ala.
Southern Bible College	Pentecostal	Houston, Tex.
Southern Bible Training School	Undenom.	Dallas, Tex.
Southern Christian College	Undenom.	San Antonio, Tex.
Southland Bible Institute	Undenom.	Pikeville, Ky.
Southwestern Bible College	Pentecostal	Okla. City, Okla.
Tennessee Temple Schools	Baptist	Chattanooga, Tenn.
Trinity College	Undenom.	Clearwater, Fla.
West Coast Bible College	Pentecostal	Clovis, Calif.
Western Baptist Bible College	Baptist	Kansas City, Mo.
Western Bible Institute	Undenom.	Denver, Colo.

Westminster Bible Institute	Cong. Methodist	Tehuacana, Tex.
William Carter College	Undenom.	Goldsboro, N. C.
Winston-Salem Bible College	Church of Christ	Winston-Salem, N. C.
Zion Bible Institute	Pentecostal	Providence, R. I.

APPENDIX D

NON-COUNCIL PROTESTANT PERIODICALS

ACTION of Men for Missions, Greenwood, Ind.
ADVANCE, Springfield, Mo.
ADVENT CHRISTIAN NEWS, Live Oak, Fla.
ADVENT CHRISTIAN WITNESS, Concord, N. H.
ADVOCATE, Circleville, Ohio
ALABAMA BAPTIST, Birmingham, Ala.
ALASKA BAPTIST MESSENGER, Anchorage, Alaska
ALLIANCE WITNESS, New York, N. Y.
AMBASSADOR LIFE, Memphis, Tenn.
AMERICAN BAPTIST, Jacksonville, Texas
AMERICAN CHRISTIAN REVIEW, Indianapolis, Ind.
ANDEAN OUTLOOK, Cochabamba, Bolivia, S. A.
ARKANSAS BAPTIST NEWSMAGAZINE, Little Rock, Ark.
ASSOCIATE REFORMED PRESBYTERIAN, Due West, S. C.
BANNER, Grand Rapids, Mich.
BAPTIST AND REFLECTOR, Nashville, Tenn.
BAPTIST BEACON, Phoenix, Ariz.
BAPTIST BIBLE TRIBUNE, Springfield, Mo.
BAPTIST BULLETIN, Chicago, Ill.
BAPTIST COURIER, Greenville, S. C.
BAPTIST DIGEST, Wichita, Kansas
BAPTIST MESSAGE, Alexandria, La.
BAPTIST MESSENGER, Oklahoma City, Okla.
BAPTIST NEW MEXICAN, Albuquerque, N. M.
BAPTIST PROGRAM, Nashville, Tenn.
BAPTIST RECORD, Jackson, Miss.
BAPTIST SENTINEL, Bellflower, Calif.
BAPTIST STANDARD, Dallas, Texas
BIBLE PROTESTANT MESSENGER, Linwood, N. J.
BIBLICAL RECORDER, Raleigh, N. C.
BIBLICAL RESEARCH MONTHLY, Los Angeles, Calif.
BRETHREN EVANGELIST, Ashland, Ohio
BRETHREN MISSIONARY HERALD, Winona Lake, Ind.
BRIDEGROOM'S MESSENGER, Atlanta, Ga.

CABLE, Palo Alto, Calif.
CALIFORNIA SOUTHERN BAPTIST, Fresno, Calif.
CALL TO PRAYER FOR MISSIONS, Marion, Ind.
CAMPUS AMBASSADOR, Springfield, Mo.
CAMPUS LIFE, Wheaton, Ill.
CAPITAL BAPTIST, Washington, D. C.
CBMC CONTACT, Lombard, Ill.
CHILD EVANGELISM MAGAZINE, Grand Rapids, Mich.
CHINESE CHRISTIAN DIGEST, Los Angeles, Calif.
CHRISTIAN BEACON, Collingswood, N. J.
CHRISTIAN COURIER, Hamilton, Ontario, Canada
CHRISTIAN CRUSADE, Tulsa, Okla.
CHRISTIAN ECONOMICS, Los Angeles, Calif.
CHRISTIAN ENDEAVOR WORLD, Columbus, Ohio
CHRISTIAN HERITAGE, Hackensack, N. J.
CHRISTIAN HOME AND SCHOOL, Grand Rapids, Mich.
CHRISTIAN INDEX, Atlanta, Ga.
CHRISTIAN LEADER, Chicago, Ill.
CHRISTIAN LEADER, Hillsboro, Kansas
CHRISTIAN LIFE, Wheaton, Ill.
CHRISTIAN LIVING, Elgin, Ill.
CHRISTIAN READER, Wheaton, Ill.
CHRISTIAN SCIENCE MONITOR, Boston, Mass.
CHRISTIAN STANDARD, Cincinnati, Ohio
CHRISTIAN UNION WITNESS, Indianola, Iowa
CHRISTIANITY TODAY, Washington, D. C.
CHRISTLIFE MAGAZINE, Moline, Ill.
CHRIST'S AMBASSADORS HERALD, Springfield, Mo.
CHURCH HERALD, Grand Rapids, Mich.
CHURCH OF GOD EVANGEL, Cleveland, Tenn.
CHURCH PRESS, Glendale, Calif.
CMS JOURNAL, Oak Park, Ill.
CO-LABORER, Nashville, Tenn.
COLLEGIATE CHALLENGE, San Bernardino, Calif.
COMMAND, Lansing, Mich.
COMMISSION, Richmond, Va.
COMPASS, New York, N. Y.
COMPASSION, Chicago, Ill.
CONGREGATIONAL CHRISTIAN, Orange, Mass.
CONQUEST, Kansas City, Mo.
CONSERVATIVE BAPTIST IMPACT, Wheaton, Ill.
CONTACT, Nashville, Tenn.
CONTACT, Huntington, Ind.
COUNSELOR, Wheaton, Ill.
COVENANT COMPANION, Chicago, Ill.
COVENANTER WITNESS, Sterling, Kansas
CRUSADE FOR CHRIST, Calgary, Alberta, Canada
CRUSADER, Manila, Philippines
CRUSADER MAGAZINE, Grand Rapids, Mich.
CRUSADES, Upland, Ind.
CUP, Hermosa Beach, Calif.

319

DECISION, Minneapolis, Minn.
DESERET NEWS, Salt Lake City, Utah
DE WACHTER, Grand Rapids, Mich.
EAST ASIA MILLIONS, Philadelphia, Pa.
EL HERALDO DE SANTIDAD, Kansas City, Kansas
ELO BULLETIN, Wheaton, Ill.
END TIMES MESSENGER, Calgary, Alberta, Canada
EPISCOPAL RECORDER, Philadelphia, Pa.
ETERNITY, Philadelphia, Pa.
EUROPEAN, Levittown, Pa.
EVANGELICAL BEACON, Minneapolis, Minn.
EVANGELICAL INTERNATIONAL STUDENTS, Washington, D. C.
EVANGELICAL MENNONITE, Fort Wayne, Ind.
EVANGELICAL VISITOR, Nappanee, Ind.
FAITH AND FELLOWSHIP, Moorhead, Minn.
FIRM FOUNDATION, Austin, Texas
FLASHLIGHT, Pasadena, Calif.
FLORIDA BAPTIST WITNESS, Jacksonville, Fla.
FOREST HOME LIFE, Forest Falls, Calif.
FREE WILL BAPTIST ADVOCATE, New Bern, N. C.
FREE METHODIST, Winona Lake, Ind.
FULL GOSPEL BUSINESS MEN'S VOICE, Los Angeles, Calif.
GENERAL BAPTIST MESSENGER, Poplar Bluff, Mo.
GIDEON MAGAZINE, Nashville, Tenn.
GLOBAL CONQUEST, Springfield, Mo.
GOOD NEWS BROADCASTER, Lincoln, Nebr.
GOSPEL ADVOCATE, Nashville, Tenn.
GOSPEL BANNER, Elkhart, Ind.
GOSPEL CALL, Pasadena, Calif.
GOSPEL HERALD, Scottdale, Pa.
GOSPEL TIDINGS, Omaha, Nebr.
GUIDE, Rexdale, Ontario, Canada
HAWAII BAPTIST, Honolulu, Hawaii
HEARTBEAT, Nashville, Tenn.
HERALD OF HOLINESS, Kansas City, Mo.
HIGH, Chicago, Ill.
HIS, Chicago, Ill.
ILLINOIS BAPTIST, Carbondale, Ill.
INDIANA BAPTIST, Indianapolis, Ind.
JUNIOR CALL, Marion, Ind.
KING'S BUSINESS, La Mirada, Calif.
LAKELAND COLOR PRESS, Minneapolis, Minn.
LATIN AMERICA EVANGELIST, San Jose, Costa Rica
LEADER, Elgin, Ill.
LIBERTY, Washington, D. C.
LIGHT AND LIFE EVANGEL, Winona Lake, Ind.
LIGHTED PATHWAY, Cleveland, Tenn.
LUTHERAN NEWS, New Haven, Mo.
MENNONITE BRETHREN HERALD, Winnipeg, Manitoba, Canada
MESSAGE OF THE CROSS, Minneapolis, Minn.
MESSAGE OF THE OPEN BIBLE, Des Moines, Iowa

MICHIGAN BAPTIST MESSENGER, Detroit, Mich.
MISSIONARY BANNER, Elkhart, Ind.
MISSIONARY BROADCASTER, Chicago, Ill.
MISSIONARY LIFE, Wheaton, Ill.
MISSIONARY STANDARD, Greenwood, Ind.
MISSIONARY TIDINGS, Winona Lake, Ind.
MISSIONARY WORKER, Peoria, Ill.
MISSION MESSENGER, Saint Louis, Mo.
MOODY MONTHLY, Chicago, Ill.
NATIONAL STATESMAN, Kalamazoo, Mich.
NAVIGATORS LOG, Colorado Springs, Colo.
NORTH ATLANTIC CHRISTIAN, Hartford, Conn.
NOW, Longview, Texas
NSSA LINK, Chicago, Ill.
OHIO BAPTIST MESSENGER, Columbus, Ohio
PACIFIC COAST BAPTIST, Portland, Ore.
PARK ST. SPIRE, Boston, Mass.
PENTECOSTAL EVANGEL, Springfield, Mo.
PENTECOSTAL HOLINESS ADVOCATE, Franklin Springs, Ga.
PENTECOSTAL TESTIMONY, Toronto, Ontario, Canada
PILGRIM HOLINESS ADVOCATE, Indianapolis, Ind.
PILLAR OF FIRE, Zarephath, N. J.
POWER FOR LIVING, Wheaton, Ill.
PRESBYTERIAN JOURNAL, Asheville, N. C.
PRIMITIVE BAPTIST, Thornton, Ariz.
PSYCHOLOGY FOR LIVING, Pasadena, Calif.
PTL QUARTERLY, Englewood, N. J.
RELIGIOUS HERALD, Richmond, Va.
REVIEW AND EXPOSITOR, Louisville, Ky.
REVIEW AND HERALD, Washington, D. C.
ROCKY MOUNTAIN BAPTIST, Denver, Colo.
SAINTS' HERALD, Independence, Mo.
SIGNS OF THE TIMES, Mountain View, Calif.
SOWER, Chicago, Ill.
SPIRIT, St. Louis, Mo.
STANDARD, Chicago, Ill.
SUCCESS, Denver, Colo.
SUNDAY DIGEST, Elgin, Ill.
SUNDAY SCHOOL COUNSELOR, Springfield, Mo.
SUNDAY SCHOOL JOURNAL, Winona Lake, Ind.
TAYLOR UNIVERSITY MAGAZINE, Upland, Ind.
TEACH MAGAZINE, Glendale, Calif.
TEACH N TRAIN, Nashville, Tenn.
TEAM, Springfield, Mo.
TEEN POWER, Wheaton, Ill.
TEEN TIME, Winona Lake, Ind.
THE BAPTIST HERALD, Forest Park, Ill.
THE BIBLE ADVOCATE, Stanberry, Mo.
THE CHRISTIAN CHRONICLE, Abilene, Texas
THE CHURCH ADVOCATE, Harrisburg, Pa.
THE CHURCH OF GOD, Queens Village, N. Y.

321

THE COMMISSION, Richmond, Va.
THE CONGREGATIONAL CHRISTIAN, W. Mansfield, Mass.
THE CONGREGATIONALIST, Milwaukee, Wis.
THE DEFENDER, Kansas City, Mo.
THE HERALD OF LIFE, Kensington, Conn.
THE LOOKOUT, Cincinnati, Ohio
THE LUTHERAN WITNESS, St. Louis, Mo.
THE MENNONITE, Newton, Kansas
THE PENTECOSTAL HERALD, St. Louis, Mo.
THE PRIMITIVE METHODIST JOURNAL, Shenandoah, Pa.
THE RESTITUTION HERALD, Oregon, Ill.
THE RESTORATION HERALD, Cincinnati, Ohio
THE SOUTHERN METHODIST, Orangeburg, S. C.
THE VOICE, Chicago, Ill.
THE VOLUNTEER GAZETTE, New York, N. Y.
TWENTIETH CENTURY CHRISTIAN, Los Angeles, Calif.
THIS DAY MAGAZINE, St. Louis, Mo.
TIE, St. Paul, Minn.
TODAY, Chicago, Ill.
TRAILS, Wheaton, Ill.
TRANSLATION, Santa Ana, Calif.
TRANSMITTER, Winona Lake, Ind.
TRINITY, Van Nuys, Calif.
UNITED BRETHREN, Huntington, Ind.
UNITED EVANGELICAL ACTION, Wheaton, Ill.
UNITED EVANGELICAL, Myerstown, Pa.
VENTURE MAGAZINE, Wheaton, Ill.
VIEW, Los Angeles, Calif.
VISION, Los Angeles, Calif.
VITAL CHRISTIANITY, Anderson, Ind.
VOICE, Los Angeles, Calif.
WAR CRY, San Francisco, Calif.
WAR CRY, Atlanta, Ga.
WAR CRY, Chicago, Ill.
WAR CRY, New York, N. Y.
WATCHMAN-EXAMINER, New York, N. Y.
WESLEYAN METHODIST, Marion, Ind.
WESLEYAN MISSIONARY, Marion, Ind.
WESLEYAN YOUTH, Marion, Ind.
WESTERN RECORDER, Middletown, Ky.
WHITE WING MESSENGER, Cleveland, Tenn.
WORLD HARVEST MAGAZINE, South Bend, Ind.
WORLD MISSIONS BULLETIN, Indianapolis, Ind.
WORLD VISION MAGAZINE, Monrovia, Calif.
WORD AND WAY, Jefferson City, Mo.
YOUNG AMBASSADOR, Lincoln, Nebr.
YOUNG CALVINIST, Grand Rapids, Mich.
YOUNG MISSIONARY, Marion, Ind.
YOUTH IN ACTION, Winona Lake, Ind.
YOUTH LIFE, Cleveland, Tenn.

APPENDIX E

NON-COUNCIL COMMUNICATIONS MEDIA

1. RADIO BROADCASTS

Airmail from God	Los Angeles, Calif.
Akron Baptist Temple	Akron, Ohio
Alpha Broadcasting Company	Detroit, Mich.
American Lutheran Church	Minneapolis, Minn.
American Mission to Greeks	Ridgefield, N. J.
Revivaltime	Springfield, Mo.
Back to the Bible Broadcast	Lincoln, Neb.
Bethany Bible Broadcast	Chicago, Ill.
Bible Fellowship Hour	Montrose, Calif.
Biola Hour	Los Angeles, Calif.
Bible Meditation Hour	Columbus, Ohio
Bible Study Hour	Philadelphia, Penn.
Boone Biblical College Hour	Boone, Iowa
Calvary Baptist Church	New York City
Calvary Hour	Goshen, Ind.
Calvary Memorial Church	Philadelphia, Penn.
Central Baptist Church	Quincy, Mass.
Central Union Mission	Washington, D. C.
Christ Memorial Church	Columbus, Ohio
Christ Truth Radio Crusade	Upland, Calif.
Christian Brotherhood Hour	Anderson, Ind.
Christians Hour	Cincinnati, Ohio
Church By the Side of the Road	Ionia, Mich.
Church of God	Cleveland, Tenn.
Cup of Cold Water Ministry	Redondo Beach, Calif.
Faith of Our Fathers	Springfield, Mo.
Faith Temple	Fort Smith, Ark.
Faith Temple	St. Petersburg, Fla.
Far East Broadcast	Whittier, Calif.
First Assembly of God	Memphis, Tenn.
First Baptist Church	Pontiac, Mich.
First Christian Church	Canton, Ohio
First Church of the Open Bible	Rockford, Ill.
First Covenant Church	Minneapolis, Minn.
Fraser Gospel Hour	Philadelphia, Penn.
Old Fashioned Revival Hour	Pasadena, Calif.
Gospel Tabernacle Hour	Sioux Falls, S. D.
Grace Baptist Temple	Philadelphia, Penn.
Grace Evangelistic Hour	Huntington Park, Calif.
Harbor of Light	Uniontown, Penn.
Heaven and Home	Glendale, Calif.
Herald of Truth	Abilene, Tex.
Hour of Decision	Minneapolis, Minn.
John Brown University	Long Beach, Calif.

Keys to Better Living	Lincoln, Neb.
Light and Life Hour	Winona Lake, Ind.
Lutheran Hour	St. Louis, Mo.
Lutheran Gospel Hour	Pasadena, Calif.
Your Radio Pastor	Jamestown, N. D.
Mennonite Hour	Harrisonburg, Va.
Men's Bible Class	Huntington, W. Va.
Message to Israel	Pachogue, N. Y.
Messiah Lutheran Church	Philadelphia, Penn.
Metropolitan Chapel	Buffalo, N. Y.
Moody Church	Chicago, Ill.
Morning Cheer	Philadelphia, Penn.
Morning Sunshine	Elyria, Ohio
New Life Broadcast	Noblesville, Ind.
Park Street Church	Boston, Mass.
Pentecostal Holiness	Oklahoma City, Okla.
People's Church	Beloit, Wis.
Psalm of Life	Minneapolis, Minn.
Radio Bible Class	Grand Rapids, Mich.
Radio Revival	Birmingham, Ala.
Radio Revival	Chattanooga, Tenn.
Rock of Ages	Newport News, Va.
Showers of Blessing	Kansas City, Mo.
St. James Lutheran Hour	Wheeling, W. Va.
Southern Evangelism Hour	Charlotte, N. C.
Spanish World Gospel Hour	Winona Lake, Ind.
Sudan Interior Missions	New York City
Temple Time	Grand Rapids, Mich.
Temple Time	Providence, R. I.
The Voice of Comfort	Tulsa, Okla.
Trans World Radio Hour	Chatham, N. J.
Twentieth Century Reformation Hour	Collingwood, N. J.
Morning Meditation	Sunbury, Penn.
Radio Revival	Los Angeles, Calif.
Voice of China and Asia	Pasadena, Calif.
Voice of Prophecy	Takoma Park, Md.
Village Church	Western Springs, Ill.
Voice of Comfort	Brockton, Mass.
Wings of Faith	Canton, Ohio
Word of Life Hour	Orange, N. J.
World Evangelistic Hour	Springfield, Ohio
World Missionary Fellowship	Miami, Fla.

2. RADIO STATIONS

WMUZ	Detroit, Mich.
KPIQ	Portland, Ore.
WCBC	Baltimore, Md.
KGER	Long Beach, Calif.
KPEL	Pueblo, Colo.
KMAR	San Francisco, Calif.

KBFG	Detroit, Mich.
WMRF	Flint, Mich.
WMUS	Muskegon, Mich.
WRBS	Baltimore, Md.
WMHE	Menomonee, Wis.
WARE	Peru, Ind.
WMBI	Chicago, Ill.
WCMR	Elkhart, Ind.
WAPO	Chattanooga, Tenn.
KAIR	Tuscon, Ariz.
KBIF	Fresno, Calif.
KBLE	Seattle, Wash.
KCCV	Kansas City, Mo.
KCTA	Corpus Christi, Tex.
KHEP	Phoenix, Ariz.
KRDU	Dinuba, Calif.
KWIL	Albany, Ga.
WAFC	Staunton, Va.
WMIT	Black Mountain, N. C.
WFUR	Grand Rapids, Mich.
WGCB	Red Lion, Penn.
WIVV	Hato Rey, P. R.
WJBL	Grand Rapids, Mich.
WWJC	Duluth, Minn.
WTOF	Canton, Ohio
WKIV	Orlando, Fla.
KCVR	Lodi, Calif.

APPENDIX F

QUESTIONNAIRE

I. Is your church and/or denomination a member of the National Council of Churches? .... Are you happy in this relationship? Why or why not? ....

II. Is your church and/or denomination involved in the Ecumenical Movement? .... Are you in favor of merger with other churches in the National Council? ....

III. Should the corporate Church be actively involved in politics? .... How much time and energy should it spend promoting the United Nations, the Peace Corps, the War on Poverty, Civil Rights, Social Welfare, Rent Control, Government Subsidies, Unionism, Tax Reform, Price Fixing, etc.? .... Why or why not? ....

IV. How can a local congregation keep partisan political issues (including endorsements and propaganda) out of the pulpit, church programs, and denominational media? ....

V. What is your local church doing in the light of (1) attacks on Biblical teachings, (2) the "new theology," (3) the "new morality" (divorce, extra-marital sex relations, homosexual behaviour, teen-age promiscuity), and (4) involvement of the clergy in demonstrations, sit-ins, teach-ins, picketing and crusades promoted by far-left propaganda organizations? ....

VI. Should local churches take positive, aggressive action to counter socialistic influences and communistic propaganda in the community and in the denomination? If so, what methods should be used? ....

VII. Does the literature being used in your Sunday School or Church School contain undesirable theological and/or social doctrines? .... Why do you regard it as undesirable, and what are you doing about it? ....
Where do you find suitable educational material? ....
What is your church doing to combat Biblical illiteracy in your community? ....

VIII. What programs in your church are promoting true Protestant American principles in your local church and community? ....
What are other Protestant churches in your area doing? Give examples: ....

IX. What do you consider to be the most serious problem confronting the Protestant churches in America today? Why? ....
What can be done about it? ....

X. What do you consider to be the most helpful agencies, books, literature, broadcasts or promotion efforts in your stand for sound Christian doctrine and for the American way of life? ....
NAME / POSITION IN CHURCH / ADDRESS

326